SHELLEY'S
DREAM WOMEN

SHELLEY'S DREAM WOMEN

by

MARGARET
CROMPTON

CASSELL · LONDON

CASSELL & COMPANY LTD
35 Red Lion Square, London WC1
Melbourne, Sydney, Toronto
Johannesburg, Cape Town, Auckland

© Margaret Crompton 1967
First published 1967

Printed in Great Britain by
The Camelot Press Ltd
London and Southampton
F.1266

*I think one is always in love with something or other;
the error, and I confess it is not easy for spirits cased in flesh and
blood to avoid it, consists in seeking in a mortal image the
likeness of what is perhaps eternal.*

SHELLEY

CONTENTS

ILLUSTRATIONS

ACKNOWLEDGEMENTS

In writing this book I have been greatly indebted to the latest edition of the Shelley Letters: *The Letters of Percy Bysshe Shelley* (1964), Vols. I and II, edited by Professor Frederick L. Jones, and published by the Clarendon Press, Oxford. I am most grateful to the Clarendon Press for permission to use this text of Shelley's letters, and also for permission to quote from a note on the Tanyrallt incident.

Material about Harriet Grove, including quotations from her Diary, is reprinted by permission of the publishers from *Shelley and His Circle*, Vol. II, edited by Professor Kenneth Neill Cameron (Cambridge, Mass.: Harvard University Press, Copyright, 1961, by the Carl and Lily Pforzheimer Foundation, Inc.).

Others to whom I am much indebted are Messrs Ernest Benn, Ltd., publishers of the Julian edition of Shelley's works; Dr Leslie Hotson, editor of *Shelley's Lost Letters to Harriet*; The Bodley Head, Ltd., publishers of *New Shelley Letters*, edited by W. S. Scott.

The Gregg Press, Ltd., in association with the Archive Press, Ltd., have very kindly given me permission to quote from *Shelley and Zastrozzi* by Dr Eustace Chesser. I should too like to thank the Literary Executor of Mr W. Somerset Maugham and Messrs William Heinemann, Ltd. for allowing me to use a quotation from *Ten Novels and Their Authors*; and also *The Times* for permission to quote from their review of

The Letters of Percy Bysshe Shelley, edited by Frederick L. Jones, in their edition of 13 February 1964.

Finally I wish to acknowledge my indebtedness to the authors, editors and publishers of all the books mentioned at the end of this volume. I must particularly mention the two early biographers, Professor Edward Dowden, author of *The Life of Percy Bysshe Shelley* (Kegan Paul, Trench, 1886) and Mrs Julian Marshall, author of *The Life and Letters of Mary Wollstonecraft Shelley* (Bentley, 1889).

PART ONE

HARRIET
GROVE

*She whom I found was **dear but** false to me.*
SHELLEY

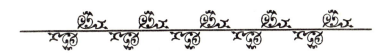

✧ I ✧

HARRIET GROVE was the first of the dream women—those impossible beings conjured up in a world of fantasy—who were to haunt Shelley all his life.

He and she were first cousins. Their mothers were sisters, the two Miss Pilfolds, Charlotte and Elizabeth, of Sussex. Charlotte in 1782 had married Thomas Grove, member of an ancient and prosperous Wiltshire family. Nine years later, in 1791, Elizabeth had made an equally advantageous match to Timothy Shelley of Field Place, Horsham, later heir to a baronetcy.

On the face of it the two families had much in common and a marriage between Bysshe and Harriet, apart from the drawback of being first cousins, might have seemed desirable. Bysshe Shelley, the romantic hero of his own imagination, was certainly much attracted by his cousin. Physically he and she were very much alike: both had the same soft brown hair, fair pink-and-white complexion, large luminous blue eyes, the same small well-set head and grace of bearing. An attractive pair, undoubtedly, to look at. Whether they were so suited in other more important ways was open to doubt.

The first recording of a meeting between the two is an early one. Shelley, at the age of eleven, spent the Easter holidays of 1804 with his relations, the Groves, at their estate, Fern, in Wiltshire. Shelley was then in his last year of preparatory school at Sion House Academy, Isleworth. His life was following a predictable course. His father intended that, after a satisfactory career at Eton and Oxford, his elder son should follow in his own footsteps and become a Member of Parliament. This plan was all cut and dried, without Shelley himself having much say in the matter.

For the time being Shelley appeared to accept what his elders

3

thought best for him. His life at that time, after all—apart from the torments of school—was a happy one. He was the elder son, with four adoring younger sisters as companions, and a younger brother too young to count. He had the satisfaction of belonging to the 'landed gentry', and to one of the richest and most important families in the county of Sussex. His father owned an attractive house and estate, to which he was the lawful heir.

And yet, though conscious of these advantages, there were already moments when Shelley secretly rebelled. He had in him already the seeds of a socialistic outlook, allied to a streak of wildness, of idealistic unpredictability, totally unshared by his very conventional father. He could not accept his blessings passively but felt impelled to question them. He was fond of his parents but there were times when they drove him to a wild impatience. It seemed to him that they lacked all vision. His mother he described as 'mild and tolerant—yet narrow minded'. No doubt his verdict on his father would have been still less flattering. Sir Timothy was a strict advocate of the respectable, and respectability was not a virtue which appealed to Shelley.

In a way he had more in common with his eccentric grandfather, the first baronet, Sir Bysshe. Sir Bysshe too was unconventional and cared not a rap for public opinion. Sir Bysshe was wayward and colourful, and pursued fantastic schemes, regardless of opposition. He and his grandson recognized in each other these same seeds of originality, of refusal to conform. And both grandfather and grandson united in despising the unfortunate Timothy. Here, however, the likeness ended. Shelley did not really care for his grandfather in spite of their bonds of similarity. He found him coarse, and rather callous, and lacking in human feeling. He had no sympathy either with Sir Bysshe's worldly ambitions to amass wealth and to found a great family of power and influence, while Sir Bysshe's matrimonial and other affairs somewhat shocked him.

Sir Bysshe had married twice (his grandson insisted that it was three times) and on both occasions he had made sure of adding to the family fortunes by marrying a wealthy heiress, the first being Mary Michell, a Sussex woman, who was the mother of Timothy. He had then cultivated the friendship of the Duke of Norfolk, made himself a devotee of the Whig cause, and in 1806 gained for himself a baronetcy. He never cared very much for his children and only spasmodically for his grandson. As time went on he became miserly and still more eccentric. The last years of his life were spent in a small home, Arun House, Horsham, overlooking the river. Here he died in 1815, aged eighty-four, and on his death over £12,000 was found to have been hoarded in banknotes, and hidden all over the house, stuffed into sofas, clothes and books.

Meanwhile his eldest son Timothy had benefited by having handed over to him the estate of Field Place, which Sir Bysshe had inherited from his brother. Field Place, though renovated more than once, is still standing. It is in the village of Warnham, about two and a half miles west of Horsham. It is an attractive square gabled house in peaceful surroundings, standing at the end of a tree-shaded drive, which in spring is gay with daffodils.

Here Shelley was born in the year 1792 and here he spent all his early years. There is no record of a meeting between him and Harriet in their early childhood though, as the two families were close and intimate, such a meeting seems more than probable. At the age of six Shelley started daily lessons with the minister at Warnham and at ten he was sent as a boarder to the Sion House preparatory school at Isleworth. His cousin, Thomas Medwin, had already preceded him there but there is no evidence of any close relationship between them, nor does Medwin appear to have offered him much protection in the rather stormy years which followed.

Shelley, though in many ways high-spirited and self-confident, had an unfortunately girlish appearance and gave the impression of being gentle and shy. He was, as was inevitable, hopelessly bullied by the other boys and his life became something of a torment. He kept aloof and was long-suffering up to a point: beyond this point his self-control deserted him and he became extremely angry, even dangerous, and was in the habit of throwing things, sometimes still smaller boys, at his tormentors. He had, however, one friend. Who this friend was is uncertain, and Shelley does not appear to have met him again in after life. But from Sion House he wrote to his mother in a eulogy of admiration and devotion for this paragon among boys—a eulogy which characteristically was received by his mother without comment.

School life, however, even apart from this glowing friendship, was not altogether barren. Shelley's imagination was a lively one and his intellect of unusual depths. Already he was showing poetic talent and he read insatiably, chiefly the sixpenny books obtainable at that time containing romantic tales of mystery, magic and love. Another subject which fascinated him was the study of science, a lifelong obsession. He loved to indulge in experiments, sometimes of a startling and destructive nature. On one occasion he blew up the school palings, and on another it is said that he abruptly blew off the lid of his desk during lesson hours.

Holidays usually were spent at Field Place but in 1804 there took place instead the Easter visit to the Grove relations at Fern, their Wiltshire estate. Here he found a large family of cousins ready to welcome him. Harriet, who had been born in 1791, was one of a family of eleven, all but two or three of whom survived childhood. Their life was comfortable and prosperous. The estate of Fern, four miles from Shaftesbury, had been in the family since 1583.

Harriet was now nearly thirteen, Shelley almost twelve. It is from a letter written in later life by a younger brother, Charles Grove, and printed in Hogg's *Life of Percy Bysshe Shelley* (1858) that we learn of Shelley's visit:

> The first time I ever saw Bysshe was when I was at Harrow. I was nine years old. . . . He accompanied us to Fern, and spent the Easter holidays there. The only circumstance I can recollect in connection with that visit was that Bysshe . . . thought it would be good service to play carpenters, and, under his auspices, we got the carpenters' axes, and cut down some of my father's young fir-trees in the park. My father often used to remind me of that circumstance.

For a prospective father-in-law it was not exactly an auspicious beginning. Charles too was evidently much impressed by the episode which loomed in his memory to the exclusion of all else. 'I did not meet Bysshe again after that,' he wrote, 'till I was fifteen, the year I left the navy.'

2

In 1808 Shelley and Harriet Grove began to correspond with one another. There is no record that after 1804 they actually met again until 1809, though it is obvious from Harriet Grove's diary that, as the months went by, she was becoming increasingly preoccupied with thoughts of the Shelleys at Field Place.

This diary, for the years 1809 and 1810, is fortunately still in existence. It is written in two small leather volumes, bound in red. Each daily space is limited as each page contains a week's entries. Harriet's handwriting was small and neat but occasionally her entries overflow on to the empty right-hand pages which are really intended for weekly expenses. The diary is, as Professor Frederick L. Jones points out, 'a valuable and fascinating document',* telling us a great deal about this first love affair of Shelley's, and giving us 'a delightful glimpse at English country life among the landed gentry in the early nineteenth century'.†

By 1809 there were nine surviving Grove children, five brothers and four sisters. Harriet, now seventeen, was the youngest but three. She had grown into a pretty and attractive girl, very like both Shelley and his sister Elizabeth in appearance. Both families had inherited the exceptional good looks of their Pilfold mothers. Shelley's cousin, Thomas Medwin, gives us a eulogistic description of Harriet in his *Life of Percy Bysshe Shelley* (1847): 'I still remember Miss Harriet Grove,

* Kenneth Neill Cameron (editor): *Shelley and His Circle*, Vol. 2.
† Ibid.

B

and when I call to mind all the women I have ever seen, I know of none that surpassed, or could compete with her. She was like one of Shakespeare's women—like some Madonna of Raphael.' In temperament she was vivacious and light-hearted, an ordinarily conventional girl of sheltered upbringing, kind and generous, with a gregarious disposition.

The diary, as is natural, is much taken up with her family and family affairs, the movements of her brothers and sisters, and her meetings with aunts, uncles and cousins, of whom she had a plentiful supply. But through it all, as an ever recurring motif and secret joy, there are these allusions to Shelley, to Field Place, to her future hopes, which she hardly dared to put into words. 'Heard from Bysshe' and 'Wrote to dear Bysshe' occurs almost every other day, alternated with 'Wrote to my Dearest Aunt Shelley'. The Horsham home is described as 'that delightful place' and it is obvious that she is longing for another meeting. After a time some of the more outspoken endearments are crossed out—perhaps for motives of secrecy from prying eyes. Some can be deciphered, some not. Even the most modern methods of magnification and ultra-violet light have failed, as Professor Jones tells us, to decipher some sentences, some allusions. But still there are the cryptic remarks left in, from which we can deduce much, of 'hoping to see the person I wish' and 'walked with my Mother and talked to her upon a subject that always interests me'.

In April 1809 at length the much-longed-for meeting materialized. On 10 April, Mr and Mrs Grove, Harriet, and her elder sister Charlotte, all went to London on a visit to the second son, John. John was a surgeon, aged twenty-three, financially independent, and he lived with a housekeeper and a cat in Lincoln's Inn Fields. He himself was very friendly with the Shelleys and both father and son frequently visited him. Sure enough, on this occasion too, when the Groves had only been in London for about six days, Shelley and his father arrived to join the party.

Shelley by now was at Eton. He had grown into a tall lanky youth, graceful in all his movements, but stooping already from his habit of poring over books—the outward appearance which he was to keep for the rest of his short life. With his small head and shock of chestnut hair, his intelligent vivid face with the large eager blue eyes, the gentleness of manner and feeling, and—the one discordant note—his harsh shrill voice, he was a young man who could not fail to be noticeable and noticed. At Eton he was known as 'Mad Shelley'. 'He stood apart from the whole school,' wrote a contemporary, 'a being never to be forgotten.'

From the first he had been a rebel against conformity, a boy determined, at whatever cost, to remain true to himself and his own ideals. Already he saw himself as a reformer of society, a champion of noble causes, a fighter against tyranny. He might be shy and something of an oddity, careless and untidy in dress, and with a dangerous excitability of temper, yet he incited in some an ungrudging admiration. His life at Eton was not altogether a happy one; by the unimaginative and more orthodox elements he was still bullied and baited. But he did have some friends. There were moments of serenity, long country walks, long communings with nature, long heart to heart talks with kindred spirits. 'I loved Shelley,' one wrote, 'for his kindliness and affectionate ways . . . he was not made to endure the rough and boisterous pastime at Eton. . . . He had great moral courage, and feared nothing but what was base and false and low.'

At work he had forged ahead with his classical studies which always absorbed him. Science again, as at Sion House, was a mixed blessing. There were more troubles over his experiments, particularly when on one occasion he flung his tutor against the wall with a fierce electric shock. He was twice threatened with expulsion and only saved this fate by his father's intervention. He cared nothing for games, boating being the only sport which appealed to him. Already, even as a schoolboy, he longed to become a writer and had already embarked on a novel. Yet, in spite of his lonely habits, he was not unsociable. What he appreciated were congenial companions who would listen to him with sympathy. And probably too, as his early biographer, Edward Dowden, romantically suggests, he already dreamed of the 'ideal' love.

In Harriet Grove, during those Easter holidays of 1809 when they met at her brother's house in London, he found an admiring and sympathic audience. All his life there was nothing he liked better than pouring out his ideas and precepts into the receptive ears of a spellbound woman disciple. Harriet Grove was the first of these, adored and adoring, a willing listener. He loved her with a romantic and headstrong devotion.

Their longed-for meeting had, unfortunately, to be concentrated into the short space of four days, which was the length of the Shelleys' visit. When they arrived Mr Shelley, according to Harriet, appeared cross 'for what reason I know not'. But this slight shadow on her happiness seems to have passed off and is not mentioned again. She and her beloved Bysshe made the most of their time together. They went to the theatre and saw *Richard III* and a farce, *Mother Goose*, also another evening play. There was an expedition to Clapham where two of the Shelley sisters, Hellen and Mary, were at school. This resulted in a mutual admiration society among the girls. 'Saw my cousin Shelleys,' wrote Harriet in her diary, 'who I think the Nicest Girls I ever saw.' While Hellen Shelley, in a letter written many years later, wrote of Harriet: 'How fresh and pretty she was,' described her as her brother's 'early love' and how her assistance was invoked on this occasion to 'keep the wild boy quiet'. Shelley, in the height of good spirits, had apparently upset the port wine, hospitably supplied by the headmistress, all over the tray cloth. Later, as they all walked in the garden, there as 'much ado to calm the spirits of the wild boy'.

But all too soon it was over. The diary entry on 20 April is a regretful one: '(Dear) Bysshe (has) left us.' Letter writing between the two was started up again at once with increased fervour, cancellations of endearments in the diary became more frequent, and on the 24th there is a sentimental reminder of Shelley: 'Charlotte made me a present of the Pink Dress (dear) Bysshe chose for us.'

Harriet and her family did not leave London until nearly a month later when they went on to Salisbury for another family visit. Here, so Harriet wrote, they were even gayer than in town. In their large family circle life was full of social activities—visiting, dinner parties, paying formal calls, dancing. But home beckoned. 'We are returned to Fern again. I am not sorry.'

It was a beloved house to them all, but now disaster threatened. Only four days after their return the discovery was made that the whole front of the building was cracked. It was in too bad a state for repairs to be considered; there was no alternative but to pull down the whole house and build it up all over again. Harriet was much distressed. It was tragic to have to leave 'dear old Fern'. On 26 June, Harriet's eighteenth birthday, the whole family installed themselves at the Parsonage House, less than two miles away. Harriet and twenty-six-year-old Charlotte walked there, the others went in a conveyance described by Harriet with a somewhat wild effort at spelling as 'the Pheaton'. The Parsonage for the next few months was to be their home, but hardly a day passed without some of the family either walking or riding over to the beloved Fern, to look over the farms and tenants, and to watch the new house in the process of being built. The rebuilding was to be a lengthy business but Harriet had a shilling bet with her younger sister Louisa that the 'new Fern' would be finished and ready for them within two and a half years.

Meanwhile the animated correspondence with Shelley still continued. John Grove, who had already stayed at Field Place in January, was invited to visit there again by Shelley's sister, Elizabeth. Harriet, envious of his good fortune, began a correspondence with Elizabeth herself. By July, 1809, she was optimistically writing in her diary: 'I think we have a chance of going to Field Place. It makes me very happy.' But by 4 August this faith was weakening: 'I am afraid Mr Shelley won't ask us to Field Place this Summer'—and in September there was a restive cry from the heart: 'I long for Mama to hear from Aunt Shelley.'

Much to her disappointment it seemed that the longed-for invitation was not to materialize. Although always preoccupied with thoughts of Shelley she was forced to carry on with her usual activities, the busy social round, as though it was this, and this alone, which engrossed her entire attention. She had a happy disposition so possibly it did not irk her too much. She was fond of her brothers and sisters and enjoyed their society, there was much coming and going among them, and great interest in their careers. There were, too, quieter days and nothing much to record in the diary beyond: 'Wrote a great many letters', 'Took a very pretty walk', or 'Nothing particular happened today.' On 6 September her future husband, Mr William Helyar, whom she was to marry two years later, is mentioned for the first time. Four days later he dined at the Parsonage. But though his visits are mentioned in the diary at fairly regular intervals after this, it is always with complete unconcern and no hint of any incipient romance.

Nevertheless, in the eyes of the Grove parents, it is probable that as a prospective suitor Mr Helyar was eyed with more favour than was the youthful and incalculable Bysshe Shelley. William Helyar was thirteen years older than Harriet. His father owned a near-by estate at Sedgehill and another near Yeovil, Somerset. His uncle was the rector of an adjoining Wiltshire village, Tollard Royal. It was to Tollard in fact that the Groves moved in October 1809 as the Parsonage House they were occupying was needed for the new incumbent. Tollard was three miles south of Fern so they were still within easy distance for the almost daily inspections of the new building site. They attended Tollard church and Harriet, an enthusiastic church-goer, frequently remarks in her diary on the excellence of her future uncle-in-law's sermons.

The year 1809 drew towards its end with, alas, no invitation for Field Place but plenty of other distractions to while away the time. A favourite brother, William, who was in the Navy, came home on leave in November. And, by the next month, Christmas festivities were approaching. 'Put Beads upon our Gowns,' wrote Harriet. A day or two later a popular annual function, the Shaftesbury ball, is recorded: 'A most excellent Ball more than 20 Couple. Danced thro' two with Mr Wm. H—.'

3

In 1810 Harriet started a new diary. Inscribed on the fly-leaf are the words: 'Harriet Grove, given her by her Mother, Jany. 1st, 1810.' The first six days of the diary unfortunately are missing but allusions to Field Place are soon forthcoming. Harriet had evidently decided that Bysshe's sister, Elizabeth, was the member of the family whose friendship was most worth cultivating, in order to bring about fruitful results. So, on 8 January, we get the entry: 'Wrote a long letter to Eliz^th Shelley.' The very next day there was a letter from her brother John—the member of the Grove family most favoured by the Shelleys—calculated to arouse her envy: 'A letter from (dear) John who has been at Field Place and been very gay there and liked his visit very much.'

Two months passed with no alleviations of her suspense. Her usual life went on with no particular excitements. She had evidently finished her formal education before 1809 as there is no mention of any studies in either diary. She could sing and draw as was the custom of the times, and play the piano a little. She liked reading and in the diary there is mention of Fielding, Richardson, Scott, interspersed with Maria Edgeworth and other lighter practitioners of literature. Her family, as always, was her mainstay and comfort: 'Walked out with my two Dear Sisters', 'Met some cows which frightened us, Louisa we lost owing to it for some time, which frightened us even more than the Cows.' But, by February: 'Dearest Louisa went to School. I miss her very much'; and, two days later, a rather weary and cryptic comment: 'Charlotte heard from Wm. who says he thinks I shall never be married that I do not care whether I ever do or not. He says he thinks I never liked anyone so much as (——), that is a thing no one will *ever know* but myself.'

In March, however, there was a change in her fortunes. She was cheered and most agreeably surprised by receiving a parcel

and letter 'from my Greatest Friend (———)'. It is thought that
the parcel contained a copy of Shelley's latest poem as three
days later we learn that a poem was shown to Charles and
Charlotte who, unsympathetically after the habit of brothers
and sisters, dismissed it as 'nonsense'. However, it did seem as
though plans were now afoot for a visit to Field Place and
Harriet's anticipation was mounting. Her only doubts were
over her mother's attitude. After a little more prompting in
the form of another diplomatic letter from Harriet to Elizabeth, the Shelleys apparently had done their part and sent the
longed-for invitation. But Mrs Grove was hesitating. 'I fear
owing to some fancy my Mother has in her head,' Harriet
wrote in anguish on 25 March, 'we shall not go for which I
feel the greatest sorrow as I had made up my mind for the
pleasure of spending a few days at Dear Field Place.'

Were the Grove parents dubious from the first of furthering
the budding romance between the two cousins? It seems
possible, but two days later Mrs Grove relented: 'At last
they say they will go to Field Place for one day—it makes me
so happy.' The omens now at last seemed favourable. Shelley
had sent Harriet a copy of his first published work *Zastrozzi*,
a short and high-flown Gothic romance. Some say Harriet
herself had had a hand in the writing of it. Charles Grove
professed scorn. But Harriet, ever Shelley's champion, was
delighted, and deeply offended with her brother for his lack
of appreciation. All heightened the excitement which mounted
in her mind at the thought of the approaching visit.

But when the desired event on 16 April at length took
place strange doubts and mystifications began to obtrude
themselves. 'Got to dear F.P. (———),' Harriet wrote: 'they are
all very glad to see us.' But there is a rider, added in perplex-
ity: 'I cannot tell what to make of it—very strange'; and
another cryptic comment, 'Still more odd', was added the next
day. The grave, watching demeanour among her elders evidently daunted her, shaking her confidence. She did not realize
at first that this was to be the vital moment of decision, the
planned opportunity for the families to make up their minds.
Was the courtship to be allowed to continue—or should the

young couple be tactfully separated into a diplomatic estrangement? It seems that the parents on both sides must finally have accepted the situation, at least provisionally, and given their consent to an informal engagement.

Hours of happiness followed. Charles Grove wrote years later: 'Bysshe was at that time more attached to my sister Harriet than I can express.' Harriet and her two brothers, Bysshe and his sister Elizabeth, made up youthful expeditions to Horsham, to Strood by moonlight, to Horsham again. The short visit was over almost before it had begun and Harriet found herself leaving 'the pleasentest [sic] party in the world' to stay instead at Cuckfield with her mother's brother, Captain Pilfold.

The contrast was painful. 'What a disagreeable place after the one we have just left.' Under the circumstances she had no patience with her elder sister Charlotte's romantic interest in a Cuckfield neighbour, Colonel Sergison. Although admitting that he was entertaining, 'I think he drinks too much,' Harriet wrote tartly. Charlotte might be 'half in love' and insist on walking in Colonel S.'s park but Harriet, her mind better employed, was just not interested: 'Very pretty I daresay but my thoughts won't let me think about it.' She lived for the moment when they would move on to her brother John's in London. On 21 April the much desired move took place and four days later 'dear Aunt Shelley' and her cousins, Bysshe and Elizabeth, arrived to join them.

This time it was to be a ten days' visit. For the first time Harriet and Shelley were to have a succession of long blissful days together without interruption. They walked in the fields, went shopping, 'had great fun'. Suddenly she dropped the name 'Bysshe' and decided that in future—perhaps in order to establish a greater and more private intimacy—she would call the loved one 'Percy'. Her longing for his undiluted society grew more pronounced. Elizabeth Shelley's unflagging high spirits in the background—or possibly too often in the foreground—began to seem something of an intrusion. 'Elizabeth as noisy as ever'—'Elizabeth talks and is in as great spirits as ever.' Diplomatically Harriet hurt her foot and made the most

of the injury: 'Staid at home all day on account of my Foot
the rest of the party went to the Play all but Mama and
Percy'—'All the party went out but me (and Dearest P.).'
On one evening all the family danced while she played for
them. They visited the opera and more than once the theatre.
But on 5 May the joyful days were over: 'The Shelleys left us
very sorry.'

This was to be the last time, though she did not know it, that
she and Shelley were to meet in these happy circumstances. As
yet no realization dawned on her of what was to come. She
and her family stayed on with brother John in London for
another fortnight. Harriet had some music lessons from a Mr
Graham, a young protégé of the Shelley parents, and she paid
visits with her mother. They were both laid low with colds but
recovered to attend a water colour exhibition. Uncles came and
went—the two Pilfold brothers and Mr Shelley himself,
although not on the best of terms with the Pilfolds. Mr
Shelley looked unwell but he was, so Harriet registered with
satisfaction: 'So pleasent [sic], I am quite happy to see him so.'

Evidently the Shelley parents were gratified to accept her as
a future daughter-in-law, no doubt hoping against hope that
her even temperament and conventional background would be
the very things needed to steady the ebullient Bysshe. Mr
Shelley handed over to Harriet a letter from Elizabeth. On his
next visit a few days later he seemed 'in great spirits'. They all
seemed to be on the best of terms.

4

On 19 May the party broke up. Charlotte Grove went off
with her uncle Pilfold on a three months' visit to Cuckfield,
where no doubt a great attraction was the presence of Colonel
Sergison. Harriet and her parents returned to Tollard.

A sad time was now in store for them. They had not been
home for more than a week or two when they heard that the

youngest Grove daughter Louisa was ill with whooping-cough at her school in Bath. A few days later she was fetched home by the Grove parents. She was kept in bed, forbidden to eat meat and—as was the medical custom of the day—continually 'bled' to reduce her fever. Harriet was constantly in attendance: 'Dear Louisa told me she liked me to be with her.' There were baffling ups and downs in her illness. One day she was much better, the next the fever would return: 'I long for her to be quite well again—She is quiet.' The surgeon and the doctor bled her assiduously, five times in all—but, perhaps not surprisingly, she grew steadily weaker. Harriet sat up with her all night but on 19 June Louisa died.

Harriet temporarily was shattered. Already she had lost a much loved younger sister, Marienne, a year younger than herself, who had died in January 1806, from burns when her muslin dress caught fire. Charlotte and Louisa were the only two sisters Harriet had left. But Charlotte was some years older and the younger Louisa had always been her favourite. Family ties made up the great absorption of her life and the loss was a blow which needed fortitude and courage. She tried to find it in ministering to her mother. Mrs Grove, too, had been overcome by the blow and seemed to be sinking under her sorrow. It was arranged that mother and daughter should go away together for a six weeks' holiday to Muddiford to recover from the shock.

As by now Harriet had practically eradicated all mention of Shelley from her diary it is more difficult to tell how the romance between them was prospering. On 13 August of that year, 1810, she and her mother returned home to face the normal routine of life once more. It must have been cheering for them to find that the rebuilding of the new Fern was progressing admirably and the roof was in the process of being put on. Daily visits started again in lively anticipation now of before long being resettled into their own beloved home.

In the middle of September Harriet received by post another offering of Shelley's literary efforts. This time it was the *Original Poetry of Victor and Cazire*—a joint work by Shelley and his sister Elizabeth. Unfortunately, however, this slim

volume created uproar in the Grove family. Charlotte, now
home again from her Cuckfield visit, discovered to her horror
that a poem Shelley had written lampooning her visits to
Cuckfield, as an effort to attract the attention of Colonel
Sergison, was printed word for word and published for all to
see:

> So [Charlotte] is going to [Cuckfield] you say,
> I hope that success her great efforts will pay
> That [Sergison] will see her, be dazzled outright,
> And declare he can't bear to be out of her sight.

Quite justifiably Charlotte was exceedingly annoyed. Even
though she and Harriet may have been shown the poem and
laughed at it in London, its publication was another matter, and
had been never dreamed of. Mr Shelley too, it seems, was involved
in the general indignation, for Harriet on 25 September writes
anxiously in her diary: 'My Father had a letter from Mr
S[helley] which I am sorry for, as it gives more trouble.'
Whatever the ins and outs of the matter, it was all doubly
unfortunate in the way of raising doubts in the minds of the
Grove parents about the stability of their future son-in-law.

This may have been enhanced still further when only a short
time later the offending volume of poems was withdrawn from
circulation. The publisher, Stockdale of London, had suddenly
noticed for the first time that one of the poems, far from being
original, had been lifted bodily and entire from the renowned
Monk Lewis. It was a poem ostensibly written by 'Cazire'
(Elizabeth). Shelley had had 1,500 copies of the work printed
at Horsham, before finding a publisher. Outraged now by
this development he ordered the whole edition to be immediately destroyed. About one hundred copies only escaped this
fate—copies which were already in circulation and sent out for
reviewing, only one or two of which probably are still in
existence. It was an ignominious ending to Shelley's first poetic
effort and no doubt did nothing to enhance his reputation with
Harriet's family.

For the rest of the year Harriet in her diary was careful to
make no reference at all to 'Percy' and her latent romance. She

must have been going through a period of much uncertainty and heart-searching but the diary does not reflect this in any way. Instead it seems that her social life became more and more hectic and absorbing. Paying calls, meeting neighbours, dancing, singing, playing games—the days were seldom unoccupied. Brothers came and went. There were sessions of reading novels aloud: *Sir Charles Grandison* was a popular favourite. She played chess with her family, failing that there was always battledore and shuttlecock. It is possible that, realizing that the romance with Shelley was going sadly awry, she flung herself into these varied activities with a feverish intensity in order to try to forget him.

In October he had gone to Oxford and he had come under the influence of Thomas Jefferson Hogg. From being a tentative Christian he now described himself as an atheist, and his letters to Harriet reflected views and opinions that became increasingly and alarmingly unorthodox. There is no doubt that Harriet took fright. First she consulted her mother, and later on her father. She was intelligent and open to discussion, but by nature and upbringing her bias was towards the comforting and the conventional. Shelley's outbursts of atheistic disbelief left her worried and uneasy. She was too very much under the influence of her family.

Her brother Charles, writing years later in 1857, gives us what is probably the true explanation of the breaking of the engagement:

> In the course of that summer [of 1810] . . . a continual correspondence was going on, as I believe there had been before, between Bysshe and my sister Harriet. But she became uneasy at the tone of his letters on speculative subjects, at first consulting my mother, and subsequently my father also on the subject. This led at last, though I cannot exactly tell how, to the dissolution of an engagement between Bysshe and my sister, which had previously been permitted, both by his father and mine.

Mr Grove, an extrovert and something of a Philistine, fond of sport and hunting, was, one can surmise, secretly much relieved by this outcome of events. He had never really approved of his young nephew by marriage. Perhaps he could not easily forget the decapitated fir trees in his park. Harriet's doubts, added to her mother's and his own, speedily settled the matter. The engagement must be off, all correspondence must cease. Elizabeth, championing her brother and rushing to his defence, tried to re-unite the lovers. But Harriet would have none of it.

There seems no doubt that the match would have meant the joining together of an ill-assorted couple with widely conflicting views. Shelley, as he said afterwards, felt that he had to have a wife who could 'feel poetry and understand philosophy'. Harriet had only a superficial understanding of either. Shelley had no use for the ordinary 'social' life of everyday people—this life made up Harriet's world. Shelley by nature was a rebel—Harriet was a conformist. But, quite apart from these differences, Shelley, with his head in the clouds, did not see life in terms of realities. Instead of a real person he saw only the image he had built up in his mind. His imagination was so powerful that he felt he could cast other people to a pattern of his own choosing. When, inevitably, he discovered his mistake, disillusion was bound to follow. Harriet perhaps was astute enough to realize this and to be warned in time.

There existed too, of course, for Harriet, Mr William Helyar. Mr William Helyar, over the months, and seldom noticed in the diary, had been gradually establishing himself as a second suitor. Unknowing of the secret engagement to Shelley, he had been becoming increasingly attentive, in a way that gratified the parents, and by which Harriet herself could not fail to be impressed. For, all things considered, Mr Helyar was so much more suitable than Shelley. His feet were firmly planted on the ground, he was older, and wiser, and steadier, and well established in life—everything in fact that was most to be desired in a prospective husband. It is very probable that it was the presence of Mr William Helyar which, more than anything, influenced Harriet to take heed in time and to break decisively with Shelley. It was this new relationship too which acted as a panacea to any incipient heartbreak which otherwise might have followed.

For, search as we may in Harriet's diary, there is no sign of any real grief, or indeed of any lowering of spirits, after the final rupture. The December entries tell of dancing, games, and endless social activities. On Christmas Day they went to church and had 'a most excellent sermon'. On the 29th she describes 'a great deal of laughing teaching my Brothers the rigadoon step'. And the diary ends on a note of excited anticipation as she and her family looked forward to the annual Shaftesbury ball.

She was only just eighteen, after all. The affair with Shelley had always been tenuous, uncertain—perhaps, even on her side, more imagined than real? The important years were still before her. Not very long afterwards, towards the end of 1811 (though not until *after* Shelley's own marriage to Harriet Westbrook) she married William Helyar. In 1820 he inherited the estate of Coker Court in Yeovil, Somerset, from his father. Later he became Justice of the Peace for Somerset and Devon and, in 1829, High Sheriff of Somerset. He and Harriet had a large family of four sons and four daughters. History does not relate whether or not they lived happily ever after but Harriet survived to the good age of seventy-six, dying in December 1867.

5

For Shelley himself the break with Harriet caused an emotional upheaval not altogether easy to analyse. It is true that he professed himself to be heartbroken. But his youthful tendency to self-dramatization was all-pervading. Now, as in the future, his romantic infatuations were largely play-acting. The role of the deserted and disillusioned lover was a role which fitted well into the saga of fantasy which made up his life. It seems too that it was a role for which he had been preparing himself for some time. As early as November 1810 he had published anonymously a book of poems entitled *The*

Posthumous Fragments of Margaret Nicholson, the last one of which, somewhat prematurely, was addressed to Harriet:—

> Art thou indeed forever gone
> Forever, ever, lost to me?

Harriet's 'cooling off' process, encouraged by the attitude of her family, and lasting probably several months, had evidently not been lost on Shelley. He could not fail to realize that his unorthodox theories and his gradually mounting opposition to Christianity held no appeal for her, and indeed caused her considerable distress. The differences between them had been much accentuated since his arrival at Oxford in the autumn and his subsequent friendship with Hogg. Hogg was a more mature and sophisticated person than Shelley with definite and unconventional views on life. He admired Shelley but also thought him rather naïve. And for Shelley's nebulous belief in a God compounded of universal benevolence he had no sympathy at all. Shelley, listening to Hogg's practised scepticism, soon came round to his view. Religion, he decided, and explained to his father later, was only desirable for those more unintelligent beings 'not having sufficient principle to discharge their duties without leaning on some support'. It fettered 'a reasoning mind' such as his own and Hogg's. All these theories and doubts and new beliefs surged in his mind and overflowed in his letters to Harriet. And, week after week, though aware of her disapproval and increasing coolness, he was impelled to go on and on, trying to convince her, until instead of convincing he alienated her, and she was irrevocably lost.

His relationship with Harriet was not the only thing that was going wrong that winter of 1810. His publisher, Stockdale, engaged with the publication of Shelley's second novel *St Irvyne*, had heard rumours of a forthcoming pamphlet on atheism, and was becoming uneasy. Stockdale—who secretly blamed the friendship with Hogg, and Hogg's influence, and later said so—felt that it was his duty to warn Mr Shelley.

Mr Shelley took fright at once. Here was the exasperating Bysshe getting into trouble yet again. After a disturbing

interview with Stockdale in London, he wrote to Shelley at Field
Place, threatening to remove him from Oxford unless he
mended his ways and abandoned some of his 'detestable
principles'. Later, at Christmas, when Shelley joined the family
at Horsham, his father tackled him once more. Argument
flowed freely, with Charles Grove, Harriet's brother, who had
been invited to spend the Christmas holidays, a fascinated
spectator. The rupture with the Grove family over Harriet's
possible marriage to Bysshe was irrevocably complete.

There is no doubt that, faced with all these unfortunate
happenings, Shelley's nerves were in a state of disarray. He and
his father were hopelessly at loggerheads. His publisher was
proving narrow-minded and interfering. His mother failed
dismally to understand him. Elizabeth, his sister, was kind but
inadequate. And to crown all, he had lost Harriet. There
seemed little help anywhere.

His only comfort and confidant was Hogg. To Hogg he
poured out the tale of his troubles and griefs in one desperate
letter after another. The 'uncongenial jollities' of Christmas
were an agony to him. What was the good of Hogg telling him
not to despond, not to despair: 'I cannot avoid feeling every
instant as if my soul was bursting—oh! how much rather
would I expire in the struggle—Is suicide wrong? I slept with a
loaded pistol and some poison last night but did not die.'
Hogg's cool and reasoned advice to acquiesce in giving up
Harriet only incensed him still further: 'Forsake her! forsake
one whom I loved! can I? never—but she is gone, she is lost
to me forever, forever.'

At first he did not blame Harriet herself. It was worldly
prejudice and bigotry which had separated them, the spirit of
intolerance. Just because he happened to hold advanced and
unorthodox opinions, how unfair and ludicrous that this should
discredit him as a potential lover or husband. He could not
accept defeat without making one last fight for Harriet's
understanding. Late in December or early January he arranged
a last meeting with her. It was useless. She wrote him a letter
to say that she could not correspond with an atheist, and
impressed on him her duty to her father. Elizabeth's efforts,

C

too, to bring about a reconciliation proved equally abortive. A few days later, to put the seal on his despair, he heard for the first time the news of Harriet's intended marriage to Helyar: 'She is gone, she is lost to me forever—married to a clod of earth, she will become as insensible herself, all those fine capabilities will moulder.' Hogg must realize that it was intolerable: 'Let us speak no more on the subject.'

Elizabeth, deeply anxious for her brother, followed him around as he took his dog on solitary walks, usually carrying with him a gun. All the family at Field Place felt the shadow of his despair and—what appeared to them—his disgrace. Mr Shelley was shocked and aghast to discover, chiefly from the Grove family, the extent of his son's disbeliefs. To the Grove parents these disbeliefs appeared an outrage against respectability, and a more than adequate reason for their disapproval of his marriage to Harriet.

Shelley himself, faced with all this opposition, hardened in his views and began for the first time to feel that it was Harriet herself who was chiefly to be blamed for the betrayal. It infuriated him that she should tamely have acquiesced in her family's opposition, that she should have allowed them to influence her opinions, and even to choose the type of man that she should marry. Once she had seemed to be his adoring and admiring disciple, sympathizing with his ideas, deferring to his views. Now, it seemed, all that was forgotten. He was bitterly disappointed in her for stubbornly remaining herself, instead of consenting to play the role he had assigned to her. Later, in an early draft of his great poem *The Revolt of Islam* he was to write (though afterwards cancel), 'She whom I found was dear but false to me . . .' of Harriet Grove.

Now, this January of 1811, his grief already hardening into disillusion, he began to put her out of his mind. There was much else to distract him, the rupture with his parents, his friendship with Hogg, life at Oxford threatening to become still more hectic. And also—though how far this influenced him it is difficult from this distance of time to say—he had already met Harriet Westbrook.

PART TWO

HARRIET
WESTBROOK

Whose eyes have I gazed fondly on,
And loved mankind the more?
Harriet! on thine:—— thou wert my purer mind;
Thou wert the inspiration of my song.

SHELLEY

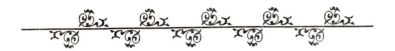

I

SHELLEY had first met Harriet Westbrook when he visited his sisters' school with the Groves while still at Eton. He had been seventeen then and Harriet only fourteen. Unfortunately there is no portrait of Harriet in existence but we have the testimony of many people to confirm that she was exceptionally pretty with a pink and white complexion, a graceful figure, and hair imaginatively described by Hellen Shelley as being 'like a poet's dream'.

Shelley, his attentions at that time engrossed by his cousin Harriet Grove, was uninvolved emotionally by this first encounter. This new Harriet was a favourite schoolfriend of his two beloved sisters, Mary and Hellen, and for that reason alone he would willingly accept her. Otherwise the fact that her name too was 'Harriet' would probably be the feature to impress itself most on his mind.

What Harriet Westbrook thought of Shelley at this first meeting is perhaps more pertinent. Socially he was in a different world from hers and it is understandable that he appeared in a glamorous light. He was young, good-looking, romantic in appearance, and the heir to a baronetcy. Harriet had been very carefully brought up by a father who had no advantages of birth, but who had made a great deal of money. Mr Westbrook had been a coffee-house proprietor and vintner. He had amassed a large fortune, particularly from a coffee-house off Grosvenor Square, and he had now settled in the fashionable parish of St George's, Hanover Square, where he had succeeded in getting himself accepted in good society.

Harriet led a very sheltered life. No risks were taken. Her upbringing was stereotyped, ultra-conventional. Mr Westbrook was a man of strict moral standards, an upright man of integrity. He was determined to give Harriet every opportunity of social betterment and he sent her as a boarder to the select school on the south side of Clapham Common. Here she would mix with people like the Shelley sisters and pave the way for an advantageous marriage. Harriet herself was attracted by the idea of marrying a clergyman. She was a solitary type of girl who did what she was told and was easily influenced by other people. Her mother was still living but seemed to play a curiously negative role in the family. The chief influence in Harriet's life at this time was that of her one surviving sister, Eliza, twelve years older, and a woman of powerful personality with a managing disposition. This unfortunate weakness of Harriet's for allowing herself to be dominated by Eliza was an important contributive factor towards the tragedy which was to come.

But in those early days of their acquaintanceship Shelley was unaware of these wheels within wheels. By January 1811 the romance with Harriet Grove had ended in disillusionment. He was once more at a loose end, his mind seething with rebellious ideas, his relations with his parents as unsatisfactory as ever, his future undecided. He was struggling along at Oxford and his second novel *St Irvyne* had just been published. Some time during that January he called with Charles Grove at the Westbrooks' home in Chapel Street, off Park Lane, on the pretext of delivering to Harriet a present from his sister Mary. His impression of Harriet at this second meeting seems to have been a favourable one. But he saw her chiefly in a role suited to his own imagination: as a potential disciple, a docile and willing listener, someone who would hang on his words, adopt his ideas as her own, and administer balm to his damaged self-esteem. To make sure of her continued interest, and in the hope that she would write to him, he ordered his publisher to send her a copy of his novel *St Irvyne*.

At Oxford Shelley's fortunes were already reaching a point of crisis. In February 1811 he and his friend and fellow rebel, Thomas Jefferson Hogg, published their controversial pamphlet, *The Necessity of Atheism*. A prominent local bookshop window was filled with copies of the offending booklet; a passing Fellow observed them with horror, stormed into the shop, and insisted that all copies should be burnt forthwith.

Shelley, suspected as chief perpetrator of the outrage, was
summoned before the authorities of University College and
asked either if he would disavow the authorship or renounce
his views. He would do neither. Hogg, eager to join in the
fray, was sent for and also implicated. He too refused in any
way to disavow what he and Shelley had written. The result
was both he and Shelley were expelled.

It was a great shock. Shelley, his head in the clouds, and
his ideas and ideals more real to him than reality, had not
anticipated that what appeared to him to be truthfulness and
honesty should land him in such straits. Hogg had never
before seen him so upset: 'He sat on the sofa, repeating, with
convulsive vehemence, "Expelled, expelled!" his head shaking
with emotion, and his whole frame quivering.' It is to Hogg,
in fact, that we are mainly, if not entirely, indebted for our
knowledge of Shelley's brief sojourn at Oxford. These reminiscences of Hogg's, written years later at the age of sixty-five,
should be accepted with reservations—certainly with the
proverbial grain of salt. Some critics even go so far as to call
them 'semi-fiction'. They are not altogether truthful—letters
are altered, events misrepresented. It is this account of Hogg's,
followed by so many biographers, that has made the truth
about Shelley difficult to arrive at. Yet Hogg's reminiscences
do hold the essential core of truth. 'Hogg,' said Trelawny
later, 'has painted Shelley exactly as I knew him.' It is a larger
than life and dramatic portrait, heightened to give colour and
mystery. But the spark is there, the authenticity:

> His figure was slight and fragile, and yet his bones and joints
> were large and strong. He was tall, but he stooped so much, that
> he seemed of a low stature. His clothes were expensive—but
> they were tumbled, rumpled, unbrushed—His complexion was
> delicate, and almost feminine, of the purest red and white—His
> features, his whole face, and particularly his head, were, in fact,
> unusually small; yet the last *appeared* of a remarkable bulk, for
> his hair was long and bushy—His features were not symmetrical
> (the mouth, perhaps, excepted), yet was the effect of the whole
> extremely powerful. They breathed an animation, a fire, an
> enthusiasm, a vivid and preternatural intelligence, that I never

met with in any other countenance—a softness, a delicacy, a gentleness.

Shelley, according to Hogg, was a misfit at Oxford, as in after days, in the ordinary usages of social life. He had no idea of time, was unpunctual and untidy, and passed his days oblivious of the chaos surrounding him. Absorbed in his scientific experiments, he did not notice the damage he was creating: the furniture stained by mineral acids, the holes in the carpets, the blackened floorboards.

His whole existence was dominated by the world of the imagination and by an absorption in chasing after intellectual truths. His early biographer, Edward Dowden, stresses this eternal questioning 'Whence? Whither? Wherefore?' and Shelley's engrossment in poetry and philosophy. He was always reading, pursuing knowledge, a book in his hand at meals, in bed, out walking. Food was a matter of little interest. He hated college gatherings and public feeding. He could subsist on bread alone, a loaf stuffed in his pocket and—as often as not—a circle of crumbs would be left on the floor where he had partaken of his latest meal. He liked vegetables and fruit and had a sweet tooth for sugar and honey. Thirst was quenched by cold water and plentiful cups of tea. In spite of a violent temper when roused he was, on the whole, sweet natured and particularly loving to children and animals. Hogg tells of his springing forward to the rescue of an overladen donkey, met on one of their walks. On another occasion, when they met with a cold and hungry little girl, Shelley insisted on buying milk for her, and kneeling down to feed her himself. He loathed cruelty and loathed injustice. 'In no individual, perhaps,' says Hogg, 'was the moral sense more completely developed than in Shelley.'

But now, in this March of 1811, both Shelley and Hogg were in trouble. At eight o'clock in the morning of 26 March they climbed to the top of a coach and left Oxford in disgrace for London. Their fathers had been informed of what had happened and both fathers were outraged. Whatever else was to ensue, they decided that the two young men must at once be separated. Lawyers were consulted and Mr Hogg's lawyer discovered that during their last weeks at Oxford Shelley and Hogg had distinguished themselves by mixing with nobody, dressing differently from everyone else, and never dining in College. Their chief trouble, it was deduced, was a youthful conceit and desire to impress on the rest of the world their unarguable superiority.

Mr Hogg decided, perhaps with wisdom, to accept the situation philosophically. His son would now have to study law without the benefit of a university education. Mr Shelley was not so easily consoled. Here were all his carefully laid plans for Bysshe's future—the brilliant Oxford career, the Member of Parliament son following in his father's footsteps, the county magnate—all, all gone hopelessly awry. He exchanged anguished letters with Mr Hogg and then rushed up to London to interview the miscreants himself. He would, he decided, make Bysshe apologize to the University and recant his atheistic views, and then return to Field Place to pursue his studies under chosen tutors. But he had counted without Bysshe's determination. There was a stormy interview, frantic argument, and Bysshe refused utterly to bow to his father's wishes. In despair at the situation Mr Shelley handed the situation over to his lawyer. The lawyer was William Whitton, a man not conspicuous for either sympathy or understanding. The stalemate was complete.

Shelley and Hogg had found lodgings at 15 Poland Street, a turning off Oxford Street. Here they were together for three weeks and at the end of that time Hogg left for York, to pursue his legal studies according to his father's wishes, and Shelley was left alone.

He was eighteen and a half and totally ignorant of life. Mr Shelley has been blamed for leaving him alone in London, to find his own lodging and to work out his own salvation, but Mr Shelley's position was not an easy one. The clash of temperaments between himself and his son, their totally opposed outlook on life, made compromise almost impossible. Shelley was lonely but he held doggedly to his independence. He did not fancy a political career and felt that it would only shackle his mind. The political state of the country did not inspire him: the mad King George III on the throne, a Prince Regent pursuing his own ends of indulgence and pleasure. Why, Shelley reasoned, could not his father give him a small allowance and allow him to pursue life in his own way? Instead, it seemed, there was no hope of financial help, even though he was heir to an immense estate. Feeling that he must make money somehow, he thought of becoming a surgeon like his cousin, John Grove. But, after attending a few lectures at St. Bartholomew's Hospital, this idea was abandoned. His uncle Pilfold at Cuckfield sent him a little money occasionally. But, financially, the situation was becoming increasingly desperate.

It was in this mood—compounded of a mixture of loneliness, bravado, humiliation, and longing for understanding—that Shelley again met Harriet Westbrook.

2

Shelley's sisters at the Clapham school had taken his part over the breach with their father. He visited them at every opportunity, his pockets bulging with cakes, and in return they did their best to help him financially by handing over some of their pocket-money. Here Harriet Westbrook was useful as a go-between. As her home was in London she was allowed more freedom and sometimes, on the way to her father's house, she would call at the lodgings in Poland Street to give the money to Shelley.

From this beginning, gradually and with increasing momentum, the Westbrook sisters became more and more friendly. They both wrote to Shelley, called on him, took him to church. When their father was away they invited him to dinner. Both girls, in spite of the difference in their ages, fell under the Shelley spell.

Shelley himself was nothing loath. He had been lonely in London since Hogg's departure and here was some very welcome company. He regaled all his experiences to Hogg at

great length. 'The youngest,' he wrote, 'is a most amiable girl,
the eldest is really conceited but very condescending.' We
cannot be altogether certain whether Eliza was herself inclined
to be attracted by Shelley or whether, from the first, she
looked upon him solely as a desirable match for her younger
sister. She certainly did not let the grass grow under her feet.
When Harriet was back at school she and Shelley visited her
together and all three walked on the common. Later, when
Harriet was ill at home, Shelley was sent for: 'My poor little
friend has been ill,' he told Hogg: 'her sister sent for me the
other night. I found her on a couch pale; her father is civil to
me, very strangely, the sister is too civil by half—she began
talking about *l'amour*; I philosophized, and the youngest said
she had such an headache that she could not bear conversation.
Her sister then went away, and I staid till half past twelve. Her
father had a large party below, he invited me—I refused.'

Harriet was gentle, kind, clinging. Shelley poured out to her
his troubles and his problems, dazzled and fascinated her with
stories of his family, of his family estates, of his life in Sussex.
Also he aired his views on atheism, hoping to rope her in as a
convert. The unfortunate and immediate effect of this friendship was an eruption at Harriet's school. The mistresses disapproved and the pupils were shocked. Shelley, to them, had
become a notorious character, peculiar for his atheistic views,
and disgraced by his expulsion from Oxford. It was unthinkable
that Harriet should become his disciple. They began to
persecute Harriet, to ostracize her, in an effort to bring her to
her senses. A mistress, in a frenzy of disapproval, on one
occasion seized a letter of Shelley's from Harriet's hands and
tore it to pieces. There were threats of expulsion. Only Hellen
Shelley remained friendly and loyal.

Not surprisingly, Harriet became more and more unhappy.
She had never liked the school very much and now she hated it.
Wild thoughts went through her head as she searched for a
means of escape. Marriage with Shelley? Suicide? She had
always been attracted by the idea of suicide. All her life she
kept the notion there, intact, at the back of her mind: a means
of escape, a way out.

Shelley, too, by now, was concerned at the way things were going. When Harriet went back to school he wrote to Hogg of her returning to her 'prison house'. But he disapproved of marriage and, in spite of this growing intimacy, he did not really want to marry Harriet. With no money his own life anyhow was difficult enough. He missed Hogg and longed to join him in York. He longed too to come to some understanding with his father. £200 a year, he decided, would satisfy him. Hogg thought it should be more but Shelley was adamant that £200 would be enough. In May, trying to enlist his uncle Pilfold's support, he left London for Field Place.

The visit was not altogether a success. Although the meeting with his father bore fruit and, aided by the intervention of his uncle and the Duke of Norfolk, the £200 a year was promised, Shelley soon found that he was restless away from the Westbrooks. He made short expeditions to London by stage-coach whenever the opportunity arose and, in the intervals, correspondence with them, kept up at a feverish pace, was his only sustaining interest. Eliza, afraid that his family might discover their intimacy and put a spoke in the wheel, wrote cryptically of keeping their friendship secret. At Field Place Shelley's mother, keeping the conversation determinedly on the level of trivialities, talked mainly about the weather, and about field sports.

Shelley, searching for drama, began to concoct in his head a fantastic scheme for his friend Hogg and his sister Elizabeth to meet, to fall in love, and to marry. Many letters were exchanged with Hogg on the subject and Hogg became quite enthusiastic. As, however, he was not likely to be welcomed by Mr Shelley, a secret visit was planned. Hogg was to be hidden in a room upstairs. 'You must sleep upon a mattress,' Shelley wrote, 'you must only walk with me at midnight.' By secreting himself in this way, Hogg might have the opportunity of watching Elizabeth from a window. But in the end these strange proposals were considered to be rather unreasonable and they had to be modified. It now seems certain that Hogg *did* come on a visit, when Shelley's father was away, and with Mrs Shelley's connivance. Possibly he never came to Field Place but stayed in Horsham. At all events he caught one short glimpse of the adored one, Elizabeth, by peering at her through the window of Warnham Church during a service—and with that he had to be content.

With Hogg unavailable and nobody congenial to talk to at Field Place, Shelley went to Cuckfield to stay with his uncle Pilfold. Here a momentous meeting awaited him. He became acquainted with a Miss Elizabeth Hitchener, a neighbouring school-teacher, who included two of Captain Pilfold's small daughters among the pupils at her school.

Miss Hitchener was a young woman of twenty-nine, tall, dark and spare, with black eyes and hair, and looking younger than her years. Shelley was delighted with her. He was interested in women of all ages, particularly if they showed any signs of intelligence. Miss Hitchener's family was humble, her father once a smuggler was now an innkeeper, but she was determined to raise herself. Her mind was above the ordinary, intellectual and inquiring. It seemed that she held liberal opinions which coincided with Shelley's own. Here was someone, he felt, who might collaborate with him in succouring oppressed humanity, in putting the world to rights. She had long discussions with him about all the subjects which most interested him: religion, philosophy, philanthropy. She sharpened his intellect, drew sparks from him. Some people in the neighbourhood thought her eccentric and conceited but Shelley did not agree. He magnified her intellectual powers out of all resemblance to the reality. 'I perceive in you,' he told her, 'the embryon of a mighty intellect which may one day enlighten thousands.' But this absurd conception of her was on a par with his aspirations to reform the world single-handed— conceptions which had their birth in fantasy.

For Shelley was still determined to pin down a policy of human betterment by his own reasoning. It all seemed so possible if only he could find the formula. A nobility of aspiration was there but a nobility marred by arrogance. He was only to grow gradually in the humility, wisdom and tolerance which were so much more apparent in the last few years of his life. It was a long apprenticeship and there were terrible lessons ahead.

On returning to Field Place Shelley did not forget Miss Hitchener but sent her books to feed her mind, and another hectic correspondence was started.

His future was still undecided and he was torn between his loyalties to Hogg and to Harriet. His own inclination would have been to join Hogg in York but he was warned that if he did this he would forfeit his allowance. So instead he went to Wales, to stay with his cousins, the Thomas Groves, on their estate Cwm Elan, hoping perhaps in this way to see the Westbrooks who might be coming to their country house at Aberystwyth.

By now he was, so he told Miss Hitchener, in a state of nervous illness. There may have been scenes with Harriet before he left for Wales. It is certain that the correspondence between them while he was away grew more and more intense. Unfortunately the letters are not now in existence but they wrote to each other almost daily and everything that happened, all the vicissitudes of his own feeling, the vicissitudes of Harriet's feeling, were duly reported in detail by Shelley to Hogg. 'If I know anything about *Love* I am *not* in love.' In view of what happened afterwards it is a strange and revealing confession. But Shelley was gradually being stampeded into a situation which he did not really want but which was largely the result of the ambivalence in his own nature: his theoretical belief in 'freedom' and sexual licence at war with his fundamental chivalry and fair-mindedness. He did not 'believe' in the ties of marriage but Harriet and Hogg between them were converting him. Harriet sent him a novel, *Adeline Mowbray* by Mrs Opie, which made plain the appalling disadvantages of a 'free union' from the point of view of the woman. Hogg, with his legal mind, pointed out the legal snags. Shelley, genuinely attracted by Harriet, was in a ferment of irresolution and restlessness. He disliked Cwm Elan anyway—'This place is a very great bore'—had little in common with his cousins, and for once was oblivious to the charms of nature. It was perhaps with a feeling of relief that, on receipt of a despairing letter of summons from Harriet, he rushed back to London.

Harriet had threatened to commit suicide. Her father, she said, was trying to force her to return to school and she felt desperate. Shelley's advice to resist, and the letter he had himself written in remonstrance to Mr Westbrook, had been abortive. It was all highly dramatic and Shelley thrived on drama. He wrote excitedly to Hogg: 'She has thrown herself upon *my* protection.' Harriet did not appear to him as an unhappy schoolgirl, at loggerheads with life. Instead, she was a dream maiden of the fairy-tales, persecuted and oppressed, pining for release. He felt chivalrous, responsible, a knight errant.

It is true, however, that hideous doubts reared themselves at times. What was he doing—rushing into marriage? He wrote a strange letter to Charles Grove, pointing out that having irrevocably lost Charles's sister, Harriet, he was now in the mood for self-sacrifice. In this mood he had obeyed Harriet Westbrook's summons. Knowing it to be a perilous decision he adapted the words of Macbeth:

> Hear it not, Percy; for it is a knell
> That summons thee to heaven or to hell.

He proposed immediate marriage. But now Harriet too had doubts. Shelley was only nineteen and she herself was only sixteen. Her temperament was not a self-confident one and she probably doubted her own capabilities as a wife. Perhaps, too, she realized that her own upbringing, sheltered, conventional, middle-class, ill-fitted her to be the helpmeet of such an unpredictable being as Shelley. 'My unfortunate friend Harriet,' Shelley wrote to Hogg, 'is yet undecided—not with respect to me but herself.' The attitude of Shelley's family was another depressing factor for Harriet to take into account. They disapproved. Harriet Grove would have been ideally suitable— but Harriet Westbrook? Mr Westbrook was certainly very wealthy but he was in trade. He owned taverns. Most of his money had been made by selling drink. The Shelley family ignored the friendship, hoping nothing would come of it. The Westbrooks, on the other hand, gave Harriet every encouragement, for to them Shelley seemed ideally suitable. Was

he not a baronet's grandson, heir to a £300,000 estate!
Eliza had no intention of letting Shelley slip through her
fingers. (In years to come Shelley was to accuse her of engineer-
ing the marriage.) Harriet, genuinely in love with Shelley, and
realizing that the alternative to a wedding was a return to the
hated Clapham school, gave her agreement to the marriage.

The decision once made, events moved swiftly. Perhaps
because of the known hostility of the Shelley family the couple
decided to elope. Shelley had breakfast one August morning
with Charles Grove at the Mount Street Coffee House, just
round the corner from Harriet's home. Here, before long,
Harriet joined them. They hired a coach and all three moved to
a tavern in the City of London where they waited all day for the
7 p.m. evening coach to Edinburgh. Then there were fare-
wells to Charles Grove, and Harriet and Shelley set out on their
journey.

The journey in those days was a long one. They were three
nights and two days on the road. Shelley, before leaving, had
borrowed £10 from Hogg and £25 from Thomas Medwin's
father, the Horsham lawyer. It was not very much and already
the financial situation was beginning to worry him. He seized
spare moments on the journey to write letters. There were two
to his father, not daring to mention his forthcoming marriage,
but hinting that the £50 due on his allowance would be very
acceptable. There was also a note to Hogg, asking if he could
manage another £10 loan. The most expansive letter was
written later, in October, to his friend, Miss Hitchener. It was
a difficult letter to write because in some way Shelley had to
excuse himself for acting so suddenly and surprisingly against
his previously held convictions. He could only do this by
disloyally putting most of the onus for the marriage on
Harriet. 'Blame me if thou wilt, dearest friend,' he plunged
desperately, 'for *still* thou art dearest to me.' Perhaps he
hoped, by this ambivalence and absurd flattery, to get Miss
Hitchener to take a charitable view of what had happened.

Meanwhile Harriet was excited and happy. Her mind once
made up, she had no regrets. On their arrival in Edinburgh she
and Shelley at once interviewed the minister. They found

lodgings in a pleasant house at number 16 George Street. Some evidence had to be falsified over their previous residence in order to get the necessary licence. This done, the marriage took place in Edinburgh the next day, 29 August 1811, Shelley describing himself as a 'farmer' of the county of Sussex.

3

By now there was alarm and consternation at Field Place. Mr Shelley and his lawyer, William Whitton, hurried up to London for lengthy interviews with Mr Westbrook, his solicitor, and Eliza. As the marriage was now a *fait accompli* there was little that Mr Shelley could do about it. He could not even disinherit his errant son—the estates were entailed. He decided, however, that he would give no financial help of any kind and the £200 a year allowance was stopped. Shelley's letters, written with the hopes that the latest quarter's instalment would soon catch up with him, fell on deaf ears.

It was an unfortunate beginning to the honeymoon. However, for the time being Shelley got over the difficulties by persuading the landlord of the George Street lodgings to give them credit until a 'remittance' arrived. This the man agreed to do but only on condition that Shelley treated him and his friends to a celebration supper. Further familiarities that the man suggested, such as washing the bride in whisky, Shelley indignantly repulsed. The only hope for further financial supplies seemed to lie in the direction of Cuckfield. Luckily Captain Pilfold did not often see eye to eye with his wealthy brother-in-law at Field Place. He ruled that it was 'too bad' that the allowance should have been stopped and did his best to remedy the situation. Friendly letters arrived at intervals with welcome donations of money.

Shelley and Harriet, their anxieties temporarily allayed, were now perfectly happy, and happier still when Hogg, due for a vacation, decided to join them in Edinburgh. Shelley

D

already had a fatal propensity for liking a third party attached
to his married life, an idiosyncrasy which he repeated to the
end. He welcomed Hogg as a boon companion, and an intellectual stimulant, and insisted that he should be given a
room in the same house as himself and Harriet. 'We have met
at last once more!' he exclaimed excitedly, 'and we will never
part again!'

Hogg, for his part, was immediately and forcibly bowled
over by the charms of Harriet. It was the first time he had seen
her: the 'lovely young bride, bright as the morning . . . radiant
with youth, health and beauty'. 'She was always pretty,' he
wrote of her, 'always bright, always blooming, smart, usually
plain in her neatness, without a spot, without a wrinkle,
not a hair out of its place.' He was always to have a curious
attitude towards Shelley's women: a desire, because Shelley
was the man he most admired, to share in everything he
possessed, even the women he loved. After Harriet it was to be
Mary, and later still Jane Williams. Shelley, lofty in his
thinking, believed in a mutual ownership of life's benefits.
Also, theoretically, he believed in free love. But the possibility
that Hogg might take advantage of these views and attempt a
mutual ownership of Harriet apparently never occurred to him.

The three now embarked on several weeks of enjoyment.
There was a great deal of talk and a great deal of sight-seeing.
They walked for miles, inspecting the sights of Edinburgh,
arguing and laughing, and returning to their lodgings, exhausted, to consume quantities of tea. Studying too was not
neglected. In an effort to live up to her brilliant young husband
and to turn herself into an intellectual, Harriet was translating
a noted French novel. She also read aloud for the benefit of the
two young men: the works were moralistic, chosen by Shelley,
but he soon became bored and slept. Hogg was more appre-
ciative, drinking in every word with a certain amount of
cynicism, but entranced by the reader. In this way the days
passed, anxieties were kept at bay, but the financial bogy in
the background was still unscotched.

Shelley could not believe that his father would not relent.
He wrote him one appealing letter after another, couched in the

most tactless terms, letters which were handed over unanswered, often even unopened, to the rigid and unsympathetic William Whitton. Even Mr Westbrook, it seemed, had hardened his heart. He had approved of the match but had been annoyed by the speed and secrecy with which it had been carried out: besides which, he felt that the responsibility of providing the income should rightly devolve on the bridegroom—or his family.

There was nothing for it but to leave Edinburgh—which, anyhow, due mainly to Shelley's inherent restlessness, was already losing its charm. A few weeks had been enough to convince him of the sordid 'commercialism' of the city, underneath its surface attraction. Probably, if only subconsciously, he was also realizing the wisdom of moving nearer to home and family before a financial crisis arose.

It was decided to move to York with Hogg whose vacation was now over. Accordingly the three set out on the journey south—travelling, for Harriet's comfort and in spite of their impecunious state, by the slow and more expensive method of post-chaise, with frequent stops for nights on the road. Shelley found the journey trying. He was fretted by the incessant bother of changing horses and by the narrow confines of the chaise: also by Harriet's remorseless reading aloud, which went on inexorably, hour after hour. 'Is it necessary,' Shelley begged, 'to read all that, Harriet, dear?' At Berwick, when the chaise was due to start, Shelley had vanished. Hogg found him eventually, by the sea wall, gazing out on a dreary sea 'with looks not less wild and dreary', and he was at length persuaded to resume the journey. York, disappointingly, failed to impress. They were unlucky in their lodgings which were dingy and unattractive. Before long Shelley, having failed by correspondence both with his father and grandfather to get any promise of financial help, decided that he must leave for Sussex immediately to make a personal appeal.

On Shelley's departure Hogg and Harriet were left alone together in the gloomy York lodging house. Hogg, emotionally overwrought by abortive efforts to make love to Harriet, now seized on this unlooked for opportunity to renew his efforts.

He was, so he persuaded himself, only proving himself true to
Shelley's theories. But Harriet felt otherwise and was shocked
and upset. She kept Hogg at arm's length, reading aloud
determinedly whenever danger threatened, or leading the
conversation round to talk of the absent Shelley, thus making it
abundantly clear that she held rigidly to her marriage vows.
Before long, too, she received a letter of friendly warning and
advice on the situation from Hogg's mother. The Hoggs were
in a state of dismay, discovering that the incalculable Shelley
had left his young bride alone with their son in York. They
knew nothing of Harriet, what sort of a girl she might be, and
perhaps they were doubtful of their son's strength under
temptation. But their concern was needless. Harriet was only
sixteen but her letter in reply was dignified and polite. She
felt confident of dealing with the situation herself and was not
in need of support. All the same she wrote to her sister Eliza,
who was soon to come on a visit, and suggested that she should
arrive as soon as possible.

Already Harriet was savouring the difficulties of her married
life. She loved Shelley wholeheartedly but temperamentally she
was no match for his unpredictable genius. Like Harriet
Grove, she was by nature conservative, conformist, conventional. Shelley had again made the same fatal mistake of trying
to harness a loyal, loving, but essentially ordinary human being
to his fiery bohemian chariot. But then he had never loved
either of the Harriets for themselves. He had looked upon them
solely as promising material to be moulded by himself into the
ideal woman of his dreams. Months later he was to write to the
second Harriet: 'Our connection was not one of passion and
impulse—It is no reproach to me that you have never filled
my heart with an all-sufficing passion; perhaps you are even
yourself a stranger to these impulses—' These are revealing
words, revealing their mutual non-compatability and their mutual
tragedy. In poor Harriet's case the tragedy was to prove lethal.

In advance of the appointed time, and much to Hogg's disgust, Eliza duly arrived at York. Soon afterwards Shelley
himself reappeared. His visit to his family in Sussex had met
with no success. All his pleas for financial help had been

referred to William Whitton who refused even to see him. Added to this, his mother now was unfriendly, frightened by his excitable manner, the violence of his requests, and his absurd accusations of immorality against her. According to Mr Shelley, his wife and daughter Elizabeth were now so nervous of the unpredictable Bysshe that they ran upstairs for safety even if they heard a dog bark. If his son remained in Sussex, Mr Shelley informed Whitton that he would have to enlist the protection of special constables. Only uncle Pilfold of Cuckfield still showed some friendliness and invited Miss Hitchener to dinner to meet his nephew. It was a slight balm to Shelley's frustration and despair when Miss Hitchener, at any rate, showed some sympathy over his marriage.

But now, back at York, Shelley was faced with a new and unexpected problem—the problem of Hogg. Harriet, who up to this time had kept Hogg's unwelcome attentions a secret, now told Shelley everything that had happened in his absence. Shelley was very angry and, in spite of his much vaunted theories, felt that his friend had been 'treacherous'. He tackled Hogg and found to his dismay that Hogg seemed to be genuinely and deeply in love. They went for a walk together in the fields round York, thrashing the matter out. Hogg begged for forgiveness and Shelley forgave him.

The next days were painful. Shelley relieved his feelings by recounting the whole story to Miss Hitchener, the 'sister of his soul', in one agonized letter after another. He realized that the delightful *ménage à trois*—himself, Hogg and Harriet—which had been such a comfort to him, providing as it did both love and intellectual sustenance, was irretrievably ruined. There was nothing for it but to separate. He and Harriet would have to go one way, Hogg another. His disillusionment was profound. Hogg, who had been abject to begin with, later became more intransigent. He even suggested a duel. Shelley, shocked and distraught, pointed out that his own life was valuable to him, neither did he wish to take Hogg's. He, Eliza and Harriet decided to leave York at short notice. Without even saying a definite farewell to Hogg, they packed their things, and travelled north to the Lake District.

4

It was the beginning of a restless life of wandering which was to last for many months. The Lake District, at this juncture, appealed to them for more than one reason: the Lake Poets had settled there, among them Southey whom Shelley much admired: and the Duke of Norfolk, whom Shelley felt to be the only friend who might successfully intercede with his father, owned an estate in Cumberland.

The three went first to lodgings and then managed to rent part of a little rose-covered house, Chestnut Cottage, at Keswick. They were without Hogg but now instead of Hogg there was Eliza, whose visit seemed likely to become a permanency. At first Shelley appeared satisfied with this arrangement. He admired Eliza and Eliza admired him. Her allowance from her father was useful and that, together with occasional gifts of money from uncle Pilfold, at that time provided their only income. Eliza was of a managing disposition and held the purse strings; she kept the money in an old stocking and doled it out, together with admonitions and advice. Harriet accepted these ministrations with meekness and gratitude. To her Eliza was beautiful and all that could be desired. 'Words can never sufficiently express her goodness and kindness to me,' she was to write later; 'she is my more than mother.' Hogg, however, had not been favourably impressed. According to his description Eliza's face—admittedly 'lovely'—was deathly white and marked with the scars of smallpox: he likened it unflatteringly to 'a mass of boiled rice, boiled in dirty water'. Her eyes were 'dark, but dull, and without meaning; the hair was black and glossy, but coarse— The fine figure was meagre, prim, and constrained.' Possibly, however, Hogg was prejudiced. He would not easily forget that it was Eliza who had backed up Harriet in the rejection of his advances.

The Lake District at first seemed to be all that was desirable.

Hogg was soon put out of the forefront of Shelley's mind and, though a fevered correspondence continued, the friendship cooled. Miss Hitchener had completely taken Hogg's place as confidante in chief. Shelley described to her at length their happy life in Keswick: the writing, studying, long walks. If only Miss Hitchener could be persuaded to join them! 'Your letters,' he wrote to her, 'are like angels sent from heaven on missions of peace.' Their correspondence was, according to him, 'the day-dawn' of his existence. But, in spite of messages from Harriet, backing up Shelley's invitations, Miss Hitchener was still chary of committing herself too whole-heartedly to this new and fascinating friendship. Her visit was still postponed to the future.

Meanwhile Shelley had written to the Duke of Norfolk to tell him of the difficulties with his father and the Duke, good-natured if rough, had called at Field Place to confer with Mr Shelley 'on the unhappy difference with his son'. The Duke also sent a most cordial invitation to Shelley, his wife and sister-in-law, to stay with him at his country home, Greystoke, in Cumberland.

This was an event, a feather in Shelley's cap, likely to impress Mr Shelley. Mr Westbrook, too, was more amiably disposed and sent a small sum of money which covered the expenses of the visit. Shelley hired a carriage for the fourteen-mile journey and the visit, which was originally to be for four days, was so successful as to be prolonged for over a week. There were other guests present, among them a Mr and Mrs Calvert, who were to prove staunch and afterwards intimate friends. Shelley, who enjoyed good conversation, and who was feeling the loss of Hogg's stimulating mind, shone in this congenial company. Eliza, too, fitted in well, the Duke professing himself 'quite charmed' by her presence. The upshot of the Duke's kindness, and his efforts on the Shelleys' behalf, was a promise from Mr Shelley of £200 a year allowance, and a similar promise of £200 from Mr Westbrook. Otherwise a complete reconciliation between Shelley and his father was still abortive. The Duke advised a letter of apology but Shelley's apology could only be qualified: he was adamant that he could not relinquish his opinions, either religious or political.

However, the fortunes of the young Shelleys were looking up. They now had £400 a year of their own, in addition to Eliza's allowance. It was comparative wealth. Shelley, generous by nature, felt liberal and unconstrained. At Greystoke he had been so much in his element that he had even overlooked writing the usual long screeds to his friend, Miss Hitchener. He came back to find that her letters to him had been mounting up in his absence. Already three of them had accumulated, long turgid epistles, a mixture of flattery and philosophy, written in sentences of formidable length, with full stops only a rarity. To Shelley these letters were precious and valued beyond measure. He set out at once to answer them in outpourings of impassioned eulogy. To him, Miss Hitchener was no longer an obscure and somewhat eccentric country schoolmistress. Instead she was 'the friend of his bosom', a sexless being certainly, but a paragon of sympathetic understanding, with an intellect towering above his own. He assured her of his undying devotion and ended his letters extravagantly: 'Adieu, my dearest friend; continue to believe that when I am insensible to your excellencies I shall cease to exist, Yours most sincerely inviolably eternally, Percy S.'; 'I bid adieu today to what is to me inexpressibly dear, your society, Ever ever yours unalterably, Percy S.'

It was soon after the return from Greystoke that, at the Calverts' house, Shelley met for the first time his great hero, Robert Southey. Southey was now thirty-seven and life had sobered him. Loaded with the responsibility of making a living, not only for his own family but for the families of others, some of the quixotic ardour of his youth had faded. Circumspection and hard work had taken the place of trying to set the world to rights. Frequently he had Coleridge's children to keep, and Lovell's as well: there were endless drains on his pocket.

The essential nobility of a man, caught by such circumstances and doing his best to make a worth-while life for others more helpless, failed to impress Shelley. To Shelley Southey was 'corrupted by the world, contaminated by Custom; it rends my heart when I think what he might have been'. This idol, like so many of the idols of his early youth, was discovered to have feet of clay. He appreciated Southey's friendliness, his invitations to Greta Hall, the kindly efforts he made to get the rent of Chestnut Cottage reduced. But Southey could not be forgiven for the abandonment of his youthful dreams, for the loss of his reforming zeal, for his subjection into middle-aged conformity. The women of his household, too, were anathema to Shelley. Mrs Southey, Mrs Lovell and Mrs Coleridge, three sisters wrapped in domesticity, and empty of any form of intellectual life, struck him with horror. It was a warning to Harriet: never, never could he bear that a wife of his should follow their example.

There was nothing for it but to look for other idols. It was in his nature to hitch his waggon to a star and for a long time, and ever since he had read *Political Justice*, a luminous star in his firmament had been the philosopher, William Godwin. The book had opened out a new way of life for him, and presented him with a creed which he was determined to make his own. As he wrote afterwards: 'It materially influenced my character, and I rose from its perusal a wiser and a better man.' Now, discovering suddenly that Godwin, whom he thought to be dead, was still alive, he wrote to the ageing philosopher in terms of respect and adulation and the fatal correspondence—which later was to bring about such an aftermath of passion and tragedy—was embarked upon.

Although Shelley did not know it Godwin's days of personal glory had faded. The doctrine he had preached in *Political Justice* had been criticized by Hazlitt as 'raising the standard of morality above the reach of humanity'. Godwin himself had found it difficult to live up to his own exhortations. He made a meagre and seedy living now, running the publication of a Juvenile library, assisted by his second wife, the virago-ish Mrs Clairmont. Shelley's second letter: 'I am the son of a man of fortune in Sussex', impressed him with its promise of benefits to come. He wasted no time in writing back to his eager young disciple and counselled him most insistently not to quarrel with his prosperous father.

Shelley by now was getting restless. His first delight in the Lake District was giving way, after the usual formula of his

youth, to dislike. The intrusion of industry into the peace of
the countryside distressed him; Keswick, he decided, was
rapidly becoming 'like a London suburb'. Harriet, loyally
acquiescent to all Shelley's vagaries, backed him up in his new-
found passion to interest himself in Catholic Emancipation in
Ireland. Between them they decided that they must work for the
betterment of the human race in some form or other, and
Ireland held the most promising prospects. This philanthropic
drive had been inherent in Shelley's nature from an early age;
when quite young at school he had decided to 'dedicate himself
to noble purposes, to be neither oppressor nor oppressed'.*
The teachings of Godwin confirmed this idealistic dedication to
the defence of the helpless, the fight against tyranny. Unfortunately there was inexperience, obstinacy, and a complete
lack of realism behind his efforts. Wiser heads than his and
Harriet's counselled him against rashly undertaking crusades
which might be too difficult to carry out. Godwin, Southey,
the Calverts—all were against the Irish enterprise.

But Shelley was in a nervous, excitable state and not in a
mood to listen to middle-aged counsel. Fired by a genuine
anguish of zeal for the ill-treated Irish, he was suffering from
nervous headaches and dosing himself with laudanum. After a
careful study of Irish history he wrote an *Address to the
Irish People*, borrowed £50 towards the expenses of the journey
from his uncle, and made an effort to obtain a loan of
£100 from the Duke of Norfolk. The more people he could
enlist in his support the more certain he felt of success.
This was another opportune moment to write to the absent
Miss Hitchener, beseeching her to join them: 'How Harriet
and her sister long to see you, and how *I* long to see you *never*
to part with you again.' The long-suffering Harriet was prevailed upon to join in this entreaty: 'Why are we separated?'
she wrote; 'should we not be more useful all together?'
But Miss Hitchener still held back, preferring to hold fast to
her school and those things which were safe and familiar,
rather than risk adventure in the perilous unknown.

During that last month of January 1812, before the final

* Edward Dowden: *Life of Percy Bysshe Shelley*.

departure from Keswick, Shelley had one of his unpleasant adventures, an adventure which strangely was repeated months later in Wales. Somebody broke into the cottage, Shelley went to investigate, and was knocked insensible. This was the story, corroborated by Harriet. Whether it really happened was afterwards queried. Just as was to be the case at Tanyrallt in later months, Shelley was considered by many people to be suffering from hallucinations. The attack, they decided bluntly, had never happened at all: it was the figment of an overwrought brain.

But whatever happened, or did not happen, the effect was unnerving. Badly shocked, the Shelleys, accompanied by Eliza, left the cottage and the last week of their stay in Keswick was spent at the home of their friends, the Calverts.

On 2 February they set out for Ireland. The journey, in a winter month, was long, perilous and fatiguing. Their ship was battered by gales and blown towards northern Ireland. Finally, after many days of an exhausting battling with the elements, they reached Dublin and found lodgings in Sackville Street.

Once safely ensconced in the forefront of the crusade, weariness evaporated and enthusiasm and self-confidence returned. Shelley was adamant that the ascendancy of the Protestants over the Catholics must be stopped and he was determined to work for a repeal of the Union. Fifteen hundred copies of his *Address to the Irish People* were hurriedly printed at five pence a copy. He and Harriet then embarked on the business of distributing these copies, their methods unorthodox as well as orthodox. Harriet is said to have giggled with enjoyment as they threw the pamphlets out of windows to people passing by below. She was very young and it was partly a joke to her, and only partly a serious matter. Social injustice, however, genuinely shocked her and Shelley was still her hero. She supported him faithfully as his efforts grew more active and as his exhortations began to carry more weight with the sceptical Irish. He was invited to lecture to large audiences who were impressed by his family background, if rather non-plussed by his schoolboyish appearance. On the whole he was well received and cuttings from local newspapers reporting his

activities were proudly sent to both Mr Shelley and Mr
Westbrook.

But in spite of minor triumphs the result of the crusade
was disappointing. The Irish, impatient and inflammable, were
anxious for violence and Shelley counselled only gradual
measures of peace and patience. He was a philanthropist and
the Irish preferred a more hot-blooded leader. Yet, in spite of
his gentle methods, his doctrines were considered by many to
be pernicious. Godwin warned him that his activities might
lead to trouble and even bloodshed.

Shelley felt baffled. He did his best, trying by gifts of
money and food to help the oppressed people who visited him.
He made some friends, notably a Mrs Catherine Nugent, also
a rebel and a philanthropist, who sewed furs for a living, and
was later to become Harriet's beloved friend and confidante.
But the plan to form an Association of Philanthropists, who
were to work for a universal freedom, foundered before ever
coming to fruition. Gradually, with all these setbacks, enthusiasm for Ireland was fading. Shelley was still determined
in some way to achieve a higher level of living and to form if
possible a group of like-minded individuals who would fall in
with his liberal ideas. Finally it was decided that some other
centre for their activities must be found. Sussex was discarded
in favour of Wales.

In all this Shelley was the ringleader. Neither Eliza nor
Harriet was a match for Shelley in argument or in intellect.
They acquiesced, accepting that they could not meet him on his
own level, neither could they inspire him with their own ideas,
or persuade him in any way against the pursuit of his. Shelley
thought frequently with longing of Miss Hitchener who, as a
sparring partner in the battle of intellects, he found so much
more stimulating than either his wife or his sister-in-law.
'Resign your school and live with us for ever!' he wrote to her
pleadingly.

In April 1812 he, Harriet and Eliza left Ireland.

5

The voyage back to England was a rough and unpleasant one. So weakened did they feel on arrival that they had to fortify themselves with meat although, in Ireland, in furtherance of a greater humanity, they had become vegetarians.

After exploring Wales for a suitable house they found Nantgwillt, a beautiful and comfortable small estate with a farm of two hundred acres, only a mile or so from the Grove cousins. They were able to rent the house for £98 but a sum of £500 was wanted for furnishing and stock. It was, for both Shelley and Harriet, the home of their dreams. 'The beauty of this place,' Harriet wrote to Mrs Nugent, 'is not to be described.' They settled in hopefully with an Irish manservant and other servants. Having done this Shelley—with an optimism peculiar under past circumstances—wrote first to his father and then to Mr Medwin, the Horsham lawyer, for financial help which was immediately refused.

It was soon obvious that their small income would not cover this new and expensive mode of living. Debts mounted up. The lump sum for the stock was unobtainable. They could not obtain security for the rent. Eliza, holding the purse-strings, rebelled secretly over the unending uprootings and wanderings. Harriet, who had followed Shelley's changing enthusiasms with unswerving loyalty, must at times have compared the comfort and stability of her old life at home with the insecurity which had dogged her path since marriage. Whatever the cause of her fatigue, she was now exhausted. For three weeks she was ill with a feverish gastric attack. The nearest doctor was several miles away and she was so weak that she had to be helped to cross the room. Worries piling up, Shelley himself became ill with an inflammatory fever.

As was his habit when things went wrong Shelley pinned his hopes on a new relationship which he idealized beyond reason or common sense. Miss Hitchener! If only Miss Hitchener could be persuaded to join them all their problems might right themselves immediately. 'You are,' he wrote, 'to my fancy as a thunder-riven pinnacle of rock firm amid the rushing tempest and the boiling surge.' She wrote back to him in equally extravagant terms—but still she hesitated. Mrs Pilfold, who was consulted, showed disapproval. Scandal had been created in Cuckfield by hints which Miss Hitchener had herself let fall about this strange relationship. Gossip had even reached the ears of Mr Shelley at Field Place. Miss Hitchener wrote and told Shelley that she was depressed by all this talk and felt it wiser to postpone her visit. Shelley—ever quixotic —wrote remonstratingly to her father: 'You have agitated her mind until her frame is seriously deranged.' Giving full rein to his passion for letter writing he also discussed the situation with his uncle Pilfold. Uncle Pilfold agreed at once that scandalous rumours were going about. Shelley wrote back indignantly, feeling self-righteous and misunderstood, and denied most emphatically that there was any question of *love*.

The altercation was temporarily abated by a financial crisis. It was becoming obvious even to Shelley that, with no money available, he, Harriet and Eliza could no longer stay at Nant-gwillt. Perhaps for the sake of their health they should go to Italy? Passports were applied for and they moved for a fortnight to the home of Mr and Mrs Grove at Cwm Elan. Shelley had little in common with his cousins and there was tedium on both sides. Eventually they abandoned the idea of Italy and moved to an unsuitable small cottage in Chepstow. But their plans now had reverted to the idea of founding a colony of twin souls with liberal ideas and ideals and they wanted a home big enough to accommodate, not only themselves and Miss Hitchener, but Godwin and his family as well. The Chepstow cottage was nothing like big enough for this purpose. So, uprooting them-selves once more, they left for Devon, and descending the precipitous Countisbury Hill on horseback, they decided to try their luck at Lynmouth.

It was a happy choice. Here, in Lynmouth, was just the house they had been looking for: a thatched-roof cottage covered in roses, and containing innumerable small rooms let out in lodgings, in scenery that was peaceful and delightful. Shelley hoped that Godwin and his entire family, as well as Miss Hitchener, might be persuaded to join them immediately but Harriet was more circumspect. The rooms, she felt, were so small that some people might class them as suitable only for servants. She advised that, to begin with, they should invite only Mr Godwin, his step-daughter Fanny Imlay, and—of course—Miss Hitchener.

Miss Hitchener was the first to arrive. At last she had made up her mind and burnt her boats. For some time past she had been writing fulsome gushing letters to both Shelley and Harriet, and gradually the thought of joining them had been occupying her mind to the exclusion of all else. Shelley's apparent infatuation for her excited her emotionally. To him it was an intimacy only of the mind and intellect—to her it meant something more. It promised a glowing and flattering relationship, not to be lightly thrown away. She felt too that Shelley, coming from such a distinguished family, must be in wealthy circumstances, and she did not realize the financial risks she was running. So she sold up her school at Hurstpierpoint, severed her connections with the life of Cuckfield, and made her way to Lynmouth.

The two months that followed were comparatively happy. From the first, however, there were hints of disillusion to come. On the way to Devon Miss Hitchener, introduced by Shelley, had spent a night at Godwin's house in London and she did not hesitate to criticize her host. Godwin, so she told an outraged Shelley, 'admired himself too much'. She was confident, bossy, expecting of deference. Once, in a letter to Godwin, Shelley had described her as 'a woman of extraordinary talents' but now, somehow, her intellect did not seem so keen as in imagination he had pictured it. Harriet, too, was not altogether sure of her feeling for this new addition to their family life. 'Very dark in complexion, with a great quantity of black hair,' the description to her friend Mrs Nugent, in Dublin, is not exactly flattering, 'she is very busy writing for the good of mankind—She talks a great deal. She is taller than me or my sister, and as thin as it is possible to be.' Eliza, too, was not impressed.

Shelley busied himself in writing poetry and he started on his poem *Queen Mab*. A sonnet written to Harriet on her birthday was full of the love and tenderness which he still felt for her. Another of his activities was the writing of broadsheets, as liberal propaganda to advocate liberty of speech. He and Miss Hitchener—described by the fascinated spectators of Lynmouth as a 'tall foreign-looking female'—sent these broadsheets out to sea in bottles, or in boxes complete with mast and sail, hoping that they might eventually fall into sympathetic hands. All Shelley's activities at Lynmouth after a time became suspect. The Irish manservant, Dan, was arrested for posting up 'seditious' papers and committed to prison for six months. The town clerk of Barnstaple wrote to the Home Office who wrote back that, though there should as yet be no prosecution, Shelley must be *watched*. The atmosphere of their happy peaceful haven became poisoned by disapproval and suspicion. By the end of August 1812 all happiness was wrecked.

These unfortunate happenings, as seemed inevitable, necessitated yet another move. Shelley by now was convinced that his own arrest was imminent. When Godwin at last arrived at Lynmouth on his longed-for visit, it was only to find that the Shelleys had packed up their belongings and departed abruptly. The landlady, so he was told, had 'loved' them. But Godwin's journey had been a tedious and hazardous one and this recommendation could not have been of great consolation.

Perhaps still with the vague hope of Nantgwillt at the back of their minds, the Shelleys had returned to Wales. Another scheme for rendering public service provided an attraction for Shelley. At Tremadoc in Caernarvonshire work on an embankment for reclaiming drowned lands had lately started. Helpers and money were desperately needed. Shelley almost immediately subscribed the sum of £100 which he could ill afford. A house, Tanyrallt, with large spacious rooms, was available to rent. All would have been well if only their domestic circumstances had had some prospect of functioning smoothly. By now, however, it was quite obvious that they had made a terrible mistake in asking Miss Hitchener to give up her life in Sussex and to come and join them. Miss Hitchener was becoming more and more difficult and impossible to live with.

It was indeed a dismal story. Poor Miss Hitchener's chief fault lay in the fact that she had failed miserably to live up to the quite impossibly idealistic role which the doting Shelley had laid down for her. Instead of proving to be 'a pinnacle of rock amid the rushing tempest and the boiling surge', she was turning out to be merely a rather tiresome and frail human being, now re-christened the 'Brown Demon'. She was, so Harriet was convinced, secretly in love with Shelley and awaiting her chance to try to alienate his affections. Eliza did not like her and resented another managing woman in the same household. 'What,' Shelley asked of Hogg, 'would Hell be, were such a woman in Heaven?'

The dilemma was all part of his disastrous habit of building up the most ordinary people into gods—only to find afterwards that, like so many members of the human race, they had feet of clay. With him the subsequent disillusionment was usually exaggerated. It could indeed verge painfully on the venomous. Miss Hitchener was now described as 'an artful, superficial, ugly, hermaphroditical beast of a woman'. She was causing rifts in the household, the other two women conspiring against her. At all costs she must be got rid of.

It is unlikely of course that Miss Hitchener was so black as she was painted. She too, if the truth be told, had had her share of disillusionment. She had imagined Shelley to be in a prosperous position, had imagined—judging by his letters—that he felt a real and lasting attachment for her. Instead there was nothing but poverty, endless wanderings, bickerings, a feeling of neglect. In Wales Shelley, busy with other things, became more and more indifferent to her. She began to realize that she was not wanted. She was faced with the break-up of her old life, of her teaching career, all to no purpose. Her health had suffered. She felt indeed—and with reason—that she had been treated abominably.

It did not reflect well on Shelley but by now he was so engrossed with the fortunes of the Tremadoc embankment that

E

he did not give much heed to self-criticism. He and the women of his household paid a visit to London, chiefly to interest influential people in the Tremadoc scheme and to collect contributions, but also in order to part, as tactfully as possible, with the unfortunate Miss Hitchener.

Shelley told Hogg that he had to promise Miss Hitchener £100 a year, in order to get rid of her. (Though oddly, as Edmund Blunden tells us in his enlightening Shelley biography, it was *she* who claimed £100 for repayment of a loan from Shelley's estate on his death!)* Hogg himself was present on the last day before the final parting which took place from a hotel in St James's Street. The coach was not coming until the evening. Harriet had a headache and Shelley was busy elsewhere. Hogg was asked to take Eliza and Miss Hitchener for a walk in the park. 'With the Brown Demon on my right arm and the Black Diamond on my left,' Hogg wrote, 'we walked—for a long time, a very long time.' After dinner the coach arrived and Miss Hitchener bade these strange people, who had so disappointed her, a dignified farewell.

Immediately on her departure they all felt better, the weight of four months incompatability was lifted, and their spirits revived. Harriet gave vent to her relief in a letter to Mrs Nugent:

> The lady I have often mentioned to you, of the name of Hitchener, has to our very great happiness left us. We were entirely deceived in her character—We were not long in finding out our great disappointment in her. As to any noble dis-interested views, it is utterly impossible for a selfish character to feel them. She built all her hopes on being able to separate me from my dearly beloved Percy, and had the artfulness to say that Percy was really in love with her, and [it] was only his being married that could keep her within bounds now. Percy had seen her twice before his marriage. He thought her sensible but nothing more—And now, thank God, she has left us never more to return.

It had all been the most ghastly mistake. Shelley was appalled now by his own 'fatuity, inconsistency and bad taste'.

* Edmund Blunden: *Shelley.*

He relieved his feelings by abusing the lady but did at last admit in confidence to Hogg that she was 'embarrassed and poor' and that he, Harriet and Eliza were 'in some degree the cause'. The £100 a year he had offered her was a sop to his conscience.

Miss Hitchener for her part returned disconsolately to Sussex. There, as was perhaps not surprising, she found that her teaching career had been blighted by gossip and that she could no longer get pupils. It was too much effort to try to build up her tarnished reputation, so instead she took a job on the continent as a governess, and later met and married an Austrian officer. The marriage unfortunately was not a success and the couple soon parted. Miss Hitchener then decided to revert to her maiden name and to make another effort to establish herself as a teacher. Helped by her sisters, she started a girls' school at Edmonton, and made a success of it. The pupils loved her and a former pupil wrote of her afterwards: 'I consider her to have been a high-principled, clever woman, with a remarkable capacity for teaching.' It is pleasant to record that time mellowed the bitter memories of Shelley's defection. Instead there grew up a pride and a glow of satisfaction at having been connected so intimately with a being so unusual, who had showed such genius in poetry, and died so young. Instead of hatred there came a renewal of tenderness and affection. She kept all Shelley's letters which later were published. In 1907 these letters were presented to the British Museum.

6

In London Shelley was making new friends. Through the publisher Hookham he met Thomas Love Peacock—tall, attractive, witty, and a classical scholar—then aged twenty-seven. He was a match for Shelley in intellect and from the first he admired Harriet. He was, indeed, later to become one of her most ardent defenders. Harriet herself was delighted with him. She was expecting a baby now and, with Miss Hitchener out of the way, she basked in all Shelley's new friendships, approving of all he did. Even Godwin, met at last in the flesh, at first took on for her the same aura of magnificence with which Shelley so determinedly invested him. They visited frequently at Godwin's house and met various members of the family. Fanny Godwin, the pathetic and humble daughter of Mary Wollstonecraft and Imlay, was a favourite with them. 'She is 19 years of age,' Harriet wrote to Mrs Nugent, 'very plain, but very sensible. The beauty of her mind fully overbalances the plainness of her countenance.' And on one occasion, to be described later, they met Mary who had been ill, and who was for many months at this time recuperating in Scotland.

Hogg, they heard, was in London, a student now in Middle Temple, and Shelley sought him out. Hogg describes it: 'I was sitting in my quiet lodgings with my tea and a book before me: it was one evening—probably about ten o'clock. I was roused by a violent knocking at the street door, as if the watch-man was giving the alarm of fire; someone ran furiously up-stairs, the door flew open, and Bysshe rushed into the middle of the room.' The past was forgiven. Shelley could not bear malice indefinitely. He invited Hogg to dinner at the hotel to meet Harriet and Eliza. Cordiality reigned again but, all the same, something this time was missing. Hogg could be received as a valued friend but no longer, for Shelley, as the intimate and confidant of his youth. None of his inmost feelings were revealed to Hogg. Godwin, the idol of the moment, was not even mentioned.

In truth Shelley, in spite of friendships old and new, was considerably preoccupied. He had come to London chiefly to raise funds for the Tremadoc scheme and his efforts were not meeting with much success. Nobody either in London or in Sussex seemed particularly concerned or particularly anxious to part with any money. 'In Sussex I meet with no encourage-ment,' Shelley wrote to a friend in Wales, 'they are a parcel of cold selfish and calculating animals who seem to have no other aim or business on Earth but to eat drink and sleep.' He himself was determined to hold fast to the cause 'which', he explained,

'I will desert *but with my life*'. He relented sufficiently towards his mother to write her a note at this time, sending his love to all the family, offering to do any errands for them in town, and justifying the 'deception' he had inflicted on them over his marriage by saying that he was now one of the happiest of men. Only one thing could make him happier: an ending to the estrangement between them.

Before long it was decided by Shelley that he, Harriet and Eliza must all return to Wales immediately. Godwin, who had been invited to dinner, was again unlucky: he arrived to find his hosts had flown, in too much of a hurry even to say good-bye.

A hard winter was ahead of the workers in Wales and the scheme for reclaiming the sea-sodden lands became more and more frustrating. Shelley became maddened by other peoples' eagerness not being equal to his own. Why, he wondered some-times, had he embarked on the scheme at all? Instead of giving up his time to the poetry he loved, here he was spending long exhausting hours in office work, visiting the exploited and ill-paid workers, taking them food, clothes and fuel, championing their cause against rapacious employers, deserting his home, deserting Harriet, wrestling with difficulties. 'I have been teazed to death for the last fortnight,' he wrote in February 1813 to Hogg, but added, 'When I come home to Harriet I am the happiest of the happy.'

There was evidently nothing yet wrong with his home life, no cloud on the horizon. Harriet still espoused his every cause, giving him unfailing support. In the evenings at home she sang to him, chiefly old-fashioned melodies such as 'Robin Adair'. She worked at Latin in order to please him. She was relieved to see that in health he was better than he had been in London; away from all the noise and bustle of city life his nerves were more rested, his temper more equable. Godwin, at further remove, no longer seemed quite the paragon of all the virtues which he had at first appeared. He expected, Harriet felt, too much deference. Possibly, too, his interest in Shelley's financial prospects had not escaped her notice. Fanny, who was modest and unassuming, was more popular. She wrote to Shelley, who

had taken her fancy, and Shelley wrote back, letters that were
teasing and playful. But he was annoyed when Fanny described
Harriet as 'a fine lady'. He wrote back that Harriet's greatest
charms were her simplicity, ease and naturalness—all the
virtues that were completely incompatible with any form of
worldliness.

To please Godwin, Shelley was reading history. He found it
depressing—'that record of crimes and miseries'. Besides history
he studied philosophy, metaphysics, religions. Christ, he
admired as an important religious teacher but Christianity
as such was still to him only a 'bribe' to good conduct, and he
despised it as a false prop which should be unnecessary. His
opinions had not changed since the Oxford days of clashes
with his father. Governments, too, came under his lash. By
nature he was a rebel. He abhorred the *status quo* and always
championed the 'under dog'. It was only gradually that
he was acquiring the wisdom and insight necessary to increase
the poetic powers which were his real driving force. In all spare
moments he worked at his long poem *Queen Mab*: the poem
which he described to Miss Hitchener as 'a picture of the
manners, simplicity and delights of a perfect state of society;
tho' still earthly'.

The Tremadoc adventure had to come to an end somehow
and the event which brought about the Shelleys' departure from
Tanyrallt in February 1813 was a weird and mystifying one.
Even now there is no exact and unarguable explanation of what
really happened. Shelley himself wrote an incoherent note to
Thomas Hookham, the publisher, the day after the event:
'I have just escaped an atrocious assassination.—Oh send the
£20 if you have it—you will perhaps hear of me no more.'
The most graphic description of this extraordinary night's
events is to be found in a letter written by Harriet to Hookham
two weeks later:

> Mr S. promised you a recital of the horrible events that caused
> us to leave Wales. I have undertaken the task, as I wish to
> spare him, in the present nervous state of his health, everything
> that can recall to his mind the horrors of that night, which I
> will relate.

On Friday night, the 26th of February, we retired to bed
between ten and eleven o'clock. We had been in bed about half
an hour, when Mr S. heard a noise proceeding from one of
the parlours. He immediately went downstairs with two pistols,
which he had loaded that night, expecting to have occasion for
them. He went into the billiard room, where he heard footsteps
retreating. He followed into another little room, which was
called an office. He there saw a man in the act of quitting the
room through a glass window which opens into the shrubbery.
The man fired at Mr S., which he avoided. Bysshe then fired,
but it flashed in the pan. The man then knocked Bysshe down
and they struggled on the ground. Bysshe then fired his second
pistol, which he thought wounded him in the shoulder, as he
uttered a shriek and got up, when he said these words: By God
I will be revenged! I will murder your wife. I will ravish your
sister. By God I will be revenged. He then fled as we hoped
for the night. Our servants were not gone to bed, but were just
going, when this horrible affair happened. This was about
eleven o'clock. We all assembled in the parlour, where we
remained for two hours. Mr S. then advised us to retire, thinking
it impossible he would make a second attack. We left Bysshe
and our manservant, who had only arrived that day, and who
knew nothing of the house, to sit up. I had been in bed three
hours when I heard a pistol go off. I immediately ran down
stairs, when I perceived that Bysshe's flannel gown had been
shot through, and the window curtain. Bysshe had sent Daniel
to see what hour it was, when he heard a noise at the window.
He went there, and a man thrust his arm through the glass and
fired at him. Thank Heaven! the ball went through his gown
and he remained unhurt, Mr S. happened to stand sideways;
had he stood fronting, the ball must have killed him. Bysshe
fired his pistol, but it would not go off. He then aimed a blow
at him with an old sword which we found in the house, and
just as he was pulling it away Dan rushed into the room, when
he made his escape.

This was at four in the morning. It had been a most dreadful
night; the wind was as loud as thunder, and the rain descended
in torrents.

This was the story—a strange one, and stranger perhaps as it
so much resembled the story of an earlier event in the Lake

District, when Shelley claimed that he had been attacked by an unknown intruder. What was the explanation—the real truth? Was there an attack at Tremadoc—or not?

The explanations are many and varied and may be listed as follows:

1. It all happened exactly as Shelley described it and there was a genuine murderous attack on his life.

2. He was suffering from delusions and hallucinations, his mind overwrought, and he imagined the whole episode.

3. There was an attack, but it was a mock one, instigated by a man named Leeson, who resented Shelley's activities in Tremadoc, and wanted to frighten him out of the neighbourhood.

4. The attack was carried out by a neighbouring shepherd farmer as Shelley had interfered with his sheep, and even shot one or two as an act of mercy when he felt they were suffering and neglected.

5. The episode was faked and engineered by Shelley himself. He was deeply in debt, and tired of Tremadoc, and he wanted an excuse to leave the district immediately.

6. Dan, the Irish manservant, who had that day been released from Barnstaple prison, was trying to frighten Shelley.

7. It was something to do with Miss Hitchener.

Peacock visited Tremadoc the following year and found that everyone in Wales was sceptical over the truthfulness of the story and put it all down to an hallucination of Shelley's. It rather appears that there was a conspiracy afloat to dismiss the episode without proper investigation. Peacock, however, apparently believed what he was told and decided that the attack was only a figment of Shelley's overwrought brain. He described it as 'a sort of semi-delusion', and Hogg agreed with him.

Dowden, Shelley's early biographer, ignored Peacock and Hogg and accepted the attack as a genuine fact. Since then biographers have differed widely in their views on what really happened. Professor Kenneth Neill Cameron in his book *The Young Shelley* (1951) went into the story carefully. He reached the conclusion that the whole episode was faked by Shelley himself—that he owed money, that Dan had warned him he was being watched by the authorities, and that he was in a state of 'trapped desperation'. He did not want to admit defeat but he had to find some convincing excuse for leaving Tremadoc without delay. There is much to uphold this explanation. Why did Shelley take his pistols to bed with him that night? And how odd that nobody else actually *saw* the assailant, and that the second attack is described as having taken place just when Shelley had sent Dan out of the room.

Nevertheless, although Shelley could act, and although he had always had an inventive capacity for fantasy, the effects of this experience on his physical and mental make-up at the time seem to have been too overwhelming to have been anything but genuine. Harriet and Eliza, the two people who knew him best, both seem to have accepted his story. Though Harriet's doubts were raised by Peacock in after months, Eliza spoke of it later as 'a frightful fact', even after the breach with Shelley. Shelley certainly was unstable but a genuine hallucination of this nature would surely have indicated actual mental derangement?

It therefore seems probable that there *was* some sort of attack that night. Professor Frederick L. Jones in his edition of *The Letters of Percy Bysshe Shelley* (1964) upholds this theory. He is "too much impressed with Harriet's circumstantial account to be able to regard the incident as purely imaginary'* and he upholds the solution given by H. M. Dowling in an article 'The Attack at Tanyrallt', printed in the Keats–Shelley Memorial Association Bulletin XII (1961). In this most enlightening article H. M. Dowling enumerates the findings of his own detailed investigations in Wales. From these findings he is convinced that there *was* a genuine first assault though he feels it possible that the second assault, by which time Shelley would be very overwrought, might have been imagined. The perpetrator of the attack is unknown but it was probably done with the connivance of the Hon. Robert Leeson, an Anglo-Irish aristocrat, and another worker on the Embankment scheme, who objected to Shelley's radical ideas, his desertion of his own class, and his revolutionary activities. He and Shelley, rival

* Frederick L. Jones (editor): *Letters of Percy Bysshe Shelley*, Vol. 1.

upper-class landlords in Tremadoc, had clashed more than once.
The object of the attack was, not to murder Shelley, but to
frighten him out of the country.

7

The Shelleys were back once more on their wanderings. It
was a life, as Edmund Blunden so pertinently puts it, of 'perpetual motion'.* So shocked were they that they left Tanyrallt
the very next day after the attack and sought refuge in the
home of a friend seven miles away.

Shelley had hankerings to return to Ireland. Not only would
Ireland be a desirable distance from the scene of the outrage,
he also had reasons for calling on a printer in Dublin who had
confiscated part of his *Queen Mab* manuscript.

So back to Ireland they went, first to Dublin to recover the
papers, and then on to the lakes of Killarney where they rented
a cottage. From Killarney Shelley sent the manuscript of the
completed *Queen Mab* to the publisher Hookham in London and
begged Hookham for a loan of money which was sent. They
might have been happy in Killarney; the country enchanted
them, and the cottage, though not blessed with every comfort,
was quiet and peaceful. After the shocks and frustrations of
Tremadoc it was just the refuge they needed. But unfortunately
Hogg came to Dublin, looking for them, and this was too much
for Shelley's composure. It was only a very short time since
they had arrived in Killarney but he and Harriet must needs
now rush off back to Dublin to intercept Hogg. It seemed an
opportunity too good to miss. However, it was not to be. Hogg
had given up hope of seeing them and had returned to London.

New plans were hurriedly made. They decided that they
would return to England too—leaving Eliza, the manservant,
and most of their belongings, stranded in the cottage at
Killarney.

Shelley could not suppress his restlessness. His nerves

* Edmund Blunden: *Shelley*.

temporarily shattered by his experiences in Wales, he was now beginning to be irked by the continuous presence of his sister-in-law Eliza. Also his mind was engrossed by thoughts of his poem, and with plans for its publication, and he felt that it would be wiser to be on the spot in London to deal with Hook-ham. Harriet loved Ireland—she had friends there, particularly her great friend, Mrs Nugent, in Dublin—but, as usual, she felt that her place was at Shelley's side. She was six months pregnant and the future was more uncertain than ever. She and Shelley had dreams of finding a permanent home but, since the Tremadoc episode, hopes of settling down for ever in their beloved Nantgwillt had become increasingly remote. Perhaps if they went to London there would be some hope of making up the quarrel with Shelley's parents; of Shelley on his twenty-first birthday, soon to come, taking his rightful place as heir to an important estate? Nothing in Harriet's marriage had turned out quite as she had expected but she was still blissfully happy. Even Shelley's unorthodox views on love, and the ties of marriage, failed to disturb her. She felt certain of his love, and in that certainty was content.

In London they stayed first at her father's house, afterwards moving to an hotel, and later to lodgings in Half Moon Street. That spring of 1813 Shelley's poem *Queen Mab* was printed in a limited edition for private circulation. There was a deeply affectionate dedication to Harriet at the beginning:

> Whose is the love that gleaming through the world,
> Wards off the poisonous arrow of its scorn?
> Whose is the warm and partial praise,
> Virtue's most sweet reward?
>
> Beneath whose looks did my reviving soul
> Riper in truth and virtuous daring grow?
> Whose eyes have I gazed fondly on,
> And loved mankind the more?
>
> Harriet! on thine:—thou wert my purer mind,
> Thou wert the inspiration of my song;
> Thine are these early wilding flowers,
> Though garlanded by me.

Then press into thy breast this pledge of love;
And know, though time may change and years may roll,
Each floweret gathered in my heart
It consecrates to thine.

It was a dedication painfully embarrassing to Shelley only a
few months later and, when that time came, he did his best to
get it removed in as many copies as possible.

First omens of disaster were ushered in by the return of
Eliza from Ireland and before long she again took up residence
with the Shelleys. Harriet wrote long letters to her friend
Mrs Nugent in Dublin telling her everything that happened.
The baby's birth was getting very near now. Harriet found
herself at times brooding over the state of the outside world.
The war with Napoleon seemed never-ending and this
oppressed her spirits; while nearer home a realization of
deteriorating relations with the Godwins added to her moods
of depression.

The household was an ill-assorted one. Harriet had not
been brought up to battle with the domestic duties of a home:
she could not cook and did not care for housework. She still
preserved her obsession for reading aloud, but Eliza, who was
not literary, thought the pastime was bad for her and took the
books away. Peacock came, giving intellectual stimulus, and
Hogg too was a frequent—and usually hungry—visitor. Meals
were disjointed affairs and often there was little that was
appetizing for Hogg to eat. Shelley himself did not suffer
for, as in the Oxford days, he seldom ate regular meals. Instead
he 'ate like the birds when he saw something edible lying
about', as Trelawny was to describe years later. Now, in
London, Shelley would as ever rush out at any moment to buy
a loaf. To assuage the pangs of hunger he carried a supply of
raisins in the pocket of his waistcoat. Another delicacy which
appealed to him was bread sprinkled with sugar and nutmeg, after
having first been steeped and squeezed in boiling water. His
goings and comings were haphazard and he had little sense of
time. He stayed up until all hours, often talking to Hogg,
sometimes playing chess. Never wearing an overcoat, and with
an open-necked shirt in the coldest weather, he was already

suffering from a cough and a pain in his side and he was afraid, at moments, of consumption. Another time, so we are told by Peacock, he was afraid of contracting elephantiasis and would morbidly examine his own skin and suddenly seize the person next to him, to see if their skin corresponded to his.

These vagaries were part and parcel of his temperament but must at moments have added to the strain of their lives. Harriet, her pregnancy in a late stage, about this time began to feel the need for a more comfortable existence. According to Hogg, she now showed the first signs of aspiring to be 'fashionable'. A little while later Shelley bought her a carriage, which he was unable to pay for. They moved from the Half Moon Street lodgings to Cooke's Hotel for the birth of the baby in June 1813. It was a little girl, fair with blue eyes, to be christened Ianthe—a little girl whose descendants are now the only living direct descendants of Shelley.

With the birth of the baby there tragically followed a swift disintegration of the young Shelleys' previously happy relationship. Harriet had set great store on a reconciliation with the family at Field Place and Shelley too had hoped that, as soon as he came of age, his financial prospects would be transformed. But although efforts were made on both sides nothing came of these efforts. Shelley was much distressed. He was deeply in debt and lived now in a constant fear of being disinherited. But his father's conditions for a reconciliation he felt to be impossible: among them, still, a declaration to University College, Oxford, that he had renounced his atheistic views. It was impossible that he should so betray his own convictions: Harriet herself agreed with him on this point. But Mr Shelley was adamant: 'What regards your avowed opinions,' he wrote, 'are in my judgment the most material parts of character requiring amendment. And as you now avow there is no change effected in them, I must decline all further communication or any personal interview until that shall be effected.'

There was no hope of being accepted at Field Place. They were still outcasts. Eliza was bitterly disappointed and showed it. Far the most worldly of the three, she deeply resented that

Harriet should have no proper position as the wife of a baronet's heir, with rich financial prospects. Part of her interest in Shelley in the first place had been due to his rank and background, and she had thought she was doing her best for Harriet's future when she had encouraged the marriage. The disappointing outcome—no proper home, an inadequate income, a sea of debts—roused her to remonstrance and mischief-making, all of which was remorselessly communicated to Harriet.

There was trouble too before long over the feeding of the little Ianthe. In the better classes the provision of a wet nurse was the usual procedure and this procedure Harriet, backed no doubt by Eliza, insisted upon carrying out. Shelley was outraged. He believed in the provisions of nature and felt strongly that mothers should feed their own babies. It was a matter of deep anguish to him that Harriet did not agree. 'I have often thought,' Peacock said later, 'that if Harriet had nursed her own child, and if this sister had not lived with them, the link of their married life would not have been so readily broken.'

Shelley's affection for Harriet was still deep enough to inspire him to write a sonnet to her on her eighteenth birthday. But resentment was mounting up and the relationship was being swiftly undermined. Harriet's unwise dependence on Eliza was the result of years of subjection. She adored Eliza who was nearly old enough to be her mother. 'How oft have I blessed that providence who had given me such a treasure,' she had once written to Miss Hitchener. Yet in her own right, we are told, she was an attractive young woman and by no means a nonentity. 'She was well educated,' Peacock said of her, 'she read agreeably and intelligently—Her manners were good; and her whole aspect and demeanour such manifest emanations of pure and truthful nature that to be once in her company was to know her thoroughly. She was fond of her husband, and accommodated herself in every way to his tastes. If they mixed in society, she adorned it; if they lived in retirement, she was satisfied; if they travelled, she enjoyed the change of scene.'

But Shelley was becoming increasingly unhappy. Perhaps he was realizing for the first time the sad but inescapable fact that he and the Westbrooks belonged fundamentally to different worlds. All Harriet's efforts at loyalty and support could not disguise the fact that she was not a rebel by nature; her tastes were not bohemian and she was not an intellectual. Eliza, whom Shelley had at first admired, now seemed to him to be everything that he most detested. Her worldliness affronted him. Months earlier he had written of her to Hogg: 'Eliza is no more a Xtian than I am, but she regards as a sacred criterion the opinion of the world.' Under Eliza's influence Harriet appeared to him to be changing; she had given up her intellectual pursuits and was more interested in clothes and frivolous amusements. The fundamental divergence between them, hitherto submerged by her youth and by her loyalty, now seemed to him to be an insurmountable barrier. He had had dreams, as he had told Miss Hitchener, of moulding 'a really noble soul into all that can make its nobleness useful and lovely'. But now he had given up all hope that Harriet would ever grow into the woman of his dreams and desires.

In desperation he turned to others for understanding. Some months earlier he and Harriet had made some new friends in London, a Mr and Mrs Newton, who believed in a 'natural' state of society, and who were both vegetarians and nudists. More recently they had met Mrs Newton's sister, a Mrs Boinville, and her young married daughter, Cornelia. These people had seemed to Shelley, in comparison to the inmates of his own home, to be everything that was most to be admired. He cultivated their society, spent hours at Mrs Boinville's house at Bracknell where she gathered together a circle of people, French *émigrés* and others, people like-minded to himself who were interested in the arts and in philosophy, and who were willing to spend hours in discussion. It was a way of life which exactly suited him and which he found entrancing.

Mrs Boinville herself, Shelley described later as 'the most admirable specimen of a human being I had ever seen'. She had 'perfect character and manners'. Her story had been a sad and dramatic one. The daughter of a rich father, she had met and married Boinville, one of the French *émigrés*. He had died tragically in a prison hospital during the Retreat from Moscow, her father dying very soon after. The shock had turned her hair completely white but her face had remained rosy, young and beautiful. Shelley thought of her as Maimuna, the sorceress in a poem *Thalaba* by Southey, a favourite poem of his:

> Her face was as a damsel's face
> And yet her hair was grey.

Her beauty, her adventurous life, her warmth, and intensity of passion for the arts, all charmed him. Besides basking in the fascination of her society, often, too, at Bracknell, he met Cornelia, her daughter. Although married to a young attorney, Thomas Turner, Cornelia spent months of every year with her mother. She too was a devotee of the arts and she too was beautiful. Shelley found her tender, trusting, womanly. She had perfect features, dark ringlets falling round her face, blue eyes, and a gentle expression. He read Petrarch with her and gradually, with her help, he was beginning to learn Italian.

With no settled home Shelley looked about desperately for some temporary place of abode. Nantgwillt was still the dream —'When we get our dear Nantgwillt,' as Harriet wrote somewhat pathetically to her friend Mrs Nugent later that year— but the dream was still remote. And in the meantime? Why not be near these new and cherished friends of his—why not be near the Boinvilles? Before long he had found a house to rent, 'merely for convenience', High Elms House at Bracknell.

⚶ 8 ⚶

Harriet now saw less and less of him, the frequent gatherings at Mrs Boinville's house—often late in the evening—engaging all his attention. Harriet found a little consolation in the society of Peacock and Hogg, both of whom were frequent visitors at High Elms. Unlike Shelley neither of them were bowled over by the charms of Mrs Boinville and her circle. Peacock found the circle over intense, laughably immersed in themselves, over serious. He was a serious scholar himself but a scholar with a strong sense of humour. His wit appealed to Harriet. She laughed with him, unable to share Shelley's passionate romanticism and, though she liked Mrs Boinville well enough, secretly resented Shelley's thraldom.

Shelley was now in dire straits over money. The disappointment of his coming-of-age had brought serious consequences. Instead of being able to pay off all his debts as he had planned, he was now held responsible for them and was being dunned by creditors. The carriage was not paid for. He still owed money at Oxford. He had promised help to Miss Hitchener, Peacock and Godwin, among others, and he was now even living in fear of arrest.

It seemed wiser to disappear for the time being. He and his little household, accompanied by Peacock, suddenly took to the road in the new carriage and set off for the north. Shelley had raised a little money for their expenses by the selling of post-obit bonds on exorbitant terms to money-lenders, a disastrous drain on the inheritance which he hoped would one day be his. They went first to the Lake District and then on to Edinburgh. Harriet, perhaps thankful to be separated from the Boinvilles, felt a renewal of happiness and wrote of her life in thoughtful and glowing terms to Mrs Nugent:

> A little more than two years has passed since I made my first visit here to be united to Mr Shelley. To me they have been the happiest and the longest years of my life. The rapid succession of events since that time make the two years appear unusually long. I think the regular method of measuring Time is by the number of different ideas which a rapid succession of events naturally give rise to. When I look back to the time before I was married I seem to feel I have lived a long time. Tho' my age is but eighteen yet I feel as if I was much older.

But the happiness in Edinburgh could not last. It seemed that they could never stay long in one place: always they must be hounded on, menaced by financial difficulties, victims of

F

their own extravagances. Soon they were back once more in England; Shelley was trying desperately again to negotiate with his father and Whitton, and at the same time promising help unlimited to the rapacious and impoverished Godwin.

It was now that the crisis with Eliza came to a head. Shelley's determination to 'save Godwin' was for her the last straw. But, instead of leaving Shelley and Harriet to themselves to work out their own salvation, she remained with them, interfering, demanding, trying to bend them to her will. She still wanted her sister Harriet to be a person important in society, with all the money and position worthy of her rank. To Shelley, as his early biographer Dowden has pointed out, 'a fashionable life meant a living death'.* The clash of two opposing ways of life was bound to lead to trouble.

Only Harriet might have saved the situation. If ever a marriage was threatened by a warning light it was now. For her the choice may have been an agonizing one—sister, husband, she loved them both—but, however agonizing, if she wanted to save her marriage, the choice should have been made. Insidiously, however, she herself was being undermined, not only by her sister's admonitions, but by her own inclinations. She had loyally championed Shelley but secretly she had much sympathized with Eliza. The two last years may have been happy ones, but they had also been exhausting. The conflict in her mind was increasing. She longed at times for serenity, security. She was not worldly but she was used to a life that was orderly and conventional. Guided now by influences too strong for her to fight against she became, as Thornton Hunt wrote afterwards, 'a tool in the hands of others, and the fact accounted for the idle way in which she importuned him [Shelley] to do things repugnant to his feelings and convictions. She thus exasperated his temper and lost her own—' In hitching her waggon to a star—and such an unpredictable star—she was beginning to discover that she had embraced a way of living which it was beyond her strength to carry through.

The long hard winter of 1813–14 dragged on in conditions of discomfort. The foggy month of December was followed by a

* Edward Dowden: *Life of Percy Bysshe Shelley.*

long period of hard frost. The Shelleys were settled temporarily in a furnished house they had rented at Windsor. It was to be their last home together, but Shelley still spent a great deal of his time with the Boinvilles at Bracknell. Mrs Boinville, noting Shelley's depression, wrote to Hogg: 'I think his mind and body want rest. His journeys after what he has never found have racked his purse and his tranquillity.' Shelley himself wrote to Hogg: 'I have sunk into a premature old age of exhaustion.' In the same letter he broke out into an unbridled diatribe against Eliza:

> Eliza is still with us—not here!—but will be with me when the infinite malice of destiny forces me to depart. I am now but little inclined to contest this point. I certainly hate her with all my heart and soul. It is a sight which awakens an inexpressible sensation of disgust and horror, to see her caress my poor little Ianthe, in whom I may hereafter find the consolation of sympathy. I sometimes feel faint with the fatigue of checking the overflowings of my unbounded abhorrence for this miserable wretch. But she is no more than a blind and loathsome worm, that cannot see to sting.

As always, his reactions were fierce and exaggerated. But it was a situation which Hogg had long ago foreseen. Hogg had never liked Eliza and, even in those first months of the marriage when they had all lived together at York, he had resented her attitude towards Shelley:

> Eliza once or twice betrayed a faint consciousness of his presence —that was all the notice she took of her sister's husband. His course therefore was plain, his peace might have been assured— It was absolutely necessary to declare peremptorily 'Either Eliza goes, or I go', and instantly to act upon the declaration. This so necessary course the poor fellow did not take; and it is certain that the Divine Poet could not have taken it, for with superhuman strength, weakness less than human was strangely blended.

Some time later Shelley was to write of the 'incurable dissensions' of this 1813–14 period. But it seemed that he was now taking the line of least resistance and accepting defeat. To ensure the children's legitimacy, and perhaps to satisfy the Westbrooks who were dubious of the legality of the Edinburgh ceremony, he re-married Harriet on 24 March 1814, at St George's, Hanover Square. A few days earlier he had been telling Hogg that Mrs Boinville's house had 'become his home'. He had his own room there, full of his most cherished books, and his visits were growing longer and more frequent. Harriet too was unhappy and her expectancy of another child brought her no comfort. She frequently sought consolation with her own family in London and when, at last and belatedly, Eliza decided that she would part company with the Shelleys and go to live on her own at Southampton, Harriet for the time being went with her.

It seemed now that Shelley hoped that the separation of himself and Harriet would be permanent. He had wild dreams of settling down indefinitely with Mrs Boinville at Bracknell. More and more he felt attracted by the peacefulness of her presence and by the appealing beauty of her daughter Cornelia. As was his habit, he idealized both women, seeing them as goddesses, as perfection personified. In their house, as he told Hogg, he had felt himself 'translated to a paradise'. At first he had imagined Cornelia to be cold and reserved but now his opinion had changed. 'She is the reverse of this,' he wrote to Hogg, 'as she is the reverse of everything bad. She inherits all the divinity of her mother.'

But it was not to be. Mrs Boinville, anxious though she had been to give shelter and succour to a wounded poet, was no marriage-breaker. It was made clear to Shelley—or possibly he realized it himself—that he must fight his battles alone. He returned to his solitary home and wrote a poem of bitter desolation: 'Stanzas—April 1814':

> Pause not! The time is past! Every voice cries, 'Away!'
> Tempt not with one last tear thy friend's ungentle mood:
> Thy lover's eye, so glazed and cold, dares not entreat thy stay:
> Duty and dereliction guide thee back to solitude.
> Away, away! to thy sad and silent home;
> Pour bitter tears on its desolated hearth.

The poem ends with an adjuration to himself for the guilt of his own feelings:

Thy remembrance, and repentance, and deep musings are not free
From the music of two voices, and the light of one sweet smile.

His feelings were in a turmoil, his dismay at the break with Harriet tormenting and inescapable. All that had happened, his defection to the Boinvilles, he persuaded himself to be the result of the change in Harriet herself. He suspected her now of a worldliness which had never been hers and even suspected her motives in marrying him. Probably, he decided, it was his rank, his money, his place in society, which had been the main attraction in her eyes. Probably all the time she had been the true disciple of the odious Eliza. In May, in a last desperate effort, and in a final flare-up of his dying love, he wrote a poem of self-extenuation, of dismay and appeal, dedicated directly to Harriet. He recalled their past blessings, begged her to change before it was too late:

Oh trust for once no erring guide!
Bid the remorseless feeling flee;
'Tis malice, 'tis revenge, 'tis pride,
'Tis anything but thee;
O, deign a nobler pride to prove,
And pity if thou canst not love.

The appeal went unregarded. Harriet herself, though utterly unaware that a final breach was so perilously near, felt that she herself had much to forgive. Shelley's defection to the Boinvilles, the solitariness of her own life, and the fact that she was once more pregnant, had all combined to reduce her to a state of sullen depression. She knew herself to be neglected and she was miserable through jealousy. Even now, when she had returned to Windsor, she was continually alone. Shelley made repeated visits to London to call on Godwin, even staying away from home in lodgings in Fleet Street to be nearer to his idol. A fatal coldness and hardness temporarily swamped the generosity of her naturally loving heart. She was

unable to make any gesture of reconciliation which might have
saved the marriage. Instead, as a temporary measure and with
no thought of permanence, she went to Bath on a visit to join
her parents.

⤳⳼ 9 ⳼⤶

It was the end of their relationship but Harriet did not
yet know it. Nothing to her could alter the deep and irrevocable bond which united her to Shelley. There was coldness
now between them—coldness, misunderstanding, a miserable
lack of sympathy—but she had no doubt but that in time it
would pass. When Shelley had finished his business in London,
when their second child was born, when the quarrel with the
family was breached, when later Nantgwillt was their home—
all these things, she felt, would contribute to the happiness
which still lay in the future. Though worried, she was not
seriously perturbed. The foundations of her life were not
threatened. She waited—sure in her heart that the deepest
loyalties of her being could not alter.

At first Shelley wrote regularly. All seemed well until,
at the beginning of July, the letters suddenly ceased. After only
four days of silence—proving the frequency of their previous
correspondence—Harriet was in a ferment of anxiety. Fearing
that some disaster might have happened to Shelley, she wrote
to the publisher Hookham for news:

6, Queen's Square
Bath.

My dear Sir

You will greatly oblige me by giving the enclosed to Mr
Shelley. I would not trouble you, but it is now four days since
I have heard from him, which to me is an age. Will you write
by return of post, and tell me what has become of him, as I
always fancy something dreadful has happened if I do not hear
from him. If you tell me that he is well, I shall not come to

London; but if I do not hear from you or him, I shall certainly come, as I cannot endure this dreadful state of suspense. You are his friend, and can feel for me.

I remain yours truly
H. S.

Shelley received her letter and wrote back cryptically. He asked her to leave everything and to come to London immediately. With the baby Ianthe she arrived in London on 14 July. But the meeting with Shelley was a tragic one. She found him completely changed towards her. He told her that their married life was over, that he had met the philosopher's daughter, Mary Godwin, and that they now meant everything to one another. He threw himself upon her charity and begged her to accept a situation which was irrevocable. He was a different man, unloving, preoccupied. The impossible had happened. The bond of love between them, which she had believed to be indestructible, had ceased to exist.

For Harriet, pregnant with Shelley's child, the shock was bitter. She kept her self-control but only, at first, because she refused to accept what had happened. She blamed Mary. Was not Mary the daughter of Mary Wollstonecraft, glamorous to Shelley for that reason alone? His feeling would pass, it must pass. She could not believe that this new passion was real, that her own marriage was at an end, that Shelley had deserted her. His frantic letters and incoherent assurances of continued solicitude made things no easier:

My dearest friend
Exhausted as I am with our interview—I cannot refrain from writing to you.
I am made calmer and happier by your assurances—my spirit turned to you for consolation—for this dearest Harriet, from my inmost Soul, I thank you—I repeat (believe me, for I am sincere) that my attachment to you is unimpaired: I conceive that it has acquired even a deeper and more lasting character. . . .

But he went on to designate the feeling that had held them together:

Our connection was not one of passion and impulse. Friendship was its basis—It is no reproach to me that you have never filled my heart with an all-sufficing passion—perhaps, you are even yourself a stranger to these impulses, which one day may be awakened by some nobler and worthier than me, and may you find a lover as passionate and faithful, as I shall ever be a friend affectionate and sincere!

—Mrs Boinville deeply knows the human heart; she predicted that these struggles would one day arrive; she saw that friendship and not passion was the bond of our attachment.

—Can your feelings for me differ in their nature from those I cherish towards you? Are you my lover whilst I am only your friend, the brother of your heart? If they do not the purest and most perfect happiness is ours—I wish that you could see Mary—

There were more agonized interviews in the days that followed: interviews between Harriet and Shelley: interviews with Godwin, Mrs Godwin and Mary: all equally abortive. Though Mary promised to give Shelley up, and though Shelley himself took an overdose of laudanum and nearly killed himself, in the end everything remained just as it was. Harriet was forced to realize that there was little that she could do to influence the course of events. The realization brought on a state of collapse. She retired to bed, grief-stricken, beaten—though even now unable to accept that Shelley himself was to blame.

Months later, apparently still of this opinion, she wrote to her friend Mrs Nugent:

Mary was determined to seduce him. She heated his imagination by talking of her mother, and going to her grave with him every day, till at last she told him she was dying in love for him, accompanied with the most violent gestures and vehement expostulations. He thought of me and my sufferings, and begged her to get the better of a passion as degrading to him as to herself. She then told him she would die—he had rejected her, and what appeared to her as the sublimest virtue was to him a crime. Why could we not all live together? I as his sister, she as his wife? He had the folly to believe this possible, and sent for me, then residing at Bath. You may suppose how I felt at this disclosure. I was laid up for a fortnight after. I could do nothing for myself. He begged me to live. The doctors gave me over. They said 'twas impossible. I saw his despair, the agony of my beloved sister; and owing to the great strength of my constitution I lived.

This was the version of her heart-breaking experience which at first Harriet clung to as her only bulwark against despair. One wonders how it was arrived at. Was it partly Shelley's own somewhat ungallant version, aimed at exonerating himself? It is not impossible though, from his subsequent letters, it does not seem likely. Though Mary may have been the first to confess her love there seems no doubt that from the beginning her feeling was matched by Shelley's own ardour. When Peacock saw him he was a being half demented by passion, torn by conflicting loyalties:

> Between his old feelings towards Harriet, from whom he was not then separated, and his new passion for Mary, he showed in his looks, in his gestures, in his speech, the state of a mind suffering 'like a little kingdom, the nature of an insurrection'. His eyes were bloodshot, his hair and dress disordered. He caught up a bottle of laudanum, and said 'I never part from this'—Again he said more calmly 'Everyone who knows me must know that the partner of my life should be one who can feel poetry and understand philosophy. Harriet is a noble animal but she can do neither.'

Peacock remarked: 'It always appeared to me that you were very fond of Harriet,' and Shelley, making no direct answer, replied: 'But you did not know how I hated her sister!'

On 28 July, only a few days later, the unmanageable situation reached its climax. Shelley and Mary, accompanied by Mary's stepsister, Jane Clairmont, left Dover in a small boat and eloped to the Continent.

PART THREE

THE GODWIN
DAUGHTERS

You cannot imagine how much all the females of my family, Mrs Godwin and three daughters, are interested in your letters and your history.

GODWIN TO SHELLEY

I

I T had been a strange and unusual household to which Shelley that spring of 1814 had re-introduced himself. Of the three 'Godwin daughters', all of whom were living at home, only Mary was really a daughter of Godwin himself. Fanny, the eldest, was the daughter of Godwin's first wife, Mary Wollstonecraft and her lover, Gilbert Imlay, while Jane Clairmont (eventually known as Claire) was a daughter of the second Mrs Godwin by a previous marriage.

Surprisingly, at the age of forty-three, Godwin had married the woman's emancipator and authoress, Mary Wollstonecraft: surprisingly, for all his life up to then, Godwin had condemned marriage and had felt love to be a matter of no very great importance. Nevertheless, he loved Mary Wollstonecraft with a genuine and passionate love and the marriage—tragically short—was a happy one. Mary, their only child, born on 30 August 1797, and now at the time of her elopement with Shelley aged sixteen, had inherited many of her mother's characteristics. She had never known her mother who had died at her own birth but she had acquired something of Mary Wollstonecraft's sensitiveness, her depths of feeling, and her rebelliousness. She could sympathize with her mother in all the emotional trials she had endured, in the vicissitudes of her life, in her intellectual aspirations, her fight for women's rights—and, above all, mourn for her untimely death.

Mary Wollstonecraft's life up to the time that she married Godwin had not been a happy one. She was less reserved than her daughter and more at the mercy of ungovernable emotions. Her childhood home had been miserable, her chief occupation protecting her mother from a violent and bad-tempered husband. It was this violent temper of her father's, as she stressed afterwards, which was the main cause of the unhappiness in her family. Her father suffered repeated failures, both at farming and in business, and finally spent the money which had been settled on his children. There was nothing left for Mary but to leave home and earn her own living—in those days a disaster and a form of social inferiority at which her independent spirit rebelled.

After first taking a post as governess in Ireland, at nineteen she was companion to an elderly lady at Bath. Bath, at the height of its popularity, was teeming with social activity but Mary Wollstonecraft did not make friends easily. Instead she retreated still further into herself and nursed her own smouldering grievances. Nothing mattered, she felt, except independence. 'Every obligation we receive from our fellow creatures,' she wrote, 'is a new shackle, takes from our native freedom, and debases the mind.' But her bondage as companion was only to be replaced by another bondage at home, nursing her mother who was dying. For a moment at his wife's death it seemed that her father might turn over a new leaf. Overcome with remorse he wept 'like a child'. But it was not long before he had installed his mistress as the new housekeeper and this time Mary left home for good.

The next years were unsatisfactory and varied. She wrote several novels. Before the age of thirty she had started a school with her sisters and given it up. Her family was a continued source of anxiety: one brother a perpetual drag on her resources, a sister marrying unhappily and under duress and, so we are told, biting her ring to pieces in the wedding coach.

Mary herself was the victim of intense and overpowering passions. She adored her great friend Fanny Blood, loved her better than anyone in the world, and abandoned everything to nurse her in Lisbon at her death. She conceived a violent admiration for the Anglo-Swiss painter and author, Fuseli, but was firmly prevented by his wife from joining his household. Another abortive love for a clergyman devastated her emotionally. Fired, however, by the revolt against tyranny of the French Revolution she at length released some of her pent-up feeling in two admirable books, *Reply to Burke* and the *Vindication of the Rights of Women*. In these books she revealed herself as a battling pioneer for women's emancipation.

The books brought her fame and freedom. In 1792 she went to Paris to live by writing but got caught up in the toils of the Revolution itself and for some time was virtually a prisoner in the city. It was in Paris that she met the American, Captain Gilbert Imlay, who was to be the father of her child, Fanny. She and Imlay lived together as lovers, eschewing marriage, partly because Mary held tenaciously to her preconceived theories of the importance of love being free and unsullied by legal bonds. It was a theory that brought her much unhappiness. By nature emotional, clinging, loyal, the lack of security and permanence which she had deliberately chosen for herself was a continual source of misery. Imlay found her conflicting moods, her probing insight, her continual suspicions impossible to contend with. After Fanny was born at Havre in 1794 he was frequently away and Mary's anguish increased. She probably realized him to be what he was—a man of shallower feeling than herself, good-natured, casual, unlikely to be faithful. Frantic with jealousy and suspicion, she wrecked what little feeling he had left for her by bombarding him with tormenting letters. Finally she discovered by cross-questioning the cook that he had a mistress, 'a little actress', and the relationship was at an end. Imlay, relieved at making his escape, deserted her.

After the hardships of her youth and the continual frustration of feeling that she had suffered, this defection of Imlay's was to Mary Wollstonecraft the last straw. She returned to England and, crazed with grief, soaked her skirts by walking up and down for half an hour in the rain, before throwing herself into the Thames from Putney Bridge.

This was, however, surprisingly to be the turning point in her life. She was dragged out and revived. Loving friends rallied round her. Maternal feeling and a natural courage re-asserted themselves. She realized that she still had her child, she still had her work, and she made up her mind to devote herself to literary pursuits in order to keep Fanny. It was then, at this crucial moment in her rehabilitation, that she crossed paths once again with William Godwin.

She had known Godwin before, some years earlier, but in

those days he had felt her too strong-minded and notorious to be attractive. Now, however, having met him again at a friend's house, she made further advances and called on him at his own home. This time he felt flattered and charmed. She was an attractive young woman, very feminine, with impulsive ways. Her portrait by Opie in the National Portrait Gallery shows her hair auburn, her eyes large and thoughtful, her mouth curved and impressionable. But there is strength in her face and an over-all serenity which is impressive. Her gifts of understanding were many and her early experiences had given her fortitude and strength.

Godwin's literary powers at this time were at their zenith. He had written his famous book *Political Justice* and he had a large following of adoring young men as his disciples. It is difficult to reconcile this scholar and man of letters, admired friend of men like Coleridge and Lamb, with the sponging, ineffectual humbug and hypocrite Godwin was in later years to become. Even now, however, there was a frigidity and crankiness which might have alienated a less warm-hearted person than Mary Wollstonecraft. She, on the contrary, could see no fault in him. He, in his turn, found 'affection melting into love'. It was a strange case of the attraction of opposites. As Mrs Marshall, Mary Shelley's first biographer, so aptly describes the relationship—'the coldest of men and the warmest of women found their happiness in each other'.*

All the same Godwin did not at first contemplate marriage. He had some strongly-felt theories about freedom for both sexes. Marriage he considered to be unnecessary and even for a man and woman to live together in the same house was, in his opinion, a mistake. In his book *Political Justice* he had pointed out the dangers of 'constant familiarity'. Mary had in the past shared some of these views but now her views were changing. She was going to have another child—Godwin's child—and she was beginning to long with increasing intensity for stability and permanence. Without stressing her own weakness she diplomatically pointed out to Godwin that it might be a mistake to risk losing cherished friends just for the

* Mrs Julian Marshall: *The Life and Letters of Mary Wollstonecraft Shelley*.

sake of a theory. As a concession to their love and after several months had slipped by—months when they lived in near-by houses, met at stated intervals and communicated with each other by notes—Godwin agreed to marry her.

Mary, who had found a new passion of interest in domesticity, and was becoming more of a normal housewife every day, was inexpressibly relieved. They joined forces, combining households to the extent of living in the same building, got married, and all went well. 'A husband,' Mary wrote, 'is a convenient part of the furniture of the house.' For the first time in her life she was ecstatically happy. The future seemed rosy and secure. Even Fanny, her love child by Imlay, had fitted well into the general scheme of things. Godwin had taken to Fanny from the first; he accepted her as his own daughter, played with her, invariably treated her with kindness and affection—a facet of his character which is perhaps the most redeeming feature in Godwin's whole history. Mary now could even run into Imlay himself occasionally and forgive completely the hurt and anguish of the past. She was preparing to write another book which was to be called *The Wrongs of Women*. This second childbirth was going to be taken in her stride. She meant to employ only a midwife and to come down to dinner the next day. There were all sorts of plans simmering in her brain; nothing seemed impossible.

But after the ordeal of childbirth things went disastrously wrong. The little girl, Mary Shelley to be, was born on 30 August 1797. Mary Wollstonecraft was only thirty-six but her health had perhaps been undermined by the trials and suffering of her youth. Complications arose and she developed dangerous symptoms. She was very ill for ten days and Godwin stayed by her bedside, hardly leaving her room. At one point there was a deceptive rally—she seemed better, Godwin dared to hope. Mary's last remembered words were of him: 'He is the kindest, best man in the world.' But his love could not save her. Her sufferings increased and on 10 September 1797, she died.

2

For Godwin her death was the most disastrous of tragedies. Mary Wollstonecraft's influence and example had gradually been having their effect in softening and moulding his strange character into something more nearly approaching her own. Now, without her, he was lost. The good was undone, dissipated for ever in the years of deterioration which followed. Godwin knew his own character only too well: 'I am bold and adventurous in opinions, not in life—Perhaps one of the sources of my love of admiration and fame has been my timidity and embarrassment—I am feeble of tact—I am extremely irresolute in matters apparently trivial, which occasionally leads to inactivity, or subjects me to the being guided by others—At all times agreeable company has an omnipotent effect upon me, and raises me from the worst tone of mind to the best.'

And now the best was gone for ever. His grief was acute and he did not know how to carry on his life. To add to his responsibility there were two very young children to be cared for: Fanny, aged three and a half years, and the new-born baby girl. As a preliminary he settled into the rooms of The Polygon, Somers Town, which his wife had occupied. For a time lady friends looked after the children until he found a suitable nurse-housekeeper. But the lady housekeeper when found was anxious to convert him to further matrimony. She became too devoted and, as her devotion was not reciprocated, a continual embarrassment. He was worried and depressed, hankering after old familiar bachelor ways, and yet anxious to do his best for the children. At length, forgetting his old diatribes against marriage, he decided that he must marry again.

The next few months were taken up with cultivating the society of ladies he had known before he married Mary, and by repeated proposals of marriage. There was a Miss Lee, who kept a school at Bath, and Maria Reveley, a favourite pupil, much admired by him for her beauty and charming manner. To his astonishment, even after repeated efforts, both these ladies refused him—Maria Reveley very soon afterwards getting herself engaged to somebody else, a John Gisborne. (In later years she and John Gisborne were to become too of the young Shelleys' most intimate friends.) Godwin's vanity was outraged by such resistance to his charms. By 1801, after months of frustration and disappointment, he was fair game for the scheming widow, Mrs Clairmont, who came to live next door to him and who cleverly introduced herself from the adjoining balcony: 'Is it possible that I behold the immortal Godwin!' Before long his subjugation was complete. On 21 December 1801, he and the strong-minded Mrs Clairmont were married quietly at Shoreditch Church.

They all went to live together at 29 The Polygon—the newly married couple, her children by her previous marriage (a daughter Jane and son Charles), Imlay's daughter Fanny, and Godwin's own little girl, Mary. Before long, there was another addition to the family, a son, William, born in 1803.

Mrs Clairmont, at the time of this second marriage, was thirty-five years old. She was good-looking and buxom, unrefined yet shrewd, inquisitive and bad-tempered, but an excellent manager, a good cook, and loyal in her admiration of Godwin. Yet, there seems no doubt that as a human being, she brought out the worst in him. She was lacking in integrity, second-rate in all her approaches to life. To Mary this second marriage of her father's brought a lifelong grief: 'I detest Mrs G.,' she wrote years later; 'she plagues my father out of his life.' 'Mrs Godwin,' wrote a friend, 'is *not* a pleasant woman, a wife far different from the one you would suppose *such* a man would have selected.'

Of his first wife Godwin had written: 'I firmly believe that there does not exist her equal in the world. I know from experience that we were formed to make each other happy.' His expectations of this second venture were pitched in a minor key. He did not dislike his new wife, at times they got on tolerably well, but at best his feeling for her was tepid. When, after a quarrel a year or two later, she suggested a separation, he wrote to her philosophically: 'You have nothing to do but suppress in part the excesses of that baby-sullenness for every trifle—The separation will be a source of great misery to me; but I can make up my resolution to encounter it—You part from the best of husbands, the most anxious to console you, the best qualified to bear and be patient towards one of the worst of tempers. I have every qualification and every wish to make you happy—'

His wife decided to stay. She remained with him through all the ups and downs of the years that followed. Although she could not win the love of Godwin's daughter Mary, and only the loyalty of Imlay's Fanny, she looked after all the children well in a material sense, and did not spare herself in the shouldering of responsibility or of hard work. Godwin, by temperament lazy and undecided, gradually handed the reins over entirely to her.

She was not faced with an easy task. Godwin's fame as a writer was rapidly declining and his financial state was precarious. She realized that, with such a large family to support, something drastic would have to be attempted in order to make some money. In 1805 she persuaded him to set up a small bookseller's and publishing firm; they were to publish chiefly children's books, a Juvenile Library, concentrating on high-class productions. One of the books they published, especially commissioned, was *Lamb's Tales from Shakespeare*, for which Godwin paid Lamb sixty guineas. In 1807 the business was moved to larger premises in Skinner Street, Holborn, and the family moved to the house adjoining the office where they were to remain until 1822.

These were chequered years, placid at times but punctuated with anxieties and upheavals. From the first the publisher's business was a failure. Godwin wrote his *Life of Chaucer* for which he received £600. But gradually the finances of the family became increasingly chaotic. Godwin himself became more and more cantankerous and quarrelsome, expecting help and attentions as his right from all and sundry, and soliciting money from his friends and acquaintances whenever possible.

Mrs Godwin did her best to reduce this chaos into order.

She took on everything—running the house, cooking the meals, looking after the children, pursuing schemes whenever possible to save the foundering fortunes of the Juvenile Library. If her temper suffered, her energy never abated, and even the lethargic Godwin was moved to admiration of her determined qualities. The children were well educated, the girls with daily governesses at home and occasional lessons from masters, the boys at Charterhouse School. Godwin himself at times took a hand in his daughters' teaching. He still favoured Fanny, Imlay's child, who had now been given the name of 'Godwin' and who was always treated as the eldest member of the family. Perhaps he was attached to her because she was the most amenable: a kind, humble, rather spiritless girl, devoting her life to the service of other people, demanding nothing for herself. Mary was more rebellious. She disliked her stepmother and disliked domesticity. Godwin she adored, and she longed for a completely intellectual life. But her stepmother's taunts at her uselessness in the house made her restless and on edge. It was so obvious too that her stepmother favoured her own daughter, Jane Clairmont, the third daughter of the family, a year younger than Mary, but already the most quick-witted, the most lively and unscrupulous and—frequently—the most unmanageable member of the household.

Mary had a delicate constitution, probably inherited from her mother. One of her troubles as a young girl was a muscular weakness of the arm for which at that time sea-bathing was recommended. In May 1811 Fanny remained at home to keep house for her father, while all the others went to Ramsgate for a holiday. Here the bathing seemed to be doing Mary so much good that she remained on for another seven months, boarding at a girls' school in the neighbourhood, to complete the cure. Possibly Mrs Godwin was glad to have her out of the house and Mary was glad to be away. Although she worshipped her father, her relationship with her stepmother was growing increasingly difficult. As she grew older Mrs Godwin became more and more jealous of her stepdaughter's superior intellect, of the fact that she was her mother's daughter (a large portrait of Mary Wollstonecraft still hung over the fireplace in Godwin's room), and of the resultant bond between Mary and her father. She therefore welcomed a later plan, hatched on Mary's return from Ramsgate, that for the further good of her health Mary should go on a long sojourn to Scotland to stay with a friend of Godwin's, a William Baxter of Dundee, who had offered to have her.

It was, from Mary's point of view, by no means an unhappy arrangement. The Baxters were cultured, kindly people and there were daughters of about Mary's own age. She sailed for Dundee on 8 June 1812, and was accompanied by a long letter of introduction written by Godwin to Baxter:

Skinner St., London. 8th June, 1812.

My dear Sir

I have shipped off to you by yesterday's packet—my only daughter. I attended her, with her two sisters to the wharf, and remained an hour on board, till the vessel got under way. I cannot help feeling a thousand anxieties in parting with her, for the first time, for so great a distance—She is four months short of fifteen years of age—I daresay she will arrive more dead than alive, as she is extremely subject to sea-sickness, and the voyage will, not improbably, last nearly a week—There can never be a perfect equality between father and child—I am not, therefore, a perfect judge of Mary's character. I believe she has nothing of what is commonly called vices, and that she has considerable talent—I do not desire that she should be treated with extraordinary attention, or that any one of your family should put themselves in the smallest degree out of their way on her account. I am anxious that she should be brought up (in this respect) like a philosopher, even like a cynic. It will add greatly to the strength and worth of her character. I should also observe that she has no love of dissipation, and will be perfectly satisfied with your woods and your mountains. I wish, too, that she should be *excited* to industry. She has occasionally great perseverance, but occasionally, too, she shows great need to be roused. You are aware that she comes to the sea-side for the purpose of bathing—She will want also some treatment for her arm—In all other respects except her arm she has admirable health, has an excellent appetite, and is capable of enduring fatigue—I trust—you will proceed on the basis of our being earnest to give you as little trouble as the nature of the case will allow—I am, my dear sir, with great regards, yours

William Godwin.

Mary stayed with the Baxters for many months. It was a happy household, quiet and self-contained. It was, too, run on conventional lines and this may have implanted in Mary that basic desire for order and conformity which was to nag at her for the rest of her life. The days were spent in long walks and drives, sea-bathing, painting lessons. One daughter of the house, Isabel, became Mary's intimate friend. Mrs Marshall, Mary's early biographer, in later years met another daughter, Christy Baxter, then an old lady. Christy talked to her of Mary, describing her as 'agreeable, vivacious, and sparkling; very pretty, with fair hair and complexion and clear, bright, white skin'. They were all fond of her and she shared in all their pursuits.

That following Christmas Mary went home for a short time and took Christy Baxter with her to Skinner Street on a visit.

By this time, in 1812, Shelley had started his famous correspondence with Godwin. On 3 November, the very day after the travellers from Scotland had arrived, Christy remembered that there were three unusual guests to dinner—Shelley himself, his wife Harriet, and her sister Eliza. It was early days in the acquaintanceship and Mary and Shelley, meeting for the first time, made on this occasion little impression on one another. Christy remembered chiefly Harriet's beauty: the brilliant complexion, beautiful hair, and the smart purple satin dress which Harriet wore. Shelley was very attentive to his lovely young wife. Otherwise, over the years, there was nothing else very much of that momentous meeting that had remained in Christy's memory.

Christy had not been an intimate friend of Mary's though on the occasion of this visit they had shared a room together. The visit had been enjoyable, Mr and Mrs Godwin both apparently making a good impression as they put themselves out to appear in their best light to their young visitor. What impressed the visitor chiefly was the independent way each member of the family carried on his or her own life. Dinner at midday was the only meal at which the entire family foregathered. Otherwise supper was a movable feast and both the Godwin parents breakfasted alone. Godwin was noticeably undemonstrative but he showed more affection to Fanny than to anyone else in the household.

Christy felt that Fanny at that time had no idea of her true position, of the fact that she was illegitimate and had no real family claims. To Fanny it seemed that Godwin was an adored father and she looked after his interests and attended unselfishly to his every want. In return he appeared to want to protect her from knowledge of a truth which later was to undermine her life. Her position in this anomalous household was a pathetic one, and perhaps for the sake of his first wife whom he had loved Godwin was determined—at the beginning at any rate—to ensure that Fanny felt loved and wanted.

But of the two girls, Mary and Fanny, as intelligent human beings, Godwin had no doubt as to which was the superior. In a letter to a friend about this time he analysed the difference between them:

> Of the two persons to whom your inquiries relate, my own daughter is considerably superior in capacity to the one her mother had before. Fanny, the eldest, is of a quiet, modest, unshowy disposition, somewhat given to indolence which is her greatest fault, but sober, observing, peculiarly clear and distinct in the faculty of memory, and disposed to exercise her own thoughts and follow her own judgment. Mary, my daughter, is the reverse of her in many particulars. She is singularly bold, somewhat imperious, and active of mind. Her desire of knowledge is great, and her perseverance in everything she undertakes almost invincible. My own daughter is, I believe, very pretty. Fanny is by no means handsome, but, in general, prepossessing.

'Very plain but very sensible,' had been Harriet's verdict on Fanny to Mrs Nugent. 'The beauty of her mind fully overbalances the plainness of her countenance.'

In June Mary and Christy returned to Dundee where Mary was to remain for another ten months. Life in Scotland went on very much as before. Mary was happy but at moments restless.

'Life,' she wrote later, 'appeared to me too commonplace an affair as regarded myself.' To make up for this deficiency she wrote stories and pursued day dreams—'castles in the air'— which, when she felt depressed or annoyed, were a well-tried refuge. She was not, however, always her own heroine. 'I could,' she said, 'people the hours with creations far more interesting to me, at that age, than my own sensations.'

3

By March 1814 when Mary left Dundee for good and returned to her own home in London, she had grown up both physically and mentally. She was now sixteen and a half and very pretty, with large hazel eyes, a wide brow, and fair hair. Underneath an air of coolness and reserve she was, like her mother, deeply emotional, a fact which, owing to this 'Madonna look' of coolness and serenity, did not immediately reveal itself. The home life which she returned to made inroads on her stoicism. After the sedate predictability of the Baxter household the semi-bohemian life of Skinner Street proved something of an outrage. They were a diverse set of people that she had to deal with: Godwin, aloof and unsympathetic, wrapped in his own unsatisfactory affairs: Mrs Godwin, increasingly bad-tempered: Charles Clairmont, precariously placed in a job with Constable's in Edinburgh: William, aged eleven, at Dr Burney's school: Jane and Fanny, both permanently at home, and neither altogether satisfactory as companions.

Of the two Mary found herself gravitating towards Jane, though probably fully aware of the greater worthiness of Fanny. But Fanny, homely, unselfish, colourless, was of the type doomed always to be overlooked or pushed to one side. Jane, on the other hand, was lively, amusing, good company— even if at times untrustworthy, inconsiderate, maddening. The

contrast in her appearance to Mary's must at this time have
been striking: Mary, of extreme fairness, and Jane, a year
younger, with eyes so dark that it was difficult to distinguish
pupils from iris, curly black hair, dark complexion, brooding
vitality. Jane, like Mary, was unhappy at home. She thought
of going on the stage and at intervals took lessons in singing.
She longed for romance, adventure, a change of scene. She was,
too, dissatisfied with her name. 'Jane', she felt, was lacking in
glamour, and adopting her other name 'Clara' she changed it
gradually to 'Clare', and finally 'Claire'.

All the three girls were intensely interested in Godwin's
friendship with Shelley. To them Shelley, young and romantic,
a poet, and the heir to a baronetcy, was a figure of limitless
attraction. 'You cannot imagine,' Godwin himself had written
to Shelley as early as March 1812, 'how much all the females
of my family, Mrs Godwin and three daughters, are interested
in your letters and your history.' Now, in May 1814, Shelley
was in London again—his marriage in disarray, with
Harriet at Bath—and calling regularly at Skinner Street.
He found much to talk about to Godwin: *Queen Mab* had
just been published: Mary Wollstonecraft was a lodestar
of inspiration to both. And, besides that, always to be
discussed, there was the business of raising money to make
Godwin's life easier.

Mary, sometimes a listener at these talks, found herself
more and more impressed by Shelley. His tolerance, his
gentleness, his genuine altruism, filled her with admiration.
Gradually they were more thrown together. Her companionship
comforted him in his distress over the breach with Harriet; she
got from him the sympathy and the mental stimulation which
meant so much to her. Hogg, in his *Life of Shelley*, describes one
of their meetings on his first visit with Shelley to Skinner
Street. Shelley had wanted to speak to Godwin but, searching
through the shop and the house beyond, Godwin was nowhere
to be found. And then:

> A thrilling voice called 'Shelley!' A thrilling voice answered
> 'Mary!' And he darted out of the room, like an arrow from the
> bow of a far-shooting king. A very young female, fair and fair-

haired, pale indeed, and with a piercing look, wearing a frock of tartan, an unusual dress in London at that time, had called him out of the room. He was absent a very short time, a minute or two; and then returned.

'Godwin is out, there is no use in waiting.' So we continued our walk along Holborn.

'Who was that, pray?' I asked, 'a daughter?'

'Yes.'

'A daughter of William Godwin?'

'The daughter of Godwin and Mary.'

Shelley was unforthcoming but the encounter impressed Hogg and remained rooted in his memory. The situation was indeed fraught with tension. Increasingly Shelley and Mary were becoming aware that the bond between them was more than companionship, more than intellectual sympathy— instead, a balancing on the edge of passionate surrender. Every day, partly to get away from her stepmother's nagging disapproval, Mary made a pilgrimage to her mother's grave in St Pancras Churchyard. Here she could take her beloved books and read in peace. Here too, after a while, Shelley followed her. What happened at these meetings in the churchyard, and who first declared their love, is not completely known. But headlong they were plunged into a passionate intensity of feeling which seemed too strong to be withstood, and which threatened to sweep them out of all control.

At first Mary tried to keep her head. They could only be friends. There must be set limits to their relationship. Shelley gave her a copy of *Queen Mab* with her name in it, and on the inner flyleaf the words, 'You see, Mary, I have not forgotten you.' While at the end of the book, in her handwriting, is the more emotional inscription:

This book is sacred to me, and as no other creature shall ever look into it, I may write what I please. Yet what shall I write? That I love the author beyond all powers of expression, and that I am parted from him. Dearest and only love, by that love we have promised to each other, although I may not be yours, I can never be another's. But I am thine, exclusively thine.

By the kiss of love, the glance none saw beside,
The smile none else might understand,
The whispered thought of hearts allied,
The pressure of the thrilling hand.*

But such frustration, such heartbreak of sacrifice, was beyond them. They could not give each other up. Shelley now saw in Mary everything that he most longed for in womanhood. The fact that she was the daughter of two of his idols—Godwin and Mary Wollstonecraft—placed her in an unrivalled position in his eyes. He idealized her too for her beauty, for her imagination and intelligence, for her love of poetry, and for her sympathy with all his most cherished aspirations. He felt that she was his twin soul, his superior in intellect, a paragon among women. Sexually too he was far more roused by her than he had ever been by the less passionate Harriet. He was now determined to spend his life at her side. On 6 July he had an interview with Godwin and told him of his feelings for Mary.

Godwin, jettisoning at one sweep all his previously held notions of free love, was outraged. He must surely have had his suspicions before this but, with Shelley as his most promising source of income, he had probably refused to look his suspicions in the face. Now he was presented with a *fait accompli*. Shelley was asking him to surrender his daughter's person—Shelley, a married man, and Mary, a girl of sixteen—and the suggestion was intolerable. He told Shelley to leave the house and not to return.

Mary was kept a prisoner in the house, under the supervision of the unsympathetic Mrs Godwin who now disliked Shelley and tried her best to keep the lovers apart. But her efforts, as events turned out, were useless. Shelley broke into the house when Godwin was out, and offered Mary a bottle of laudanum. She was to take the laudanum and he was going to shoot himself. In this way they could be reunited. Mary, weeping and distraught, begged him to calm himself and told him, if he would go home peacefully, she would always be faithful.

* Byron.

Shelley calmed down and did as he was asked. He went out, leaving the bottle of laudanum on the table. But this did not mean that he was calmly acquiescing in the separation from Mary. It was now that he wrote to Harriet at Bath, begging her to leave everything and to come to London immediately. The interview then took place in which he told Harriet that their marriage was at an end, that he loved Mary and could not give her up.

Harriet having been told, he and Mary felt themselves free to make plans for their future together. There were still the various abortive efforts to separate them, there was still much to endure, but their minds were made up. Shelley was now successfully persuading himself that he had no obligations towards Harriet beyond financial provision. She had, after all, always known his views on the impermanence of marriage. On this subject he had, so he now reminded himself, never deceived her. She should therefore realize that since their love was at an end, if indeed it had ever existed, it was now only right and proper that they should separate. Mary, with a streak of ruthlessness in her complex character, backed him to the hilt. At this time in her life she had no sympathy for Harriet and no compassion; everything that had happened to Harriet was fully deserved, her own fault for making Shelley unhappy. Even as late as 1825, after Shelley's death, Mary still wrote of the separation: 'His justification is to me obvious.' It was not until many years later, in 1839, after much tribulation and suffering of her own, that for the first time she admitted a growing sense of remorse. By that time she had begun to feel that some of her own bitter sorrows had been meted out to her by fate as an atonement for Harriet's tragic end.

But poor Harriet's final tragedy was yet to come. For the present she remained suspended in shock and disbelief while events, over which she had no control, inexorably took their course. At five o'clock in the morning of that late July day in 1814 Mary met Shelley, who had a coach waiting ready outside his lodging in Hatton Garden. With Mary went Claire. Claire did not want to be left behind and Mary, weakening, was nervous of the journey and felt that Claire's knowledge of French might be an asset. It was a terribly hot day and Mary, overwrought with emotion, flagged on the journey to Dover and had to rest at each stage. At Dartford they took on two extra horses but even so they failed to arrive at Dover in time to catch the Channel packet.

This was a serious situation. At any moment the Godwins would discover their departure and, as likely as not, set out in pursuit. Shelley decided it was dangerous to wait for to-morrow's boat. Instead, while the girls refreshed themselves with a bathe in the sea, he made arrangements with two local fishermen to take his party across the Channel that evening in a small sailing boat.

It was only to be a two-hour crossing but in the event it took much longer. A thunder squall blew up with strong winds and rough seas. Mary, seasick and exhausted, lay back in the bottom of the boat, resting between Shelley's knees. Waves rushed into the vessel and even the fishermen became alarmed. Shelley found himself reflecting on death—'It was rather a thing of discomfort and of disappointment than horror to me.' Claire remained unaffected and alert. Gradually the wind died down, the storm moved away, and the coast of France appeared in sight. In the early morning of 29 July the travellers disembarked safely at Calais.

4

There was perturbation at Skinner Street. 'Five in the morning. M. J. for Dover,' Godwin wrote in his Journal. And, sure enough, that very evening, at the Calais inn where they were resting, Shelley received the message that 'a fat lady had arrived who said that I had run away with her daughter'. The former Mrs Clairmont was in pursuit of Claire.

Claire began to waver. Perhaps, momentarily, she saw their little party in the light of a sober common sense. What were they after all? An unstable and immature young poet of twenty-one, and two precocious schoolgirls, neither yet seventeen, with little money between them, and few prospects. She spent the night with her mother, almost decided to go back, but was advised by Shelley to take another half-hour for consideration. Disastrously for them all, she decided to stay. Mrs Godwin, her patience and temper strained to the utmost, thereupon departed, so Shelley tells us, 'without answering a word'.

Shelley was quite satisfied. He looked upon Claire as a potential disciple and it never irked him to have a third party on his honeymoons. Claire, who loathed restraint and had little family affection, was game for further adventure, whatever the consequences. Only Mary must have had doubts. She did not really care for Claire. And by allowing Claire to stay with them they were accepting responsibility for her welfare when their own plans were hazardous and improvident in the extreme.

With money short, they decided to *walk* through France to Paris. There they tried to raise money from an agent attached to Hookham, Shelley's publisher. In temporary straits, Shelley sold his watch and chain. All three, it seemed, moved in a euphoria of irresponsible unreality. A small donkey was bought for the girls to ride on in turn, but the donkey proved too weak for the load, and instead they had to carry the donkey. At each new place they discovered Claire was ecstatic: 'This is beautiful! Let us live here!' Mary hardly bothered to eat and at night they were often 'too happy to sleep'. The donkey was got rid of at financial loss and replaced by a mule. The girls, dressed in black silk, rode in turns until Shelley hurt his foot and then the girls had to walk while he rode. At intervals they stopped under trees, ate bread and fruit, and drank wine. It was decided now that they should continue their journey via France to Switzerland, and then on to Germany.

At Troyes they rested for a while, Mary unwell, and Shelley with a sprained ankle. Here they decided to dispose of the mule, again at a loss. Their apartments were far from comfortable and Shelley relieved his feelings by writing another of his famously tactless letters to Harriet:

Troyes, 120 miles from Paris, in the way
to Switzerland, August 13th . . . 1814

My dearest Harriet

I write to you from this detestable town. I write to show that
I do not forget you. I write to urge you to come to Switzerland,
where you will at least find one firm and constant friend, to
whom your interests will be always dear, by whom your feelings
will never wilfully be injured. From none can you expect this
but me—

He went on, in a chatty style, to describe their adventures,
Mary's health, the desolation of the war-stricken country
through which they had passed, their plans for going on by
carriage to Neufchâtel:

We have met none of the robbers they prophesied at Paris. You
shall know our adventures more detailed if I do not hear at
Neufchâtel that I am soon to have the pleasure of communica-
ting to you in person, and of welcoming you to some sweet retreat
I will procure for you among the mountains.—I wish you to bring
with you the two deeds—as also a copy of the settlement. Do not
part with any of your money. But what shall be done about the
books?—With love to my sweet little Ianthe, ever most affectionately yours, S.

I write in great haste. We depart directly.

Having had enough of walking, they now hired a carriage.
But the *voiturier*, an erratic character, grew tired of their loitering
by the way, gave them the slip and went on ahead, intending
them to follow on foot. This they did, walking for miles, and
only consoled by the beauty of the magnificent mountain
scenery through which they passed, and which inspired Shelley
later to wonderful descriptive poetry. But such intensive
travelling had many drawbacks. They were getting sick of
'wheeled machines' and the carriage was disposed of. Like the
donkey and the mule it had become a liability. They felt
very tired. If only they could find somewhere comfortable to
settle—but one inn after another was unsatisfactory, and
apartments they rented were often filthy. At length at Brunnen
they found a promising château, engaged two rooms in it for
six months, and went out to hire some beds.

Shelley as a Boy, from a pencil sketch
by the Duc de Montpensier *(Bodleian
Library)*

William Godwin, from
a portrait by James
Northcote *(National
Portrait Gallery)*

Mary Wollstonecraft,
from a portrait by John
Opie *(National
Portrait Gallery)*

It was not until the next day that they began to think about money. Shelley carried all their money loose in a sack which he had obtained from a banker at Neufchâtel. Now the sack was emptied into a convenient receptacle and the money counted. They found, to their consternation, that their assets were now reduced to only £28.

Fortunately for Harriet she had not taken up Shelley's offer to join them in Switzerland and there had been no letter from her at Neufchâtel. If she had decided to make the journey she would have found the birds had flown. For suddenly, at an hour's notice after the counting of the money, the three pilgrims decided that Switzerland at the moment held no further attractions and that they must return as speedily as possible to England.

Even allowing for their youth, their joint irresponsibility at this juncture is startling. Claire, in her Journal, finds it 'laughable' that, after taking part of a house for six months, they should have left within two days. After waiting one day for the washerwoman to appear, and another day for the linen to dry, they set off on their homeward journey. This time they decided on yet another mode of travel and went by water, up the Reuss and the Rhine, reaching Rotterdam by 8 September.

There was a contrary wind blowing so they could not at once set sail. Instead they did some sight-seeing among the Dutch, who they found refreshingly 'sober and slow' compared to the more licentious Germans. Shelley prevailed on the captain of a ship to take them across the Channel at a cost of three guineas apiece and at length, after another stormy night at sea which 'almost killed' them, they arrived back in England, penniless, on 12 September.

The next problem was the nightmare one of finding some money. They had not even enough left to pay a boatman who took them up the river. Instead they drove from place to place in a hackney coach, calling unavailingly on all their past associates in London, including Hookham the publisher, begging for a loan. Shelley's banking account in England, until a settlement had been drawn up, was shared jointly with Harriet. It now appeared that Harriet had availed herself of most of the meagre funds available and there was nothing left for the travellers to do but to call on her for help. Accordingly Shelley paid a long two-hour visit to Chapel Street while, in the gathering darkness, the two girls waited outside for him in the coach. Harriet begrudged the money but, under the circumstances, capitulated. The boatman was paid off, a hotel in Oxford Street was found for the night, and the next day they all moved to lodgings in Margaret Street.

The weeks that followed were weeks of chequered happiness. Though happy in each other, Shelley and Mary found, to their consternation and shame, that people who had previously welcomed them now turned away in coldness. None of the Godwin family would see them. All Shelley's attempts to get in touch with his idol were met with rebuff and the information that no communication could be made except through a solicitor. Mrs Godwin was still extremely angry. Fanny was away, staying with her aunts in Ireland. Even Isabel Baxter, who had been Mary's greatest friend, was now cold and unresponsive, appearing to believe the current story going about that Godwin had shamefully sold the two girls, Mary and Claire, to Shelley for £800 and £700 apiece! Only Peacock remained faithful. Shelley was paying Peacock £100 a year to superintend his financial affairs. Now Peacock came nearly every day and went out with Shelley to Hampstead Heath, to sail boats—always one of Shelley's favourite pastimes.

It was an unfortunate thing that Shelley's generous schemes for sharing his inherited wealth took no account of the fact that at present he had no wealth to share. Nevertheless, as well as the payment to Peacock of £100 a year, he still had every intention of financing Godwin, besides keeping both Harriet and Claire. The situation was an impossible one; he was soon heavily in debt, with creditors and bailiffs on his trail. His misguided notion that Mary and Harriet might get on well together, and that Harriet should live with them as 'the sister of his soul', had been turned down by the lawyers. Settled provision must therefore be made for Harriet who was at present living at Chapel Street, almost entirely dependent on her father. Shelley visited her at intervals and wrote her a succession of extraordinary letters. These letters have a strange history.

5

For years the letters were missing, though known to exist. They were used by the Westbrooks after Harriet's death in their Chancery proceedings to prevent Shelley claiming custody of the children. But Peacock, writing his recollections forty years later, failed to find any trace of them.

It was not until Leslie Hotson was making investigations on another matter in the Public Records Office that he came upon an index entry 'Shelley v. Westbrooke'. It dawned on him that among the Shelley documents he might find copies of the missing letters. As described in his book *Shelley's Lost Letters to Harriet* (1930) the exciting discovery was made of existent copies of these letters. Light—much more light—was at last thrown upon the very baffling story of Shelley's break with Harriet.

His insensitiveness in these letters is extraordinary. There are exhortations, scoldings, a self-righteous self praise, which make the reader wonder whether Shelley might not at this time have been almost deranged. Any hint of remorse or guilt towards the wife he had made pregnant and deserted is completely absent. Instead he wrote to her as though, by deigning to remain her friend, he was conferring enormous benefits:

> I deem myself far worthier and better than any of your nominal friends—Me you may keep as a most stead-fast and affectionate friend, but I have a certain price. It is confidence and truth.— You think that I have injured you—Even now when a violent and lasting passion for another leads me to prefer her society to yours, I am perpetually employed in devising how I can be permanently and truly useful to you.—My attachment to Mary neither could nor ought to have been overcome. Our spirits are united. We met with passion, she has resigned all for me.

There was more in the same tone. In spite of all that had
happened he expected Harriet to put her complete faith in
him, to hand over her future to his vague promises and generous
intentions. Instead she went to a lawyer and her family
proposed to take action in the courts. This incensed him to
further admonitions:

> I was an idiot to expect greatness or generosity from you, that
> when an occasion of the sublimest virtue occurred, you would
> fail to play a part of mean and despicable selfishness. The pure
> and liberal principles of which you used to boast that you were a
> disciple, served only for display. In your heart it seems you were
> always enslaved to the vilest superstitions, or ready to accept
> their support for your own narrow and worldly views. You are
> plainly lost to me for ever. I foresee no probability of change.

Harriet, stung to anger, wrote bitterly in self-defence. For
several weeks of that September and October of 1814 the
wrangle by letter continued. Harriet, pregnant with Shelley's
child, hit out blindly. She abused Mary, tried to implicate
Godwin. Shelley, outraged at having lost a 'disciple', maddened
by his own financial predicament, hounded by the bailiffs,
was equally implacable:

> I desire to renew no intercourse of whatsoever nature with you—
> You have lost a friend whom you will with difficulty replace—
> Your contumelious language towards Mary is equally impotent
> and mean—I consider it an insult that you address such Cant
> to me. Harriet, if you still continued what I once hoped you
> would never cease to be, if you deserved my affection, with what
> eagerness would I devote myself to your pleasure. Desert the
> selfish and the worldly wretches with whom you seem to pride
> yourself in making common cause, and I will be your friend.

Why, he persisted, was she not grateful for his continued
interest in her? He was willing to 'superintend the progress' of
her mind, to assist her in 'cultivating an elevated philosophy'.
The irritation of his visits, he noticed, produced 'more pain
than advantage'. 'Collect yourself I entreat you: remember
what I am: recall your recollections of my character.'

Her hints about financial settlements only proved to him her unworthiness: 'You have little need to fear that I shall fail in real duty.' And then, as an afterthought, in a postscript: 'I hope that you will attend to the preservation of your health. I do not apprehend the slightest danger from your approaching labour—Your last labour was painful, but auspicious—I see Hookham tonight. I am in want of stockings, hanks and Mrs W's posthumous works.'

This correspondence might almost appear farcical if the situation was not so tragic. But Harriet was irredeemably unhappy; and Shelley himself, driven frantic by the exigencies of his life, was now broken in physical health and suffering from an attack of lung trouble.

For two or three weeks, from October to early November of that year 1814, he was a fugitive from home and living in fear of actual arrest. He dared not sleep at his lodgings and he and Mary were only together at home on Sundays, the one day of the week when they were legally safe from bailiffs. For the rest of the time they had to be content with snatched meetings in parks or museums, in tramping the streets, in an exchange of feverish letters of love and longing. 'My love, my own one—' 'My beloved Mary—' 'Oh, my dearest love'—there is no doubt, reading these pathetic notes, of the reality of the feeling which bound them. Shelley at this time usually slept and had his meals at Peacock's home, but by day he haunted lawyers and moneylenders, trying to raise money.

'Money affairs,' he wrote to Harriet on 12 October, 'are in a desperate state. If November arrives without further success I must go to prison—I have not any money to send you.' He urged her to spin out her quarter's allowance from him as economically as she could. He did not want her to be dependent on her father, 'that selfish fellow'. Eliza too drew down his opprobrium: 'Your sister is absent from Town?—I wonder that her professed affection for you permitted her to leave you in the terrible state of dejection in which your letter of Sunday was written.' He felt battered on all sides. Mary, like Harriet, was pregnant and far from well. At times they were actually short of food. Mary's Journal describes the privations and difficulties of their lives at this time: 'People want their money, won't send up dinner, and we are all very hungry.' Half starving, Shelley would rush round to Peacock's to fetch cakes for them. They moved into cheaper lodgings and Shelley sold his microscope and other things 'to buy bread'.

The last hope now was Harriet herself. Could not she perhaps provide them with funds and Shelley would pay her back? The last of the Hotson letters is written to Harriet on 25 October:

> I cannot raise money soon enough—Unless you can effect something I must go to Prison—I depend wholly on you—Write to me and send the money soon—Write quickly—send a porter with the letter—if possible let it contain the £30. I am certain to repay it in a fortnight. These vexations have induced my antient illness—so exhausted as scarcely able to walk—If once in prison, confined in a damp cell, without a sixpence, without a friend—I must inevitably be starved to death. We have even now sold all that we have—you will shudder to hear that before I could sell the last valuable Mary and her sister very nearly perished with hunger—My dear Harriet, send quick supplies.

It is believed that Harriet accepted and answered this appeal. By 9 November anyhow it appears that the danger of arrest was over and Shelley rejoined Mary and Claire in their new lodgings in Nelson Square.

In December Harriet's second child—a son—was born. Mary heard the news with a feeling that was not untinged with bitterness. Harriet, Shelley's legal wife, had given birth to a son and heir. Her own child, shortly to be born, would have no legal status. In spite of the great love binding her and Shelley together it seemed that the advantages still lay in Harriet's hands. She could not help being aware too of Shelley's pride and pleasure in the birth of his heir. It was a knife turning in the wound of her insecurity. He wrote, as she remarked in her Journal . . . 'a number of circular letters of this event, which ought to be ushered in with ringing of bells etc., for it is the son *of his wife*—' It was the first manifestation of the acidity which was always latent in her written musings—understandably perhaps, as the difficulties of her life mounted one upon another.

For, quite apart from her resentment over Harriet, she had always the more acute uneasiness caused by the presence of Claire. There was, it seemed, to be no escape from this termagant 'step' sister. Having once cast her lot with Shelley and Mary, Claire was now determined to stick with them at all costs. On no account would she return to Skinner Street. Her perpetual presence was, however, becoming to Mary an increasing irritation. She was an unsettling element, demanding attention—Shelley's attention chiefly—and, as far as Mary was concerned, an unwelcome intruder.

Shelley's own feelings towards this third party in his unorthodox household were at this time ambivalent. He was stimulated by Claire's admiration and liveliness, while at the same time appalled by her lack of depths and by her 'insensibility and incapacity for the slightest degree of friendship'. She fastened on him, took advantage of his kindness, argued and quarrelled with him, kept him up late at night. She hoped perhaps to attract him to herself while at the same time realizing that the hope was a slender one. She knew in her heart of hearts that she could not displace Mary but she envied Mary her luck. For Shelley, as Claire herself looking back years later would have acknowledged, was the one man in her life who never let her down, who remained unfailingly kind through nightmare days of storm and strain.

Shelley, now, taking the blame in their quarrels, roused her to an unwonted sincerity of admiration: 'How I like good, kind, explaining people.' She was not the person to hesitate to make the most of her opportunities. Mary was pregnant, unwell, unable to get about. So Claire constituted herself as indefatigable companion and helpmeet. Everywhere that Shelley went she went too. She made the excuse that Shelley was nervous of being left alone, that he still feared for his life and a possible attack from his old enemy Leeson from Tremadoc. So together they tramped the streets, explored the byways of London, once even got locked into Kensington Gardens.

Mary was forced to look on helplessly. Shelley, aware perhaps of his own emotional weakness, gave himself stern advice in his Journal: 'Beware of weakly giving way to trivial sympathies. Content yourself with one great affection—never suffer more than one even to approach the hallowed circle.' But he looked upon Claire as a disciple, another charming young woman to mould to the desired pattern. He was flattered by her attentions and felt that he could influence her for good. His patience with her vagaries—the hysterics, nightmares, sullen moods, selfish demandings—never wavered. But, with the unconscious cruelty of the idealist out of touch with reality, he did not apparently stop to consider how this state of affairs might react on Mary.

⚜ 6 ⚜

Early in 1815, providentially for them, there was a change in their fortunes. In January Sir Bysshe Shelley died. Immediately, Shelley's hopes were raised. He was, after all, his father's heir, and the heir to a baronetcy. Surely now there would be something forthcoming of the family fortune which he could rightly call his own?

Soon after seeing the death in the papers he and Claire rushed off to Sussex for the reading of the will. Leaving Claire at a neighbouring village, Shelley presented himself at Field Place and was refused admittance. He accepted the position philosophically, sat down on the door-step, and passed the time by reading *Comus*. At one juncture the family doctor came out of the house to inform him that his father was still very angry and had not forgiven him.

However, the upshot of the family negotiations—a complicated matter of entailed and unentailed estates—was that Shelley became the recipient of £1,000 a year, plus a considerable lump sum to pay off his debts. After his previous penury this was wealth indeed. Shelley immediately decided that Harriet must have £200 a year, and he sent off to her in addition a sum of £200 for immediate expenses.

Mary, at home, was receiving visits from Hogg and from her

stepbrother, Charles Clairmont. Charles had lost his job in Edinburgh and was now living at Skinner Street, restless and adventure-seeking as ever. He came, full of gossip, with news of the Godwins. They were still, it appeared, unforgiving towards Claire and talked of immuring her in a convent. The aunts in Ireland, who planned to have Fanny later to teach in their school, were shocked by the family scandal, and were dubious lest Fanny's name too should become contaminated. Poor Fanny herself was in the doldrums. It had saddened her that neither of her 'sisters' had made her their confidante. Instead they had left home abruptly with Shelley, who had been her treasured friend, and there was nobody now for her to turn to. She was maid-of-all-work at home, timid and subservient, with very little to look forward to. Mary and Claire felt nothing but impatience towards her. In their eyes she was *too* weak, *too* humble altogether. Why did she not strike out on her own, take a firm line for once, disobey orders and come and visit them?

Mary was expecting her baby's birth in two months' time. Before this happened she and Shelley decided to move lodgings once more into a better district. It seems, however, from Mary's Journal, that all the necessary arrangements were made on the spur of the moment with an improvident lack of organization: 'Wednesday. Feb: 8th. We are to move today, so Shelley and Claire go out to look for lodgings. Hogg and I pack, and then talk. Shelley and Claire do not return until 3; they have not succeeded; go out again; they get apartments at Hans Place; move.'

Fortunately the move was accomplished just in time. A week later Mary's little girl was born prematurely. Neither she nor Shelley was in very good health and at first the baby, a seven-months child, was not expected to live. With the Godwins absent from home, at last Fanny could bear no longer the enforced separation from her 'sisters': she came to call and stayed the night. By 2 March, only ten days or so after the baby's birth, there was yet another 'bustle of moving', into still another lodging house. The condition of the baby had been improving. They had imagined that all was well. But now, only four days after the latest move, Mary woke up in the morning to find that the baby was dead.

The death was a great shock to her. Her first impulse was a strange one: 'Send for Hogg. Talk.' The very next day she was left alone by Shelley and Claire who went 'to town'. 'Stay at home,' Mary wrote in her Journal, 'and think of my little dead baby. This is foolish, I suppose; yet whenever I am left alone to my own thoughts, and do not read to divert them, they always come back to the same point—that I was a mother, and am so no longer.' Fanny came, wet through, and fortunately stayed the evening. But a few days later again Mary wrote: 'Dream that my little baby came to life again; that it had only been cold, and that we rubbed it before the fire, and it lived. Awake and find no baby.'

The rackety life which they had been leading for so long was affecting her nerves and this loss plunged her into a deep depression. She fretted over Shelley's continual absences with Claire, and she fretted over the separation from her adored father. Mrs Godwin had relented sufficiently to send her a present of linen for the baby but otherwise there was no truce with Skinner Street. It seemed that there was nobody to sympathize with her distress except Hogg, and Hogg made the most of his opportunities.

An extraordinary episode now took place in which it seems possible that Mary and Hogg became lovers while Shelley accepted the situation with approval. There is one particular letter of Shelley's to Hogg himself which seems to confirm this supposition:

26 April 1815

My dear Friend

I shall be very happy to see you again, and to give you your share of our common treasure of which you have been cheated for several days. The Maie* knows how highly you prize this exquisite possession—Do not fear. We will not again be deprived of this participated pleasure.

It does not seem that the 'affair' meant very much to Mary. Perhaps indeed she was only trying dutifully to carry into

* A pet name of Shelley's for Mary.

practice Shelley's concepts of free love and his rebellion against social inhibitions. In Shelley's eyes, theoretically, at any rate, such behaviour did no harm to existing and deeper unions. Is it possible that, looking back, he was ashamed of his indignation when Hogg had tried similar tactics with Harriet? Now, maybe, he was determined to live up to his own precepts and to make no such gaffe a second time.

Strange episode as it was, it was soon to be over. Shelley was the one love of Mary's life and Hogg was only a makeshift. The more immediate problem now was the problem of Claire's future. How could her life be planned so that she was no longer so dependent on them? Her continued presence, Mary could see only too plainly, was ruining their happiness, and Shelley was gradually coming round to the same conclusion. Mary's Journal tells its own story:

> *March 11th.* Very unwell—Talk about Clara's going away, nothing settled; I fear it is hopeless. She will not go to Skinner Street; then our house is the only remaining place, I see plainly. What is to be done?
> *March 14th.* Shelley and I go upstairs and talk of Clara's going; the prospect appears to me more dismal than ever; not the least hope. This is, indeed, hard to bear.

It was a trial and a tribulation. The effect of Claire's continual presence in Mary's life can be gauged by her remark years and years later in the time of her widowhood, when her daughter-in-law offered to leave the two together: 'Do not leave me alone with her; she has been the bane of my life ever since I was three years old.' Her diary now showed more and more signs of the strain that she was enduring. Sarcasm abounds: 'Shelley goes out with his friend,' 'Shelley and the lady walk out.' There were few alleviations to the difficulties of her life. Godwin was still expecting financial help and did not hesitate to send demanding pleas by his stepson, Charles. Shelley himself was still tied up with Harriet, visiting her at times, sometimes finding her in 'a surprisingly good humour', and arranging, for identification purposes, that his son Charles should be brought into court.

By May it had been suggested that Claire should try to find employment as a companion or governess. An advertisement brought only one answer, and that was unsatisfactory. A friend of Godwin's, a Mrs Knapp, was approached with the hope that she might have Claire to live in her house, but this plan too came to nothing. Claire herself remained apparently untroubled and buoyant, and was further cheered by winning a money prize of unspecified amount in a lottery. Finally she took matters into her own hands and decided that she had better make herself scarce before any more Mrs Knapps appeared on the scene. She needed, she said, a change of air and a holiday. 'Shelley and his friend,' Mary wrote thankfully in her Journal, 'have a last conversation.'

The next day Claire departed in good spirits by herself for cottage lodgings in Lynmouth, Devon. She was not without courage. Before long she had written to Fanny—a letter of ebullience and confidence:

> You told me that you did not think I should ever be able to live alone. If you knew my constant tranquillity, how cheerful and gay I am, perhaps you would alter your opinion. I am perfectly happy. After so much discontent, such violent scenes, you will hardly believe how enraptured I am with this dear little quiet spot. I am as happy when I go to bed as when I rise. I am never disappointed—

And Mary, meanwhile, had made a thankful and revealing entry in her diary: 'I begin a new journal with our regeneration.'

7

The next months were perhaps to be some of the happiest of Mary's life—a short space of time in which she had Shelley to herself. Their first thought was to find a house of their own, after weeks of living in lodgings. They were both fond of

travel and, before starting the search in earnest, they had a
holiday together in Devon. Then again, strangely, they separated. Even now Mary had to endure moments of agonized uneasiness. While she waited at Clifton, Shelley wandered about,
searching for houses on his own, interviewing solicitors in
London. The haunting thought occurred to Mary that even
now they might not yet be rid of Claire. A letter she wrote to
Shelley in July 1815 is full of the uncertainties of her position
and reveals plainly her longing for security and peace of mind:

> My beloved Shelley—
> What I am now going to say is not a freak from a fit of low
> spirits, but it is what I earnestly entreat you to attend to and
> comply with.
> We ought not to be absent any longer; indeed we ought not.
> I am not happy at it. When I retire to my room, no sweet love;
> after dinner, no Shelley; though I have heaps of things *very
> particular* to say; in fine, either you must come back, or I must
> come to you directly. You will say, shall we neglect taking a
> house—a dear home? No, my love, I would not for worlds give
> up that; but I know what seeking for a house is, and, trust me,
> it is a very, *very* long job, too long for one love to undertake in
> the absence of the other. Dearest, I know how it will be; we
> shall both of us be put off, day after day, with the hopes of the
> success of the next day's search, for I am frightened to think
> how long. Do you not see it in this light, my own love?
> —Pray, is Clara with you? for I have inquired several times
> and no letters; but, seriously, it would not in the least surprise
> me if you have written to her from London, and let her know
> that you are without me, that she should have taken some such
> freak.
> —Dearest, best Shelley, pray come to me; pray, pray do not
> stay away from me!

There is more in the same strain. Perhaps the ghost of a
deserted Harriet, fretting and lonely at her father's house in
Chapel Street, sat at Mary's elbow. What could she know of
the future when the past held such inconstancy? The very
urgency of her feeling threatened at times to break her iron
control.

To her unbounded relief, a house was found. Before long they were settled at a house at Bishopsgate, not far from Windsor. There they were happy for several months and here their little son, William, was born on 24 January 1816. Altogether it was a period of tranquillity, badly needed by Shelley, who had been told by his doctor that spring that he might shortly die of consumption. Peacock came to stay and took him in hand. Peacock decided that his illness was partly due to his starvation diet. Vegetarianism, he decided 'entered for something into his restlessness'. Certainly, he felt, it did not agree with him: 'it made him weak and nervous and exaggerated the sensitiveness of his imagination'. Instead of tea and bread and butter Peacock insisted upon well-peppered mutton chops. The resulting apparent improvement in Shelley's health he took as being the good effect of his ministrations. Shelley, whose liking for Peacock at this time was only qualified, attributed the improvement to other sources. It was due, as he explained in a letter to Hogg, to the fact that he was 'so much more free from the continual irritation under which I lived, as to devote myself with more effort and consistency to study'. And, in the same spirit of optimism, to the same correspondent a month later he wrote: 'No events, as you know, disturb our tranquillity.'

Nevertheless there was trouble in store. Godwin's demands for money were becoming more and more rapacious and the year 1816 was to prove the most tragic and disturbing of Shelley's life.

He and Mary, in spite of their happiness in each other, could not fail to realize that, in the eyes of other people, they stood guilty and condemned. Shelley, a married man, had deserted his young wife at a time when she was pregnant and most needed him, and had run off with a girl of sixteen, little more than a child. Even the Newtons and the Boinvilles could not countenance such behaviour and withdrew their friendship. Apart from Peacock and Hogg, none of their former associates stood by them. In March 1816 Shelley published his poem *Alastor* which was overlooked and neglected by the critics. It seemed to Shelley that they were faced with the coolness and enmity of almost everyone. Feeling soured and despairing, he began to make wild plans to eschew society completely and to retreat with Mary to some solitary refuge in Scotland or Cumberland.

These schemes were disrupted, however, by the reappearance of Claire. Claire, in the intervening months of the Shelleys' peaceful sojourn at Bishopsgate, had not been idle. The idyll of Lynmouth had been short-lived and before long she had joined her brother Charles in London. Her recurring fancy to go on the stage took possession of her once again and she cast about in her mind as to the most likely means of achieving this end. She must, she decided, conscript the help of someone famous, someone with power, someone who stood out from the rest of the world. Why not the poet Byron? It was an eventful decision, and one that was to have far-reaching and shattering consequences to her entire life.

But, once having made up her mind on a course to pursue, Claire was not easily daunted. Byron was on the Board of Management of Drury Lane Theatre. And, besides that, with his romantic aura, his shady history, and his personal glamour, Byron was, so Claire decided, a desirable end in himself. Mary had her poet, the son of a baronet, a near member of the aristocracy—why should not she, Claire, go one better and achieve as a friend a real lord, a true member of the aristocracy, and a poet who was world famous? This, whatever the perils, would be triumph indeed.

She wrote twice to Byron. The first letter, which was signed 'E. Trefusis', confessed her devotion and told him that she placed her happiness in his hands. She begged for an answer and, when none came, she wrote again, a much shorter note sent by a messenger, suggesting that she should call upon him at seven o'clock that evening.

Strangely, Byron agreed. He was not particularly interested and certainly not intrigued. His life was in disarray, his marriage had foundered, he was facing social ostracism, and his main mood was one of cynicism. But he was bored and any unexpected happening provided a momentary diversion. He met Claire, was attracted by her good looks, and agreed to a later scheme of hers that they should spend a night together at some obscure place in the country. They became lovers and in April Claire knew that she was pregnant and that Byron would be the father of her child.

She was not dismayed. What had started for her as a romantic adventure was becoming gradually an all-absorbing relationship. Triumph was here indeed. Not only had she got to know Byron, but already they were lovers, he was bound to her by her pregnancy, and there was no knowing what the future might hold. She made the mistake of letting Byron see that he held so high a place in her affections that she could not do without him. As the sharer of a passing prank he had found her amusing. Her voice had attracted him: he was beguiled enough to write a poem to her . . . 'There be none of Beauty's daughters'. He had thought her pretty and lively. But the last thing that he wanted was a serious, responsible attachment. Now, as a passionate woman, laying claims to his devotion and loyalty, he found her more than tiresome. And anyhow, England was growing too hot to hold him. He was making plans to leave the country of his birth and to go and live in Switzerland. He tried to choke Claire off by telling her that they must part.

Claire, however, was not to be so easily sidetracked. The reality of her devotion for Byron is a matter which has been open to doubt. Mrs Marshall, Mary's early biographer, thought that Claire's unpublished letters proved that she was not deeply in love. Since then some of the letters have been printed. They reveal preoccupation and deep infatuation if not real love. What seems likely is that they are proof of the deepest feeling of which Claire, at the age of seventeen, was capable. At all events, looking back at her life years later in 1827, Claire wrote to her friend Jane Williams a letter which summed up the disastrous havoc which the ill-starred affair with Byron had brought to her:

> I am unhappily the victim of a *happy passion*. I had one; like all things perfect in its kind it was fleeting, and mine only lasted ten minutes, but those ten minutes have discomposed the rest

Percy Bysshe Shelley,
from a portrait by
Amelia Curran,
1819 *(National
Portrait Gallery)*

Mary Shelley, from a
portrait by Richard
Rothwell, 1841
*(National Portrait
Gallery)*

Leigh Hunt, from a
portrait by Samuel
Lawrence
*(National Portrait
Gallery)*

Thomas Love Peacock,
from a portrait by
Henry Wallis *(National
Portrait Gallery)*

of my life. The passion, God knows from what cause, from no faults of mine, however, disappeared, leaving no trace whatever behind it except my heart wasted and ruined as if it had been scorched by a thousand lightnings.

Now, in 1816, knowing in her heart of hearts that this short period of ten minutes of happiness was already over, she tried desperately to prolong it. Perhaps as a result of this experience, she was never to fall in love again, and it did not seem at the time to be an experience lightly to throw away. Byron was going to Geneva and she got him to agree that she could join him there. He made the proviso, however, that she should not come alone.

It was at this juncture that Claire turned once more to the Shelleys. Shelley had always admired Byron. He had sent him a copy of *Queen Mab* and looked upon him as one of the greatest poets of the day. It now appeared to Claire that it would be both admirable and convenient if she could contrive a meeting between these two such kindred spirits. She got in touch with Shelley and put her plan before him. Whether she told him of her affair with Byron is not known. It is thought that Mary, anyhow, was not told.

The Shelleys were at a loose end, they had planned to leave Windsor anyway, and Shelley had always felt that to live on the continent might benefit his flagging health. Even his patience too was becoming exhausted by Godwin's incessant demands for money—so frequently combined, as it was, with insults. 'Do not talk of *forgiveness* again to me,' he wrote angrily to his persecutor, 'for my blood boils in my veins.' Mary's life threatened to become embittered from the same cause. And besides this, according to Peacock, Shelley had received lately one of his hallucinatory warnings (which appeared to occur at intervals during his life) to the effect that he was in danger, that some plot was afoot, laid by his father and uncle, to entrap him and lock him up.

So, all things considered, the idea of going to Geneva with Claire and joining forces with Byron did not seem uncongenial. Claire had her way, and both Shelley and Mary agreed to the plan.

I

8

On 3 May 1816 they all set out for Geneva. The Napoleonic wars were over, Napoleon was safely and finally incarcerated, and travel on the continent was the rage of the moment. They settled at the Hôtel d'Angleterre in a suburb on the edge of the lake, where the view was perfect and the climate golden. Byron had not yet arrived. There was no congenial society but they were happy at the change of scene. 'Our time passes swiftly and delightfully,' Mary wrote in her Journal.

A fortnight later Byron joined them. He arrived in style, in an enormous Napoleonic coach which he had had especially made for such an occasion. Besides bedding it included a library and a dining-room. He was accompanied by a staff of three menservants and a private physician, the Italian Dr Polidori. As was intended, the arrival caused a great deal of stir and commotion and, to add to the dramatic effect, Byron signed his age as 100 in the hotel visitors' book.

He was pleased to make the acquaintance of Shelley but Claire was a more tiresome adjunct to the party. Byron continued the liaison but his attentions were only half-hearted. Unable to be loyal to any woman he wrote of her disparagingly to his half-sister, Augusta Leigh: 'As to all these mistresses, Lord help me, I have had but one. What could I do? A foolish girl, in spite of all I could say or do, would come after me— I could not exactly play the Stoic with a woman who had scrambled eight hundred miles to unphilosophize me.'

Before long, however, hotel life became too gregarious for Shelley's liking, particularly since the arrival of Byron and his retinue, and he moved with Mary and Claire to a cottage near Coligny, on the other side of the lake. A fortnight later Byron, sick of being an object of ceaseless curiosity at the hotel, took the Villa Diodati on a hill above the Shelleys' cottage. He and the Shelleys were only now separated by a vineyard and visiting took place daily. There were mountain excursions, outings on the lake, Claire entertained them with her beautiful singing voice, Byron too sang, and in the evenings they all foregathered for talk.

In spite of their dissimilarity, Byron liked Shelley. In later years he was to be one of his most vigorous champions: 'You were all mistaken about Shelley,' he told Trelawny, 'who was without exception, the best and least selfish man I ever knew.' In return Shelley was fascinated by Byron's genius and intellect. 'Lord Byron is an exceedingly interesting person,' he wrote to Peacock that July, 'and as such is it not to be regretted that he is a slave to the vilest and most vulgar prejudices, and as mad as the winds.' Byron's friendship was always to cause turmoil and schism in Shelley's mind. He revered the poet but was shocked and aghast at the man.

Meanwhile, Claire made valiant efforts to breathe more life into her dwindling 'romance'. She made as many visits as she dared alone to the Villa Diodati, ostensibly for copying Byron's manuscripts. But she could not fail to notice that Byron showed little enthusiasm for these visits and, at times, seemed even studiously to avoid being alone with her. The position was not made easier by the doctor Polidori, who would not absent himself and appeared oblivious of the possibility that he might not be wanted.

The weather had broken up and there were frequent storms. They were all cooped together indoors in the evenings, sitting in the firelight. Byron and Shelley continued their absorbing intellectual discussions and Mary listened, enthralled and fascinated, but too timid to join in. On one evening, for something to do, Byron suggested that they should each write a ghost story. There had been talk on the origins of life, on experiments by Darwin, on the possibilities of reanimating corpses, and Mary's imagination had been fired. She went to bed that night, her mind chaotic with excited visions of a monster, made by man, but dedicated irrevocably to evil. She could not sleep and was fearful and terror-struck by her own imaginings. But the very next day she began writing it down. It was to be her 'story'. Shelley saw it and was impressed by its imaginative power—so strange and unusual for so young a girl.

He told her that she must prolong it, make it into, not a short story, but a book. This caught Mary's enthusiasm. The other members of the party had made half-hearted attempts at ghost stories but only Mary was genuinely fired by creative inspiration. She worked hard at this new and absorbing occupation and decided to call the book *Frankenstein*.

Byron was concentrating more and more on poetry. He wrote *The Prisoner of Chillon* during these Geneva days and was also working at *Childe Harold*. Shelley wrote his 'Hymn to Intellectual Beauty'.

On 4 August Shelley celebrated his twenty-fourth birthday. But already the little idyll at Geneva was nearing its close. Cares, problems, difficulties, were pressing in upon the travellers once more. It was now revealed to everybody that Claire was expecting a baby. Unpleasant scandals were being spread among their English neighbours. Their movements were spied upon. There was a letter from the lawyer in England telling Shelley that he was wanted and should return to England without delay. Fanny wrote gloomy letters, full of troubles, begging that more financial help should be sent to Godwin.

Fanny's troubles particularly were a weight on Shelley's mind. He had promised Godwin a further £300 by the end of June and had been unable to carry out his promise. Fanny, now, upset on her stepfather's account, seemed to be slipping further and further into a state of depression and melancholy. All her affairs were going wrong.

She wrote to them of the 'dreadful state of mind I generally labour under' and told them 'my mind always keeps my body in a fever'. She had hoped that her aunts in Ireland would take her to teach in their school but her hopes were gradually dying. She had not a sou of her own. Her state was one of complete dependence. She missed her 'sisters', missed Shelley himself who, she had somehow persuaded herself, was a very special friend of her own. She envied them now, meeting Byron, seeing Switzerland, all the excitements of their lives in which she had no share. A pathetic note about Mary's baby is contained in one of her letters: 'Kiss dear William for me, I sometimes consider him as my child, and look forward to the time of my old age and his manhood.' She would have liked to send them books but had no money. She begged Shelley for the £300 for Godwin who was unwell and uneasy in mind. If only, she said, he could go on writing his novel, with a mind free from financial worry, the novel might turn out to be one of his best.

Shelley and Mary rushed out and bought a watch—a present for Fanny when they should return home. Family anxieties weighed increasingly on their spirits. It seemed obvious that their days in Switzerland were numbered. But, before they left, there was the problem of Claire's future to be discussed with Byron.

Byron by now was becoming noticeably more bored and impatient. He was tired of sociability, sick of Claire, and anxious to be left to himself. The forthcoming birth of Claire's baby, a baby of which he was the father, was an event-to-be which moved him very little. What should be done with the baby when it was born? He could only suggest that possibly it could be put in the care of his half-sister, Augusta Leigh. When Claire objected he was ready to agree with any suggestion the Shelley party liked to make which would involve him in the least trouble. Shelley insisted that Claire should return with him and Mary to England: that they would look after her until the baby was born, and that the Godwins need not be told. And after that, as Claire insisted to Byron, the baby must remain with either one of its parents until it was at least seven years old. Claire herself should be called the child's 'aunt'. During those early years they must never part with it.

Byron, casually inattentive, and for the moment uninvolved, agreed to all these arrangements. The Shelley party started their packing on 28 August and the next day at nine in the morning they left Geneva. When they got to England Mary and Claire went to Bath to live in lodgings until the baby arrived, and Shelley stayed in London to negotiate the sale of *Childe Harold* to Byron's publishers. As a farewell letter Claire had written to Byron, telling him that she would love him and nobody else to the end of her life. She begged him to write to her and stressed her dread that he might forget her. She signed the letter 'Your own affectionate, Claire.' Meanwhile Byron had written flippantly to his equally flippant half-sister of the 'demoiselle' who had now returned to England to produce 'a new baby B'.

✕⚶ 9 ⚶✕

After a short time at Bath, Mary joined Shelley on a visit to Peacock and his mother at Marlow. Shelley had been busy making arrangements for the sale of Byron's poem—at a good price, as demanded by the author. He had also seen poor Fanny, who was still unhappy and indignant on Godwin's behalf, and urging Shelley to supply the promised £300.

Shelley went back to Bath with Mary after the Marlow visit, a worried man, badgered on all sides: he had promised to finance Godwin but if there was one object on which his father and the lawyers were determined, it was to prevent Shelley raising money on the estate for such a purpose. At Bath he, Mary and Claire—back in their old unhappy, three-cornered household—tried to carry on with their normal lives. Shelley wrote his poetry, Mary busied herself increasingly with the writing of *Frankenstein*, while Claire, against all her better judgment, found herself writing more and more frequently, an anguished series of letters to Byron.

Depressed by her coming confinement, she was becoming gradually more bitter. Byron never replied, cared nothing for her. Shelley took up the cudgels on her behalf: he embarked on what was to be the preliminary to many letters written to try to melt Byron's heart towards Claire. 'I think her spirits begin to fail,' he wrote, and begged Byron to write or send 'some kind message'. But Byron remained unmoved. Shelley he liked and was willing to correspond with. Towards Claire he remained implacable.

But now suddenly, when already the little party at Bath had much to contend with, real tragedy threatened. For the moment

Claire was taken out of herself, forgetting her own woes. Fanny, the eldest of the 'Godwin daughters', so stricken and harassed that she had lost all sense of proportion, had been writing letters which were growing increasingly more anxious and despairing. Since returning to England Shelley had handed over part of the expected £300 to Godwin but this had not been enough. 'For *his own* and the *world's sake*,' Fanny wrote frantically to Mary, 'he [Godwin] should finish his novel and is it not your and Shelley's duty—to endeavour to prevent, as far as lies in your power, giving him unnecessary pain and anxiety?'

Her attitude—maddening after all Shelley had already done for Godwin—was becoming completely unreasonable, and even hectoring. She blamed the Shelleys too for other things—for leaving letters lying about, for allowing servants to overhear and spread gossip of matters which should have been kept private. Scandalous rumours, she told them, had been flying about and it was their fault. She would not agree with Shelley and Mary who decided that the blame, if any, could be attributed to Mrs Godwin for going about collecting false information. Fanny was made desperate by all that had been happening to her. Her aunts in Ireland had decided that the family reputation was too shady for them to have her at their school. Probably it was at this time that she discovered the true facts of her birth. Mrs Godwin was nagging and bullying her continually for being a burden to a household in which she had no legal footing. She was lonely and penniless and felt that she had not a friend in the world. Suddenly and without explanation—apart from the false excuse that her aunts had sent for her—she disappeared.

It was not until a day or two later that letters arrived for both the Godwins and the Shelleys from Bristol. 'I depart immediately,' Fanny wrote, 'to the spot from which I hope never to remove.' Mary made a note in her Journal: 'A very alarming letter comes from Fanny. Shelley goes immediately to Bristol.' From clues obtained at Bristol, Shelley, who was joined by Godwin, hurried on to Swansea. On the morning of 10 October Fanny was found dead at the Mackworth Arms Inn, Swansea. She had retired to bed early, telling the chambermaid

that she was very tired. The next morning her door had been
forced open, and her dead body found, the long dark hair about
her face, and an empty laudanum bottle by her side.

Her possessions, found with her dead body, were few and
pathetic. On the table beside her bed was the watch from
Geneva, Shelley's and Mary's last present. In her reticule was a
handkerchief, a necklace, and a small purse containing two
coins. With these there was a note, the note that Fanny had
written before she took her own life:

> I have long determined that the best thing I could do was to
> put an end to the existence of a being whose birth was unfor-
> tunate, and whose life has only been a series of pain to those
> persons who have hurt their health in endeavouring to promote
> her welfare. Perhaps to hear of my death may give you pain, but
> you will soon have the blessing of forgetting that such a creature
> ever existed as—

The final name was omitted—or destroyed. There was no
written clue to her identity and Godwin, whose first thought
was one of concealment, insisted that the body should be left
unclaimed. They would be wisest, Godwin suggested hysteric-
ally, to tell people that Fanny had gone away to Ireland to live
with her aunts. He was deeply shattered but could not face the
truth that Fanny had killed herself. For months he kept her
death a secret from his friends. Charles Clairmont, who had
gone abroad, was never told and a letter from him, a year later,
contained a message to her. Finally Godwin revealed to his
friend, Mr Baxter, that Fanny was dead, but added that she
had died of a sudden fever in Wales.

Mrs Godwin blamed Shelley. Shelley, she insisted, had
come as an interloper into their lives, all three girls had fallen
in love with him, he had played havoc with their affections,
and this was the result. Four years later she was writing to
Mrs Gisborne, still harping on this same theme. Fanny's
death, she persisted, was due to jealousy of Mary. Godwin
himself was later inclined to agree with her.

To Shelley himself the tragedy of Fanny's death came as a
terrible shock. He, Mary and Claire were plunged into a

gloom and dismay which was long-lasting. Shelley could not help dwelling in his mind on that last meeting with Fanny in London only a few weeks earlier. How blind he had been not to realize the true nature of Fanny's misery and how near she was to breaking point! Because she was loyal to the Godwins and would not betray them, he and Mary had never sufficiently appreciated her real character—her faithfulness and unselfishness amounting almost to nobility. 'There was he,' as Mrs Marshall wrote, 'offering sympathy and help to the oppressed and the miserable all the world over, and here—under his very eyes—this tragic romance was acted out to the death.'*

> Her voice did quiver as we parted,
> Yet knew I not that heart was broken
> From which it came, and I departed
> Heeding not the misery then spoken.
>   Misery, o, Misery,
> This world is all too wide for thee!

But worse was still to come. That tragic year of 1816 was not finished with yet. Shelley, his health and nerves strained to the utmost, went off again that autumn on another visit to Peacock at Marlow. Lately Shelley had revised his opinion of Peacock. Peacock—although he disapproved of the break with Harriet and talked in after years of the difficulty he found in 'keeping on friendly terms with Mary Godwin'—had proved himself a good friend to Shelley who described him now as 'an amiable man of great learning'. Shelley too had lately been a little cheered by an article in *The Examiner* in which the writer Leigh Hunt had praised a 'new school of poets'—the school of Keats, Shelley and Reynolds. Now Shelley and Leigh Hunt met for the first time, from which meeting was to ensue a lifelong friendship. In trouble Leigh Hunt was a friend in a thousand—kind, sympathetic, unfailingly patient. Scatter-brained and improvident, and something of a cadger, he was yet to be perhaps the dearest friend Shelley ever had. A few years later, it was through his efforts to meet and welcome Leigh Hunt to Italy that Shelley died.

* Mrs Julian Marshall: *The Life and Letters of Mary Wollstonecraft Shelley.*

Leigh Hunt's friendship, Peacock's astringent support, Mary's affectionate letters—Shelley now needed all the help he could muster to carry him through these melancholy days. He busied himself looking for a house to rent in the Marlow neighbourhood as he and Mary hoped to settle down again in their own home as soon as they could. Mary wrote, egging him on: 'A house with a lawn, a river or lake, noble trees, and divine mountains, that should be our little mousehole to retire to. But never mind this; give me a garden and *absentia* Claire, and I will thank my love for many favours—' Her letters were sprinkled with endearing terms: 'Sweet Elf', 'Sweetest', 'My blessed love'. It is easy to see that she was possessed by the same nagging unease of past days. Always uppermost in her mind was the longing that she and Shelley might be permitted to have a home together of their own, as in the happy months before they went to Geneva.

Shelley returned to Bath on 14 December. For some time he had been wondering and worrying why, for several months, he had heard no news of Harriet and his children. Even Peacock, who had been looking after Harriet's money affairs at one time, had now lost touch with her. Shelley had written to Hookham asking if he could discover any news. Now, only the next day after his return to Bath, Hookham's reply arrived with the appalling news that Harriet was dead. Her body had been found in the Serpentine in Hyde Park.

⚜ 10 ⚜

Harriet's death has always remained something of a mystery.

In his book *Shelley in England*, Roger Ingpen gave verbatim in an appendix the inquest proceedings on the body of 'Harriet Smith', now known to have been Harriet Shelley. The verdict given was 'Found *dead* in the Serpentine River', with the addition that: 'The said Harriet Smith had no marks of violence appearing on her body, but how or by what means she became dead, no evidence thereof does appear to the Jurors.'

In spite of this somewhat ambiguous verdict it has always been taken for granted that Harriet's death was suicide by drowning. Even on this theory, however, there is much that remains unproved and mysterious.

What had been happening to Harriet since Shelley and Peacock had lost touch with her—all the time, in fact, that Shelley was abroad at Geneva? This is not easy to trace. At one time she had certainly been living at her father's house in Chapel Street with her two children. But it seems that both the children were delicate, that London air did not agree with them, and that some time in 1816 the Westbrook family or their lawyers arranged for them to be removed to the guardianship of a vicar in Warwickshire. Without even her children Harriet was very much alone. Strangely in the Harriet story there is little mention of Harriet's mother and yet—so we gather— her mother was alive. Only Eliza was her sheet anchor and where, one wonders, was the beloved Eliza's love and support during this crucial period? And how unfortunate that even Peacock, who had been a kind intermediary in trying to get from Whitton more money for the children, had in these last months lost touch with her.

There are, however, letters in existence which Harriet wrote at this time in which it appears that she was trying to forget her own grief by helping other people. There is one to her old vegetarian friend, Mr Newton, whose wife was dying, offering a gift of fruit, or her assistance in looking after his children. We hear, through Fanny Godwin, of one or more visits Harriet paid to Bracknell, perhaps to consult Mrs Boinville.

Months earlier there had been a revealing letter to her great friend, Mrs Nugent, in Ireland:

> I really see no termination to my Sorrows. As to Mr Shelley I know nothing of him. He neither sends nor comes to see me. I am still at my Father's which is very wretched. When I shall quit this House I know not. Everything goes against me. I am weary of my life. I am so restrained that life is scarcely worth having—at nineteen I could descend a willing victim to the

Tomb. How I wish those dear children had never been born. They stay my fleeting spirit when it would be in another State. How many there are who shudder at death. I have been so near it that I feel no terrors. Mr Shelley has much to answer for. He has been the cause of great misery to me and mine. I shall never live with him again. 'Tis impossible. I have been so deceived, so cruelly treated, that I can never forget it. Oh no, with all the affections warm, a heart devoted to him, and then to be so cruelly blighted. Oh Catherine, you do not know what it is to be left as I am, a prey to anguish, corroding sorrow, with a mind too sensitive to others' pain. But I will think no more. There is Madness in thought. Could I look into futurity for a short time how gladly would I pierce the veil of Mystery that wraps my fate. Is it wrong, do you think, to put an end to one's sorrows? I often think of it—all is so gloomy and desolate. Shall I find repose in another world?

'Shall I find repose in another world?' It was a question quite obviously that haunted Harriet's mind. She felt herself unwanted, a burden to her family, a deserted woman who had lost husband, income, position, esteem. In the letter quoted above she begged Mrs Nugent to come and stay with her, but there is no evidence that Mrs Nugent ever came. Could Harriet at this time have started a promiscuous affair, spurred on through loneliness? Did she find herself pregnant? Did her father banish her from the house or did she become sick of restraint and disapproval, and leave of her own free will?

We only know that in September 1816 she left her father's house and moved to lodgings at 7 Elizabeth Street, Hans Place, Brompton, not far off. She was taken there by a friend of the Westbrook family, a Mr Alder, a plumber, who lodged at a near-by public house. Apparently the Westbrooks knew where she had gone. She remained at Elizabeth Street until 9 November when she left abruptly. After she had been missing for about a week the Westbrooks instituted a search for her, and ponds were dragged. It was not until 10 December that her body was found in the Serpentine.

A few details can be filled in, chiefly from evidence at the inquest. Mr Alder evidently knew her well; he said that she was about twenty-one years of age and, after five years of marriage, she and her husband were separated. He added that for some months she had been noticeably depressed as though 'something lay heavy on her mind'. At the lodgings she went under the name of Smith and said that her husband was abroad. She paid rent for the lodgings regularly in advance and the landlady, Mrs Thomas, noticed that she seemed very gloomy and appeared to be pregnant. Mary Jones, the maid, said that she was very quiet and spent a lot of her time in bed. There was no sign of any improper conduct, only a 'continual lowness of spirits'. On 9 November she breakfasted and dined in her apartments but told the maid that she wished to dine early—at four o'clock. She only took about ten minutes over her meal and immediately afterwards went out. When the maid went into her room at five o'clock she found it empty. She never saw or heard from 'Harriet Smith' again.

The body was first seen in the Serpentine by a Chelsea pensioner. On the morning of 10 December he was on his way to Kensington and noticed something in the water which he took to be a human body. He called to a boy on the opposite side to bring his boat and together they investigated. He found that it was indeed a body and that there were no signs of life. He felt that the body must have been lying in the water for some days.

Yet Harriet had been missing for a *month*. It is considered to be unlikely that she had been in the water all that time as, in that case, the body would have been hardly recognizable. A notice printed in *The Times* on 12 December 1816, the day after the inquest, is not very enlightening:

> On Tuesday [December 10th] a respectable female far advanced in pregnancy was taken out of the Serpentine River and brought home to her residence in Queen Street, Brompton, having been missed for nearly six weeks. She had a valuable ring on her finger. A want of honour in her own conduct is supposed to have led to this fatal catastrophe, her husband being abroad.

The inquest verdict of 'Found dead' was, however, unaccompanied by any medical evidence to say that the victim was actually pregnant. At the inquest proceedings and in *The Times* the name of Westbrook was never mentioned.

There is mystery too over the 'suicide letter' which Harriet wrote to Eliza before she died. Presumably this could not have been left behind in her lodgings as it was not mentioned at the inquest by any witness. Possibly it was delivered in some other way to Eliza, and it may have been this letter which started the search for Harriet and the directive that ponds should be dragged:

> My dearest & much belov^d Sister
> When you read this letter I shall be [no] more an inhabitant of this miserable world—Too wretched to exert myself, lowered in the opinion of everyone, why should I drag on a miserable existence? embittered by past recollection & not one ray of hope to rest on for the future—I know that you will forgive me, because it is not in your nature to be unkind or severe to any— I have not written to Bysshe—Yet should he see this perhaps he might grant my last request to let Ianthe remain with you always—My dear Bysshe—Do not refuse my last request, I never could refuse you & if you had never left me I might have lived, but as it is I freely forgive you & may you enjoy the happiness which you have deprived me of—God bless & watch over you all—you, dear Bysshe, & you, dear Eliza. May all happiness attend ye both is the last wish of her who loved ye more than all others. My children—I dare not trust myself there—My parents, do not regret me; I was unworthy of your love and care— God bless you all is the last prayer of the unfortunate Harriet S.

II

Was Harriet unfaithful to Shelley?

Except for one or two rather ambiguous phrases—'lowered in the opinion of everyone'—'unworthy of your love and care'— there is not much to suggest it in this long and tragic letter.

Peacock, Trelawny, and others, were all firmly convinced of Harriet's innocence. 'I feel it due to the memory of Harriet,' wrote Peacock in his *Memoirs*, 'to state my most decided conviction that her conduct as a wife was as pure, as true, as absolutely faultless, as that of any who for such conduct are held most in honour.' 'I was assured,' we read in Trelawny's *Recollections*, 'by the evidence of the few friends who knew both Shelley and his wife—Hookham, who kept the great library in Bond Street, Jefferson Hogg, Peacock, and one of the Godwins—that Harriet was perfectly innocent of all offence.' Mark Twain championed her. Louise Schutz Boas in her recently published book *Harriet Shelley* defends her nobly. A recent reviewer in commenting on the Shelley story calls Harriet 'the one good person in it'. And again, in a review of Professor Frederick L. Jones's magnificent edition of the Shelley Letters: 'It can be said that the person who comes out best from a study of these two volumes is Harriet.'*

If Harriet was indeed pregnant at her death Louise Boas makes the interesting suggestion that the father might have been Shelley himself. He had been visiting Harriet in London earlier that spring—at a time when there was still emotional tension between them, when he was still her husband in law, and when Harriet longed for his return. It is a feasible suggestion. One can imagine—if this was the case—the exasperation of her family, already exasperated by Shelley's instability, left already with Harriet herself and two children on their hands. There might have been heated words and recriminations. The Westbrooks might have wished her to hide herself somewhere, incognito, until the baby was born. Or Harriet herself might have decided, partly for their sakes and partly for her own, to try to manage on her own.

Harriet had strong views on the sanctity of marriage. She had been upset by Hogg's overtures and had sent for Eliza. She was friendly with Peacock but there was no suggestion of a liaison. It is difficult for us then to accept the suggestions—emanating chiefly from Godwin—that Harriet indulged in 'repeated acts of levity' with various men. A Major Ryan was frequently mentioned. Godwin also stated that she was having an affair with a Colonel Maxwell—adding, with odious unctuousness, 'Peace be to her shade.' Some of these infidelities were supposed to have taken place months before Shelley had

* *The Times*, 13 February 1964.

left her. Shelley himself, in a letter to Mary, written on 16 December 1816, appeared to believe—or to make himself believe—a story of final degradation: 'It seems that this poor woman—the most innocent of her abhorred and unnatural family—was driven from her father's house, and descended the steps of prostitution until she lived with a groom of the name of Smith, who deserting her, she killed herself.'

Perhaps the most that can be said to Harriet's discredit with any certainty is to stress the unfortunate effects of her dependence on Eliza. For if anything had disastrous repercussions on her marriage to Shelley, surely it was this? Dowden, Shelley's early biographer, wrote: 'It is certain that Shelley's friends, though differing on various other matters, agreed in believing that Eliza's influence on Harriet was used with most injurious effect.'*

Hogg was emphatic on the same theme: 'Eliza had tended, guided, and ruled Harriet from her earliest infancy; she doubtless had married her, had made the match, had put her up to everything that was to be said, or done, as Shelley's letters plainly show.' Among modern writers on Shelley, Professor Kenneth Cameron and Leslie Hotson appear to agree that such unnatural dependence on an elder sister must have retarded Harriet's development into maturity. 'She failed to develop into a wife and mother,' Dr. Hotson wrote, 'and remained Eliza's little sister to the end—Shelley struggled in vain to get rid of the sister and emancipate Harriet's spirit.'†
Between them, according to Hotson, Harriet's father and sister had made Harriet 'unfit for the burden of life'.‡ Professor Cameron in *The Young Shelley* went further. He could see signs in Harriet from her earliest years of maladjustment and a schizoid personality. He cited the extreme modesty, the continual talk of suicide, the mechanical reading aloud, the 'small, neat' handwriting. Friendly and lovable though she may have been there was a lack of 'emotional or intellectual initiative'.§ In her, Professor Cameron thought, there was an

---

* Edward Dowden: *Life of Percy Bysshe Shelley.*
† Leslie Hotson: *Shelley's Lost Letters to Harriet.*   ‡ Ibid.
§ Kenneth Neill Cameron: *The Young Shelley.*

inherent weakness of personality which 'would not withstand strain'.*

All this seems possible. Was there some family weakness inherited through Harriet's mother who, so strangely, plays no part at all in the Harriet story? Could Eliza's obsessive watchfulness have been disastrously caused through over conscientiousness and realization that it was up to her to play a mother's part? Certainly it is not true that Eliza was a monster of inhumanity. There were many who spoke well of her.

It is not true either of Harriet that, as the biographer Mrs Marshall wrote, 'She never, at any time, took life seriously.' Her letters show a feeling heart and normal intelligence. Certainly it seems that she was at a loss to know how to deal with events but—and surely this should be stressed—her life with Shelley had been no easy one. After Shelley's abrupt desertion, and his defection to Mary, there was little in life to cheer her. Her letters to Mrs Nugent show heartbreak. She and her father had never had much in sympathy and now, it is apparent, he kept her under restraint and treated her as though she was disgraced. She had few friends. Shelley himself, when he called occasionally, distressed her by what she felt a change in him to 'materialism'. True, he allowed her the £200 a year, but he was unwilling to pay anything extra for the maintenance of his two children. Harriet had had to produce Charles in the Court of Chancery that April to settle the Estate. Though up to then Shelley's claims of custody of the children had been refused, Charles was the heir, and Harriet was afraid of losing him.

The future was frightening. When Shelley and Mary went off to Geneva that summer and Shelley's visits ceased, Harriet's loneliness became still more acute. She was forced to realize now, what she had refused to accept at the beginning, that her marriage was at an end. Shelley would never return to her.

Possibly her self-control broke. Possibly her mind became unhinged and betrayed her body into extravagance and degradation. It seems unlikely from what we know of her from other people, and from the letters she wrote, but it is a possibility.

* Ibid.

K

There is the mystery of Shelley's remarks to Southey some time later when Southey remonstrated over Shelley's treatment of her: 'I am innocent of ill—the consequences you allude to flowed in no respect from me. If you were my friend, I could tell you a history that would make you open your eyes; but I shall certainly never make the public my familiar confidant.' The Egham surgeon, who attended Mary at Clara's birth, said that Shelley once spoke of Harriet as 'a frantic idiot'.

It does not seem that we shall ever know the exact truth.

12

That the effect on Shelley himself of these dreadful happenings was cataclysmic is, however, indisputable. It might be said that with these tragedies his hold on life slipped, that there was something in them in the nature of a death blow.

Up to now instead of living in a world of reality he had been playing a part in a fantasy. He had confidently imagined that everything would follow a self-appointed plan. But now things were going terrifyingly wrong. Instead of the other characters in the drama dutifully carrying out the parts he had assigned to them they were suddenly proving themselves to be unpredictable, self-willed people, over whom he had no control. It was a devastating development. He had been so sure of his own rectitude, of his own dedication to good. He had assumed the cloak of self-righteousness and seen himself as a knight in shining armour, battling on behalf of all the world's oppressed. Now suddenly faced with these two tragic deaths, one of which might with justice be partly laid at his door, the whole fabric of his self-esteem was punctured. His play-acting fell to pieces. Harriet's suicide, following so shortly after Fanny's, stripped him of all illusion and, for the first time, he found himself face to face with reality.

But he could not admit his own involvement. Any acknowledgment of self-guilt to his sensitive and self-approving nature was intolerable. He had to go on living. Besides going about, seeing to his family, he had to live with himself and his own conscience. The situation maddened him. For a time even he seemed to be mad.

That this question of Shelley's sanity has been seriously considered is proved by an article in *The Quarterly Review* for October 1861, quoted by Peacock (who, however, did not agree with it):

> 'The man,' says Coleridge, 'who mistakes his thoughts for persons and things is mad.' And Shelley's hallucinations, though not to be confounded with what is usually called insanity, are certainly not compatible with perfect soundness of mind. They were the result of an excessive sensibility, which, only a little more severely strained, would have overturned reason altogether. It has been said that the horror of his wife's death produced some such effect, and that for a time at least he was actually insane. Lady Shelley says nothing about this, and we have no explicit statement of the fact by any authoritative biographer. But it is not in itself improbable, and, there are not wanting in his own writings indication of such a calamity. We cannot tell how much of the description of the maniac in *Julian and Maddalo* may not be taken from the history of his own mind. There are other poems which suggest the same observation.

Much more recently we have too Dr Eustace Chesser's psychological appraisal of Shelley's mind derived from the analysis of his early novel *Zastrozzi*. The sub-title of Dr Chesser's book *Self-Revelation of a Neurotic* is revealing and interesting. It is not an attempt to evaluate Shelley as a thinker or poet. Though praising 'the profundity of his insight',* Dr Chesser thinks that Shelley was 'an introspective schizoid type'† and that he 'took refuge in a dream world because reality was too much for him'.‡ The incurable impulse of his life was in fact 'a flight from reality'.§

The letters Shelley wrote after Harriet's death are unbalanced and devious, showing him at his least admirable. In January he

---

* Dr Eustace Chesser: *Shelley and Zastrozzi.*   † Ibid.
‡ Ibid.   § Ibid.

wrote to tell Byron that his late wife was dead under circumstances 'of such awful and appalling horror' that he could hardly bear to think of them. He added that her sister might truthfully be said—'not in law, yet in fact'—to have murdered her in order to obtain their father's money. And to Mary, a few days earlier: 'There can be no question that the beastly viper her sister, unable to gain profit from her connexion with me—has secured to herself the fortune of the old man—who is now dying—by the murder of this poor creature—There is but one voice in condemnation of the detestable Westbrooks.'

Hitting out wildly at others was his only refuge from intolerable thought. For a time it was his only comfort. He trumpeted his own innocence, other peoples' good opinion of him: 'Hookham, Longdill—everyone does *me* full justice,—bears testimony to the uprightness and liberality of my conduct to her.'

Although he pretended to Byron that Fanny's death had affected him 'far more deeply' than Harriet's, there is ample evidence from all his friends to show that Harriet's death shattered him to the very core of his being. Trelawny said that 'the thought of her was a torment to him during the rest of his life'. Leigh Hunt wrote: 'It was a heavy blow to him and he never forgot it. For a time it tore his being to pieces.' Peacock said: 'Harriet's untimely fate occasioned him deep agony of mind, which he felt the more because for a long time he kept the feeling to himself'—and quoted an occasion when they were walking together in the woods. After a few minutes Shelley had suggested that he might take to beer-drinking as a means of deadening his feelings. The next day he was apologetic and admitted painfully: 'I was thinking of Harriet.'

Some of his very real agony of grief is shown in his poetry written at this time. We can sense something of the self-questioning which, for the first time, had bared his quivering mind.

For, in the end, perhaps it may truthfully be said that, when the first crazed reaction to shock and horror was over, Harriet's death was of enormous benefit to him as a sentient human being. At last he was jolted from the self-righteous fantasy which had hitherto made up his world. Now, instead of soaring in high-flown realms of imagination, for a moment of time he was earth-bound, his feet planted firmly on the ground. And from now on his contact with *terra firma*, though often nebulous, was never again to be wholly non-existent. Harriet's death had taught him a lesson which was never wholly out of his mind.

It was a high price to pay. For the rest of his short life he managed to keep up a front of confidence and fearlessness. But only he knew how much of his effort to help and support others in the years that remained was a secret atonement, an expiation of recognized guilt. Only when he was quite alone, a prey to his own thoughts, did he sometimes look despair in the face. 'Stanzas Written in Dejection, near Naples', months later, were far more than the expression of a passing mood; they are words wrung from him by a bitter experience which haunted him through the years, sapping his health and even his will to live.

PART FOUR

MARY
SHELLEY

And I return to thee, mine own heart's home.

                    . . . Thou and I,
Sweet friend! can look from our tranquillity
Like lamps into the world's tempestuous night,—
Two tranquil stars, while clouds are passing by.
                              SHELLEY

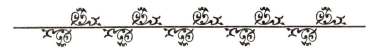

I

OUTWARDLY at any rate Mary accepted Harriet's death calmly and without compassion. There is no evidence that she wrote or said anything at this time to show any feeling of compunction at her share in the breaking up of Shelley's marriage and its tragic results.

In excuse for her attitude it is possible that she did genuinely believe that it was Harriet's own behaviour which had caused the marriage to fail in the first place. Shelley's early biographer, Dowden, quotes from a note written by Claire years later in her introduction to a transcript of letters. Alluding to Shelley's elopement with Mary, Claire wrote: 'He succeeded in persuading her by declaring that Harriet did not really care for him; that she was in love with a Major Ryan; and the child she would have [i.e. Charles] was certainly not his. This Mary told me herself, adding that this justified his having another attachment. I spoke to my mother and to the Boinvilles on this point in after years. Neither had ever seen or heard of any such person as Ryan.'

Ryan, however, did exist—though apparently only as a casual acquaintance. In spite of Shelley's explanation Mary must surely have been mystified when in the eventful court case which followed Harriet's death, and which needed all possible efforts of self-extenuation on Shelley's part, this alleged adultery of Harriet's with Major Ryan was not brought forward or even hinted at.

But there was an inflexible drive in Mary's character, remarkable in so young a woman. She had thrown in her lot with Shelley, believing what she wanted to believe, discarding what she wanted to discard, and she was determined to justify herself. Though delicate in physical health she was robust and forceful in her decisions. She would not have been human either if she had not realized that Harriet's death greatly simplified matters.

Now, for the first time, there was the possibility that she and Shelley could legalize their position and be married.

It was a prospect which excited her. Her upbringing had not been a happy one. Her father was hard, her stepmother unsympathetic, and she was the daughter of Mary Wollstonecraft. All sorts of conflicting emotions warred in a nature capable of intense and torturing feeling. But fundamentally—and strangely, considering the circumstances she had chosen for herself—there was a longing for stability. Perhaps with nostalgic memories of the Baxter household, she wanted to conform and to lead a conventional life. She disliked intensely being in any way ostracized and longed to be an approved member of society. Marriage, she saw at once, would be the first step in bringing about this desired transformation.

The immediate problem was to get the Westbrooks to hand over Shelley's children. At first Shelley had imagined that this would just be a matter of routine and that he, as the father, would be their obvious guardian. In this Mary backed him up loyally. She was quite prepared to accept Harriet's two children, Ianthe and Charles, and to bring them up as her own. She waited at the lodgings in Bath while Shelley went up to London to make the necessary arrangements.

But before long it became obvious that there were going to be difficulties. It seemed that the Westbrooks were in no hurry to surrender the children. Shelley made two efforts to call on Eliza and on both occasions found her not at home. He then wrote her a letter, making her aware of his plans: 'My friend Mr Leigh Hunt will take charge of my children and prepare them for their residence with me.' Perhaps beginning to feel that in labelling Eliza a murderer he had overstrained the truth, he now somewhat double-facedly, attempted to retract: 'Allow me to assure you that I give no faith to any of the imputations generally cast on your conduct or that of Mr Westbrook towards the unhappy victim. I cannot help thinking that you might have acted more judiciously but I do not doubt that you intended well—'

Certainly such sentiments might have been more tactfully expressed and, in the event, this letter bore no fruit whatsoever.

Shelley, now genuinely anxious over the outcome of these negotiations, consulted his solicitor who told him that if he regularized his private life by marrying Mary, all would be well. There could then be no legitimate reason to prevent him from having the children.

With rumours of a Chancery case pending Shelley and Mary wrote excited, distracted letters to one another. Shelley, who had always looked upon marriage as a 'mischievous and tyrannical institution', was nevertheless willing to follow what he called 'a mere form' and to marry Mary who had already blessed him with 'a life, a world of real happiness'. She wanted it. Her father wanted it. All friends, including Peacock and the influential Sir Lumley Skeffington, advised it without delay. Mary herself accepted the dearly-wished-for event with a coy delight: 'As to the event you allude to, be governed by your friends and prudence as to when it ought to take place, but it must be in London.'

Shelley returned to Bath but, as soon as Christmas was over, he and Mary left Claire and little William in the Bath lodgings and went again to town. As usual Leigh Hunt proved the staunchest of friends and a great deal of time was spent with his household. On 27 December Godwin, who had been assiduously writing to both Shelley and Mary, urging them to matrimony, came to call. All past coolness was forgotten. Here was a prospective son-in-law in every worldly sense desirable. From being snubbing and insulting Godwin now became 'studiously flattering'. 'P.B.S. and M.W.G.,' he wrote in his diary of 29 December, 'dine and sup.' Mary was delighted at this change of front. She had persuaded herself that a large part of the urgency of her desire for marriage was because of the reconciliation it brought about with her father. All plans had been made for the marriage to take place the next day, 30 December, at St Mildred's Church in the City. And here the marriage was celebrated. 'Call at Mildred,' wrote Godwin mysteriously in his diary, 'with P.B.S., M.W.G. and M.J. They dine and sup.'

There is no doubt that he and 'M.J.' were proud parents. It was not long before Godwin's satisfaction broke out in correspondence. He made haste to write to a not very close brother informing him of the happy event:

> My daughter is between nineteen and twenty—I went to church with this tall girl some little time ago to be married. Her husband is the eldest son of Sir Timothy Shelley, of Field Place, in the county of Sussex, Baronet. So that, according to the vulgar ideas of the world, she is well married, and I have great hopes the young man will make her a good husband. You will wonder, I daresay, how a girl without a penny of fortune should meet with so good a match. But such are the ups and downs of the world.

There was, however, no mention now of the 'downs'—of the previous elopement, of the anger and rage, of Claire's participation, and Mary's disgrace. Mrs Godwin, too, was determined to put a smiling face on this unlooked for and astounding change of fortune.

Only Claire was kept in the background. In an advanced stage of pregnancy—of which her parents were serenely unaware—she remained discreetly at Bath, awaiting the birth of Byron's child. On the very day of his marriage, 30 December 1816, Shelley wrote her a long letter describing the event, and giving his general feelings on this and other subjects:

> Dearest Claire
>
> Your letter today relieved me from a weight of painful anxiety. Thank you too, my kind girl, for not expressing much of what you must feel—the loneliness and the low spirits which arise from being entirely left—The ceremony, so magical in its effects, was undergone this morning at St Mildred's Church, in the City. Mrs G. and G. were both present, and appeared to feel no little satisfaction. Indeed Godwin throughout has shown the most polished and cautious attentions to me and Mary. He seems to think no kindness too great in compensation for what has passed. I confess I am not entirely deceived by this, though I cannot make my vanity wholly insensible to certain attentions paid in a manner studiously flattering. Mrs G. presents herself to me in her real attributes of affectation, prejudice, and heartless pride. Towards her, I confess, I never felt an emotion of anything

but antipathy. Her sweet daughter is very dear to me—We left the Hunts yesterday morning and spent the evening at Skinner Street, not unpleasantly. We had a bed in the neighbourhood, and breakfasted with them before the marriage. Very few inquiries have been made of you, and those not of a nature to show that their suspicions have been alarmed. Indeed, all is safe there—Do not answer our letter, as we shall be on our way to you before it can reach London.—I will not tell you how dreadfully melancholy Skinner Street appears with all its associations. The most horrid thought is how people can be merry there! But I am resolved to overcome such sensations—if I do not destroy them I may be myself destroyed—Adieu, my dear. Keep up your spirits and manage your health till we come back. It will be Wednesday evening at nine o'clock. Adieu, my dear. Kiss Willy and yourself for me.

Ever affectionately yours
P. B. Shelley.

P.S. Mary can't write, being all day with Mrs G.

✵ 2 ✵

A few days later, on 13 January, Claire's baby was born at Bath—Mary's only comment in her Journal, 'Four days of idleness.' The baby was a girl, later to be christened 'Allegra' but at first called 'Alba', meaning the 'Dawn', after Byron's nickname, Albé. There were no complications and Claire soon recovered her health.

Shelley wrote to Byron to tell him of the new arrival—'a most beautiful girl'. Hoping to arouse parental feeling, and to instil Byron with enthusiasm over this event, before long he wrote of the baby again, enthusing still more over the baby's appearance: its excellent health, intelligent blue eyes, black hair, exquisitely shaped mouth. Byron accepted the news with characteristic flippancy and wrote to his half-sister that he was puzzled how to dispose of 'this new production'. He would, he added, probably put it in a convent, where it might become a nun—a character, he felt, which was wanted in their family.

Shelley, meanwhile, was again in London, dealing with the complicated matter of his own children's future. In spite of his marriage, a source of so much satisfaction to Mary, the hoped-for solution of these children was no nearer settlement. Mr Westbrook had decided that Shelley was not a fit person to have young children in his care and, in order to bring Ianthe and Charles within the protection of the Chancery Court, on 2 January 1817, he had settled on them the sum of £2,000. A Bill of Complaint to the Lord Chancellor was filed and the Court of Chancery hearing was fixed for 24 January. The allegations against Shelley included the accusation of having deserted his wife to 'cohabit unlawfully' with Mary Godwin, and of having blasphemously derided Christianity and 'avowed himself an atheist'. The infants now appealed to be placed under protection of the Court of Chancery, under fit guardians.

Shelley, smarting under these accusations, filed an answer to this Bill of Complaint, and later wrote a long and spirited statement in his own defence. He insisted that he had not deserted Harriet but that they had agreed 'in consequence of certain differences—to live separate and apart from each other'. As regards the children he had only allowed Harriet to keep them at her 'urgent entreaty' and he had had every intention of later bringing them up himself and educating them. He did not dispute that he held unorthodox opinions about marriage, but insisted that everyone had a right to their own opinions. Mary Godwin, he added pungently, was now his lawful wife.

From the first the case did not go well for Shelley. The Westbrooks had engaged the most eminent counsel available. Shelley's counsel, not so shrewd, unwisely made personal attacks on the Westbrook family, claiming that they were unsuitable guardians because Mr Westbrook had 'formerly kept a coffee house', that Eliza was 'illiterate and vulgar', and that it had been with her 'management' that Shelley had eloped with Harriet in the first place. Greatly to his detriment the nine letters which afterwards disappeared for so many years—eight letters to Harriet and one to Eliza—were brought in evidence against him. In these letters of course it was made evident that the separation was entirely against Harriet's wishes. And in the letter to Eliza after Harriet's death, far from mentioning a Major Ryan, or suggesting that Harriet herself had been unfaithful, Shelley had given himself away hopelessly by writing of Mary as 'the lady whose union with me you may excusably regard as the cause of your sister's ruin'!

The Lord Chancellor could not at once give a decision on the case and they had to wait over two months for a judgment. For six weeks of this anxious period of waiting Mary joined Shelley in London. They spent most of the time with the sympathetic Hunts. The Hunts lived in Hampstead. They were bohemian and slapdash in their way of living and they had a large and boisterous family. Shelley, however, found Hunt's kindly nature comforting, and he released some of the unbearable tensions within himself by playing with Hunt's children. All children loved him. He treated them as equals, becoming a child himself.

There were many visitors at Hunt's house and—with an absorbing appreciation of the Arts to bind them—plenty of good talk and good argument. Shelley and Mary now met for the first time the Cockney school of poets. Besides Lamb, Hazlitt, Reynolds and Keats they made the acquaintance of the painter Severn and a good friend of after years, Horace Smith. Horace Smith liked and admired Shelley but Haydon, another acquaintance, described him as 'a hectic, spare, weakly yet intellectual-looking creature', and made fun of him cutting up a small helping of cabbage on his plate with as much satisfaction as if it had been a wing of chicken. Keats, too, was not impressed. This, however, may have been mainly due to the difference in their social positions. Keats, through his feelings of inferiority was proud and prickly, and he resented, even before it had been offered, the slightest hint of patronage.

But, in spite of these new friends and diversions, it seems that Shelley's nerves were in shreds, his melancholy and agony of suspense almost too great to bear. 'How much,' he said once, when indulging in his favourite pastime of sailing paper boats, 'I should like that we could get into one of those boats and be shipwrecked—it would be a death more to be desired than any other.' It was a strange death wish—could it have been a morbid longing to share Harriet's fate?—which was to occur more than once in his life.

Fits of the agonizing—and seemingly inexplicable—pain, which he suffered from all his life, left him at times weak and shaken. Dowden quotes Thornton Hunt's reminiscence of a day at Hampstead when Shelley sat reading and 'suddenly threw up his book and hands, and fell back, the chair sliding sharply from under him, and he poured forth shrieks, loud and continuous, stamping his foot madly on the ground'.

At length, on 27 March, the blow fell. The Court verdict was given against Shelley and he was deprived, on moral and religious grounds, of the custody of the two children. The Chancellor did not consider that Shelley had changed the principles which he had avowed at nineteen. Consequently his conduct had not changed either and this conduct the Chancellor considered to be 'highly immoral'. The case against 'paternal authority' would have to be finally determined in a further report. Meanwhile, although the children could not be handed over to Shelley's care, they would not be handed over to the Westbrooks either, and he would probably have the right to 'name fit and proper persons by whom the children should be educated'.

The negotiations dragged on for some months. Shelley wanted his lawyer, Longdill, to have guardianship of the children. The Westbrooks wanted them to remain where they were in charge of the clergyman in Warwick. In the end another suggestion of Shelley's, a Dr and Mrs Hume of Hanwell, was accepted. The Humes were to take the children for £100 apiece yearly. Shelley was to contribute £120 of this sum, the remaining £80 was to come from Mr Westbrook's original Chancery investments. Shelley was to be allowed to see them once a month but only in the presence of Dr and Mrs Hume. The Westbrooks' visits too were to be twelve a year, but they were allowed to see the children alone. Sir Timothy Shelley and his family could see the children whenever and as often as they liked.

3

In March 1817, before the final verdict on the children, the Shelleys moved to their new home, Albion House, at Marlow. Here they were joined by Claire, Allegra and William, and the Swiss maid, Elise. At Bath Claire had called herself 'Mrs Clairmont' but now, nearer London and her family, she reverted to her maiden title, and Allegra was described as 'the daughter of a friend in London, sent for her health to the country'. The Marlow house was taken on a twenty-year lease and here they meant to settle 'for ever'.

It was a large house, barrack-like in shape, and Gothic in detail. There were four reception rooms, five bedrooms, two nurseries, six or seven attics, and a water-closet. One of the reception rooms was large enough for a ballroom but Shelley turned it into a library. The outlook was gloomy, the house damp and sunless. It was said that at no time, because of inter-vening trees, did the sun shine into any of the rooms and, as a result, even the books became mildewed. At the back was a large garden and four acres of meadow but—unfortunately—no view of the near-by Thames.

Besides Elise two other servants were installed, a vegetarian cook, and a manservant called Harry. Shelley liked to keep open house. Ceaseless hospitality reigned and the house was always full of visitors. The Hunts, with all their family, came whenever they liked, and remained as long as they liked. Hogg, Peacock, Horace Smith and Godwin were frequent visitors. Shelley himself, though surrounded with friends, made no interruption in his poetry writing and disappeared at intervals into the woods, or in a boat on the river, to write the poem which was afterwards published as *The Revolt of Islam*.

Mary herself still pursued her own authorship in the intervals of running the house, looking after the children and guests, supporting Shelley. In some ways she was happier. As a legal wife the strain of her invidious position outside

L

marriage had been removed. But she was pregnant again and at times overtired. Besides the trouble over Shelley's children—a ceaseless cause of grief—there were still many problems to contend with. One of the greatest of these was the problem of Claire and Allegra.

It seems that by now the Shelleys had definitely decided that Claire must remain with them. The problem was a difficult one. Having made the initial blunder of taking her with them on their elopement, it was not easy for them to go back on it, and to discard her. She was trained for no career, had no money and—apart from them—no friends. The liaison with Byron had complicated matters still further. The Godwins knew nothing of this escapade or of Allegra's birth. The Shelleys, having made it up with the Godwins, were anxious to keep in their good books. It was impossible to reveal to Claire's parents that, under their supervision, Claire had become the mother of Byron's child. In the end they accepted the situation and Claire's continual presence with the best grace they could muster.

Claire herself had no desire whatever to make a life on her own or to return to the Skinner Street household. She was lively and attractive, her looks were striking, the visitors paid her attention, and Shelley himself was her never-failing friend and defender. So, satisfied with her lot, she sat back, dug in her heels, and relied upon Shelley's kindness of heart and emotional weakness to get the better of Mary's incipient hostility.

But, although the Shelleys were prepared to keep Claire and to give her a home, they were worried about Allegra. They loved Allegra, but she was Byron's child and surely, in some way, Byron should be responsible? To add to the difficulties, it was not long before they discovered that her presence was causing gossip. The inhabitants of Marlow, already aware of the Chancery suit and the scandal surrounding Shelley's name, now began to wonder about Allegra. Whose child could she be? They noticed Claire's impulsive manner towards her, the reckless displays of affection, and felt sure that Claire must be the mother. What more likely than that Shelley himself was the father? His unconventionality, his strange opinions, his

peculiar household—all lent colour to this theory. Scandalous
rumours spread through the neighbourhood.

In April and again in July Shelley wrote to Byron asking him
his intentions for 'little Alba'. 'We are,' he wrote, 'somewhat
embarrassed about her.' Not only the neighbours were curious,
there were the reactions of their visitors and servants to consider.
He hoped perhaps that Byron might be coming to England
himself before long—he had been planning to sell Newstead—
and that he would then make arrangements about the child.
Failing that, Shelley suggested 'two very respectable young
ladies in this town' who might take charge of her, and who
lived near enough for Claire to superintend her.

No reply came for some weeks and meanwhile life at
Marlow went on much the same as usual. They were increasingly dissatisfied with the house but in the summer there was
an improvement, as they were able to spend more time out of
doors. They did not mix in the social life of the neighbourhood but Shelley concerned himself endlessly with the poor of
Marlow, particularly the many lace-makers of the town who
were now out of work.

He visited them frequently, took them soup and other
comforts, gave them medical advice, and, when necessary, warm
blankets marked with the name 'Shelley' so that pawning
would be impossible. Money was supplied, too, a small sum
put by each week: the poor and needy came for their share on
Saturday evenings. On one occasion when no money was forthcoming Shelley returned from a pilgrimage in his stockinged
feet, having given away his shoes. 'Love,' he insisted, 'should
be the law of life.'

His health was better in the summer weather, in spite of the
pain in his side from which he so frequently suffered. He often
subsisted on bread and raisins, getting up early to walk or read
before breakfast, and wandering about the country, sometimes
with a wreath of wild flowers mixed with 'old man's beard' on
his head, to the amazement of the neighbours. 'He was the most
interesting figure I ever saw,' one wrote sympathetically, 'his eyes
like a deer's, bright but rather wild—He seemed quite absorbed,
and he dashed along regardless of all he met or passed.'

Mary, at last, with some struggle and difficulty, had managed to finish *Frankenstein*. She was now anxious to find a publisher and, to simplify this, she went for a short time to Skinner Street to stay with her father. The book was rejected by several publishers but at last accepted by Lackington. The book was to have an amazing popularity, lasting to the present day: a hundred years after Mary's death to be made into a film, and later published in popular guise as a paperback.

She was reticent about her writing, seldom talking of it. And even now, on this literary pilgrimage in London, she was nervy and on edge away from Shelley. 'I am very well here,' she wrote to him, 'but so intolerably restless that it is painful to sit still for five minutes. Pray write. I hear so little from Marlow that I can hardly believe you and Willman live there.' On the last day of May she returned to Marlow with relief, to find the Hunt family ensconced on one of their long visits.

Already she and Shelley were beginning to think of Italy as a refuge. Shelley was still brooding over his children and had written a poem against authority beginning 'I curse thee'. He felt that there was an undeserved shadow cast on his name and Mary's, and his reaction was one of extreme bitterness. He was now living in fear that a criminal action might follow the Chancery Suit, and that his other children too might be taken from him. The ceaseless claims on his generosity—the cadging attentions of Godwin and Charles Clairmont, besides the less blatant expectations of the impecunious Hunt—at moments drained and exhausted him.

A visit from Mr Baxter, the father of Mary's old friend Isabel, was cheering for a time. Mr Baxter, expecting the worst, was favourably impressed and delighted by Mary's new husband. He did his best to patch up the ruined friendship between the two girls, a disaster which had so depressed Mary. But Isabel's new husband, who had heard scandalous rumours of the Shelley household, was determined that there should be no reconciliation.

This visit of Mr Baxter's was interrupted by the early birth of Mary's awaited baby. A girl, to be named Clara, was born on 2 September. Mary made a slow recovery. She had been

upset by the trouble over Isabel. There was still the problem of
Allegra waiting to be solved. Claire's continual presence,
though accepted, was often irksome. The house, with autumn
coming on, was cold, damp and cheerless. And, on top of all
this, she was worried about Shelley's health which, with the
colder weather, was already worsening.

4

Shelley had at length finished his long poem *Laon and Cythna*
—later to be published as *The Revolt of Islam*—and the effort
had exhausted him. He felt that there was a danger, if he did
not take stern measures over his state of health, of early
death. In September he went to London to get medical advice.

Rest and a change of climate was the suggested treatment.
The doctor warned Shelley, too, against 'the excitement of
composition'. Again Shelley's mind flew to Italy. Byron had
written at last to say that he wished to have Allegra with him
at Venice. He vaguely wanted Shelley to send her out to him.
Here perhaps was yet another reason for visiting Italy. They
could take 'little Alba' with them.

He and Mary kept up a fevered correspondence discussing
the pros and cons of such a decision. Italy—or the English
seaside. 'We must go to Italy,' Shelley wrote, 'on every
ground. This weather does me great mischief.' And again, a
few days later: 'I think we ought to go to Italy. I think my
health might receive a renovation there—I think Alba ought
to be with her father—This is a thing of incredible importance
to the happiness perhaps of many human beings.'

Mary was obsessed by doubts of all sorts, largely financial:

> How much do I wish that I were with you! but that is impossible,
> but pray in your letters do be more explicit! and tell me all your
> plans. You have advertised the house, but have you given
> Maddocks any orders about how to answer the applicants? and
> have you yet settled for Italy or the sea? and do you know how to

get money to convey us there, and to buy the things that will be absolutely necessary before our departure? And can you do anything for my father before we go? Or, after all, would it not be as well to inhabit a small house by the sea-shore, where our expenses would be much less than they are at present?

On one thing both were decided. They must leave Marlow. 'What a dreadfully cold place this house is,' Mary wrote, shivering over a fire, with the garden looking 'cold and dismal'. 'Let us, past all doubt, quit the house.' The children were delicate—all tragically destined to die before they were six years old. William particularly felt the cold, a situation which could not have been improved by a spartan system of cold baths every day for all three of them. Mary, in Shelley's absence, was inundated by the usual visitors and, so soon after her confinement, was feeling the strain. The Hunts were tactless, getting up late in the mornings, going out walking alone, and never suggesting that she might like to accompany them. 'Peacock dines here every day, *uninvited*, to drink his bottle— He morally disgusts me!' She was out of sorts, uncertain of the future, the fits of depression inherited from her mother, Mary Wollstonecraft, increasing as she grew older. Only Shelley's presence and loving support could bring her any real peace of mind.

But that October a new trouble arose, which prevented Shelley from spending much of his time at Marlow. Once more his creditors were after him and he was in fear of arrest. Even Mary had to advise him to stay away: 'My love, you ought not to come down. A long, long week has passed, and when at length I am allowed to expect you, I am obliged to tell you not to come.' Besides debts which were partly Harriet's, Shelley owed money on behalf of Godwin, and an outstanding debt to his uncle and and old ally, Captain Pilfold. Captain Pilfold, his patience exhausted, had applied to Sir Timothy. Sir Timothy, advised by Whitton not to help his son any more, referred him to Shelley's lawyer, Longdill.

It seems certain that Shelley was actually under arrest for two days during the month of October. Mary wrote on the 16th: 'You say nothing of the late arrest, and what may be the consequences, and may they not detain you?'—adding, maddeningly—'May you not be detained many months? for Godwin must not be left unprovided.'

This preoccupation over the financial support of Godwin was, with Mary, an obsession. One of her main objections to the pilgrimage to Italy was the fear that her father might be angry and consider himself let down and deserted. 'Italy appears to me further off than ever,' she wrote, 'and the idea of it never enters my mind but Godwin enters also, and makes it lie heavy at my heart. Surely,' she went on, 'he cannot be blind to the many heavy reasons that urge us. Your health, the indispensable one, if every other were away. I assure you that if my Father said 'Yes, you must go; do what you can for me . . .' I should prepare everything with a light heart, arrange our affairs here—I know not whether it is early habit or affection, but the idea of his silent quiet disapprobation makes me weep as it did in the days of my childhood.'

His silent quiet disapprobation! There is no doubt that the traumatic experience of Mary's stern and loveless upbringing had bitten deep. No wonder that Shelley, manacled as he was by the impossible claims of what Edmund Blunden has called 'this inconceivable father-in-law',* longed at moments with bitter longing to get away from such an exasperating situation. He had been to his good friend Horace Smith and borrowed £250 and written to Mary suggesting that they should all come to London, leave the cook in charge until the house was sold, possibly even let it, furnished or unfurnished—at all events leave, without further delay, for Italy.

Still Mary was hesitating: 'Your account of our expenses is by very much too favourable. You say that you have only borrowed £250. Our debts at Marlow are greater than you are aware of. We cannot hope to sell the house for £1,200; and to think of going abroad with only about £200 would be madness, for that would not much more than carry us there—In fact I do not think we can go if we cannot find some means of raising money.'

But the letters plying to and fro, all the arguments, the

* Edmund Blunden: *Shelley.*

discussions, the problems, were leading inexorably to a final decision. It was perhaps the problem of Allegra more than anything which induced Mary finally to give her consent to the Italian project. Somehow Allegra had to be got to Italy to join her father. Byron made no suggestions, sent no money. It took weeks, or even months, to get from him any reply to their letters. Yet, strangely, all three—Shelley, Mary, Claire— were convinced that they were doing the best thing possible for Allegra's future by giving her over to her father. His title, his fame, his social position—they, who thought so little of these things in theory, seemed mesmerized by the very things they professed to despise. Byron only, they felt, could provide the wonderful, privileged life to which his daughter was entitled. So Italy it must be. All other problems would have to sort them- selves out in time.

On 16 December the house at Marlow was advertised in *The Times*. On the usual ruinous terms Shelley borrowed another £2,000 in consideration of £4,500 to be paid at his father's death. He was much preoccupied over the New Year in altering his poem *Laon and Cythna* and removing the in- cestuous relationship between brother and sister to which his publisher had objected. Finally it was finished, the name changed to *The Revolt of Islam*. There was a dedication to Mary:

> So now my summer task is ended, Mary,
> And I return to thee, mine own heart's home;
> As to his Queen some victor Knight of Faëry,
> Earning bright spoils for her enchanted dome;
> Nor thou disdain, that ere my fame become
> A star among the stars of mortal night,
> If it indeed may cleave its natal gloom,
> Its doubtful promise thus I would unite
> With thy belovèd name, thou Child of love and light.

Early in 1818 Mary's novel *Frankenstein* was published anonymously, dedicated to Godwin, and with an unsigned preface by Shelley. Shelley sent a copy to Sir Walter Scott, who professed to admire it above all his own works.

By January Shelley, exhausted, was repeatedly ill with

ophthalmia. Godwin, who had been on a last visit to Marlow, wrote expressing concern over the ophthalmia, but a concern chiefly aroused by the possibility that he might catch the infection himself. Shelley was trying to placate him, giving him all the money that he could spare, but Godwin was not satisfied: 'I acknowledge the receipt of the sum mentioned in your letter. I acknowledge with equal explicitness my complete disappointment.'

At the end of January there was rejoicing at Marlow for on the 25th the house was sold. Shelley went on ahead to London and the others joined him later, bringing with them not only Elise but a local Marlow girl called Milly. At Marlow, after they had left, their good works were remembered for years—but by some Shelley was remembered as a 'madman', with his habits of striding, reading, through the town, only stopping occasionally to buy crayfish in the market in order to throw them back into the Thames.

The Shelleys now settled in lodgings in Great Russell Street and proceeded to spend a gay and hectic month in London, sight-seeing, entertaining friends, and theatre-going. Shelley had developed a great liking for Mozart's operas and Leigh Hunt gave a description of them at Covent Garden. 'We look up to your box,' he recalled a year later, 'almost hoping to see a thin, patrician-looking cosmopolite yearning out upon us, and a sedate-faced young lady bending in a similar direction, with her great tablet of a forehead, and her white shoulders unconscious of a crimson gown.'

There is no record that Shelley saw any of his family again before leaving England: the estrangement seems to have been complete. Nor is there anything to show that he saw the two children, Ianthe and Charles. The Hunts, Horace Smith, Keats, Novello—all were frequent companions—while Hogg and Peacock as usual dined repeatedly.

Peacock at this time seemed very much taken with Claire. They spent a large amount of time together, walking in the parks, wandering about the streets of London. Mary wrote years later that if only Claire had married Peacock she might have been spared much suffering. But did Claire want to marry? After the extreme emotional upheavals of her early youth, it seemed that she had used up all capacity and desire for further emotional adventure—her heart, as she was to say in after years, 'wasted and ruined as if it had been scorched by a thousand lightnings'. Her experience with Byron had embittered and cut short her youth. As a middle-aged woman she was to thank God that she could never be young again and that that suffering could never be repeated. Now, though Peacock was such a frequent visitor, there is no record that her heart or feelings were in any way involved. She made herself amiable, singing and playing the piano at the Hunts, entertaining them all. But the only person that she really loved was Allegra. And —perhaps—Shelley? At all events she took what came, sticking by the Shelleys, making little effort to alter her way of life, sometimes cheerful, frequently discontented, carried along by the tide.

Byron had written at last to say that he wished his daughter to be called, not Alba, but Allegra. On 9 March all three children were christened at the church of St Giles in the Fields, a course which Shelley probably agreed to for possible civil advantages. Allegra's parents were described as: 'Right Hon. George Gordon, Lord Byron, the reputed father by Clara Mary Jane Clairmont.'

The serious dispute between Shelley and Godwin over money was only partially healed and heralded the final breakup. But Shelley felt he had suffered too much. Time now was short. On 10 March when the Hunts came to spend with them their final evening in England, Shelley fell into a deep sleep before the Hunts had left. Anxious not to disturb him, they went without a farewell and he awoke to find them gone.

The next morning Shelley and his little party set off for Dover where they stayed the night. The weather had been rough and stormy, there were waves 'mountain high', and they were undecided whether or not to make the journey. Finally, with a favourable wind, they decided to risk it. They were all in cheerful mood. It seems unlikely that it ever crossed their minds that Shelley might be leaving England for ever. The crossing, in spite of the weather, was accomplished in under three hours. From Calais Shelley wrote to Hunt that all was going well. Before long they were embarked once more on their journey and on their way to Italy.

5

The weather was bad to begin with but, the farther south they travelled, the more conditions improved. Rheims, Dijon, Lyons, Chambéry—soon they were high among the Alps and Shelley already seemed to be better in health. It was a delight eventually to reach Italy with 'primroses scattered everywhere' and a cloudless sky.

On the way Shelley had been keeping Byron informed of their impending arrival. Now from Milan he wrote telling him that his little girl had reached Italy at last, 'in excellent health and spirits' and with eyes as blue as the sky over their heads. He suggested that Byron should spend a few weeks with them that summer. His idea was that they should rent a house on the Lake of Como, that Byron should join them for Allegra to make his acquaintance, and then at the end Allegra might return with her father to Venice. Claire too wrote to Byron. Her letters were lengthy—Byron later rudely called them 'bad German novels'—and probably wanting in tact. Blindly, desperately, she still tried to provoke him into a renewal of interest in herself, addressing him as 'My dearest friend'.

But the plans, so hopefully made, were to go sadly awry. Shelley and Mary went house-hunting at Como and failed to find what they wanted. Byron, who had been bored by the intimacy at Geneva, had no wish to renew it. Shelley's high-mindedness and Claire's importunities together were too much for him. He had a horror of seeing Claire again and, although the Shelley party waited for him at Milan, he did not come. When he did eventually write it was without sympathy, to tell them that he was sending a messenger to Milan to fetch the child, and that Claire must resign all claims to her.

At this callous ultimatum Claire was plunged into grief and desperation. Byron would never answer her letters or write to her direct. All she saw were the letters he wrote to Shelley which, in their lack of concern for her or her feelings, added to her despair. Shelley, caught up in this difficult and unpleasant situation, did his best to intercede for Claire, without adding fuel to the flames which were already raging. His letters to Byron were sensible, compassionate and balanced—revealing a new maturity. He could not hold himself responsible for Claire, for anything she had done, for anything that she wrote. All he could do was to look at the situation with purely humanitarian eyes. Claire was a mother with a mother's feelings. 'Your conduct,' he wrote to Byron, 'must at present wear the aspect of great cruelty, however you justify it to yourself.' Or again: 'A tie so near the heart should not be so rudely snapt.'

The Shelleys had been hearing lately lurid and upsetting rumours of Byron's way of life in Venice. This, combined with his hard-heartedness towards Claire, made them now think again about the wisdom of handing over Allegra completely to her father's care. Shelley warned Claire that she should give the matter grave thought. Was she really acting in the child's best interests by parting with her? Claire, in spite of everything, her bitterness towards Byron, his cruelty towards her, was adamant. The messenger had arrived from Venice and Allegra must go back with him. It had been intended that the English maid, Milly, should go with her but now Mary made a generous gesture, offering to part with Elise. This would mean, as Shelley assured Byron, that little Allegra would be attended 'almost with a mother's care'.

On 28 April the two set off. 'Claire,' as Shelley told Byron, 'is dreadfully unhappy.' They all felt sad at the parting with Allegra. Mary had looked upon her almost as 'one of her own children' and Shelley described her as 'the most lovely and engaging child I ever beheld'. They begged Byron to write at once, and not to disappoint them, with news of the travellers' safe arrival.

Byron's own reactions are harder to analyse. His mask of

flippancy covered all signs of deeper feeling. In due course he wrote to his friend Hobhouse that his 'bastard' had arrived, adding that she was much admired and caressed by the Venetians. He had already told his half-sister Augusta that he was counting on the child proving a comfort to him in his old age. Now, though appearing gratified by the child's intelligence and beauty, he wrote to Augusta that he was astounded by her resemblance to Lady Byron! Fletcher, the valet, so he added, was 'stupified' by it. It was, perhaps, an unfortunate resemblance under the circumstances and could not have provoked Byron to enthusiasm. True, he had not given up all hope of re-uniting with Annabella, but his current mode of life was not in keeping with his aspirations. The present mistress of the Palazzo Mocenigo was a Venetian baker's wife, 'La Fornarina'. Here they lived, surrounded by cages of birds, peacocks, cranes, dogs, monkeys and quarrelsome women. It must have seemed a strange and alien way of life to little Allegra, and to the Swiss Elise who could not speak a word of Italian.

After the departure of Allegra and Elise, Claire battled agonizingly with despair. Allegra had been 'the only thing I had to love, the only object in the world I could call my very own'. It seems indeed that her love for Allegra was the one genuine and unselfish emotion of her life. Now in her efforts, however misguided, to give her child a brilliant and prosperous future, she had thrown away her own happiness.

On her twentieth birthday they all left Milan. Travel, Shelley had decided, was the panacea for all ills. He had abandoned the idea of taking a house on Lake Como for the summer and decided instead that they would move on still farther afield. From Milan they made a leisurely journey via Parma and Bologna to Pisa. Claire made efforts to drown her grief by describing the scenery and places through which they passed in her Journal. Eventually, after having been depressed at Pisa by the sight of convicts chained together in pairs sweeping and cleaning the streets, they reached Leghorn.

The chief attraction of Leghorn was a letter of introduction which they had with them to a Mr and Mrs Gisborne. Mrs Gisborne had once been Mrs Reveley and a friend of Mary

Wollstonecraft. She was beautiful, intelligent, charming, and in past days had been coveted as a wife by Godwin. When his own wife Mary Wollstonecraft had died in childbirth, the then Mrs Reveley had taken the baby Mary into her charge and cared for her for several weeks. Two years later Mrs Reveley's own husband had died. Godwin did not waste time—he proposed to her within a month, but unfortunately for him he was rejected. Mrs Reveley, in her greater wisdom, decided to marry instead John Gisborne. In 1801 the Gisbornes went to Italy, taking with them Henry Reveley, Mrs Gisborne's son by her first husband. Now, on Mr Gisborne's retirement after the failure of his business, they had settled down in Leghorn.

Immediately that the Shelleys arrived at Leghorn on 9 May they got in touch with the Gisbornes who called upon them that same day. In spite of the difference in age groups, the two couples became extremely friendly. Mrs Gisborne could talk to Mary about her mother and it was Mrs Gisborne too who particularly charmed Shelley. He was to describe her later to Peacock as 'the sole attraction in this most unattractive of cities'. Mr Gisborne, although of a literary turn of mind, was less congenial. Described by Leigh Hunt as 'placidity personified', he was, according to Shelley, an 'excessive bore' with a 'prodigious nose'. It was a nose, he added, which was 'once seen never to be forgotten and which requires the utmost stretch of Christian charity to forgive'. 'I, you know,' he told Peacock, 'have a little turn-up nose, Hogg has a large hook one but add them both together, square them, cube them, you would have but a faint idea of the nose to which I refer.'

In spite of the nose, however, the Shelleys met the Gisbornes every day. They took long evening walks together, read aloud, and gave each other lessons in Italian.

The Shelleys stayed at Leghorn for a month. Before the end of the month Shelley, ever restless, went on alone to the Baths of Lucca to find a house for the summer months. He found what he was looking for, a house with a small garden, and the others joined him on 11 June. Now indeed they found peace and solitude—the quiet which Shelley had been craving, to soothe his fevered nerves. They were surrounded by mountains with delightful walks in the woods. As the heat increased and the place filled up with visitors, they went riding early in the morning or late after dinner. Their life was uneventful with no social activities whatever.

Shelley was having a rest from creative work and instead translated Plato. He had come to the conclusion that Mary's dramatic talent was greater than his own and he was anxious that she should try her hand at a work on the Cenci or Charles I, two subjects which greatly attracted him. Mary loved all kind of literary activity but knew her limitations. She preferred to stick to her novel writing, to transcribe Shelley's manuscripts for him, to listen to him reading aloud.

In this way the days passed peacefully enough until, in August, new anxieties arose over Allegra. For some time the letters from Elise had been unsatisfactory—ill at ease and complaining—and now they heard that Allegra and Elise had left Byron and were lodging with the British Consul and his wife, a Mr and Mrs Hoppner. Claire became upset and anxious and was seized with a determination to go to Venice herself to investigate. She did not want to go alone and planned that Shelley should go with her. He could then intercede with Byron on her behalf.

6

It was a fatal decision which was to set in train a whole host of calamities. But Claire and Shelley together were too much for Mary and she resigned herself to a lonely interlude at the Baths of Lucca, with the children and servants, while Shelley and Claire went off to Venice.

Paolo, their Italian servant, was to accompany the travellers as far as Florence. They set off in an uncomfortable jolting one-horse cabriolet but at Florence Paolo obtained for them a comfortable carriage, drawn by two mules. Shelley felt better for the travelling and Florence was 'the most beautiful city I ever saw'. There were delays there with passport difficulties and Shelley seized the opportunity to write to Mary: 'Well, my dearest Mary, are you very lonely? Tell me truth, my sweetest, do you ever cry?—If you love me you will keep up your spirits—How is Willmouse, and little Ca?—They must be kissed for me—Adieu, my dearest girl—I shall write again from Venice—Adieu, dear Mary.'

Claire's plans were circumspect and involved. In order not to irritate Byron, she intended to stay by herself at Padua while Shelley went on to Venice. Shelley was then to give Byron the impression that the whole Shelley party were at Padua, and that this visit of his was merely a passing act of politeness. In this way Byron would not suspect that the whole purpose of the journey was to find out about Allegra.

But in the event Padua was too depressing. The strangeness and the solitude wore down Claire's fortitude and she was further appalled to find that the beds were full of insects. There was a rapid change of plan and she decided instead to continue the journey with Shelley to Venice. Shelley wrote to Mary a detailed account of their adventures. They set out by gondola and had an 'extremely cold' journey, with violent storms of rain and lightning, arriving at Venice at midnight. The gondolier on the journey regaled them 'without any hint on our part' with lurid stories of the extravagant 'giovenotto Inglese' who 'lived very luxuriously and spent great sums of money'. Lately, so the gondolier added, he had had 'two of his daughters over from England and one looked nearly as old as himself'. Poor Elise and Allegra! It was obvious that wild rumours over Byron's way of life were increasing daily.

After breakfast Shelley and Claire took another gondola and called on the Hoppners. The Hoppners no doubt were excited and curious at finding themselves the centre of such a drama. At all events they rose to the occasion, invited both Claire and Shelley into their home, paid them 'the kindest attentions' and 'expressed the greatest interest in the event of our journey'. Shelley was charmed by such solicitude, accepting it at its face value, and telling Mary that the Hoppners 'entered into all this as if it were their own dearest concern'.

The Hoppners had one little boy of their own, aged seven months. They had taken pity on Allegra and Elise, realizing the unsuitability of their remaining with Byron. Elise had been helpless and lost at the Palazzo Mocenigo and the Hoppners thought her too inexperienced. They were, it appears, kind if limited people with humane feelings. Their actions were prompted by good neighbourliness rather than affection for Allegra. 'She was not,' wrote Mr Hoppner years later after Byron's death, 'by any means an amiable child, nor were Mrs Hoppner or I particularly fond of her.'

Allegra herself had changed after the vicissitudes she had lived through. Alternately pampered and neglected by Byron and his entourage, she had now lost a good deal of her former liveliness and was pale and apathetic. But she was, Shelley insisted, still 'as beautiful as ever'.

Hoppner told him that Byron often expressed 'extreme horror' at the thought of Claire arriving in Venice. He advised Shelley to call on Byron alone. This Shelley did and found Byron a good deal more friendly and amenable than he had expected. He appeared in fact to be delighted to see Shelley and prolonged the interview to interminable lengths. While Claire waited impatiently at the Hoppners, Byron insisted that Shelley must go riding with him on the sands of the Lido. Great patience and tact were needed on Shelley's part. In the intervals of discussing Allegra's future, he had to listen to histories of Byron's 'wounded feelings', recitations from *Childe Harold*, and a spate of talk on literary matters. Finally, however, a happy solution was arrived at. Byron offered the loan of his villa not far off at Este and agreed that Allegra should be permitted to go there for some weeks to be with her mother.

As Shelley had given him to understand that Mary and the rest of the family were near by at Padua, it was important to summon Mary at once to bear out this story. Shelley who had been writing her a long letter at 'scrappy intervals' added the last paragraphs in the early morning. 'Pray come instantly to Este,' he wrote, 'where I shall be waiting with Claire and Elise in the utmost anxiety for your arrival. You can pack up directly you get this letter.' He gave her instructions for the

M

journey which was to start at four o'clock in the morning. He enclosed an order for fifty pounds for expenses, counted four days for the letter, one day for packing, four more days for the journey.

The letter arrived at a moment of great inconvenience and anxiety for Mary. She had asked the Gisbornes to join her lonely vigil at Lucca and they had only just arrived. On top of that, the baby Clara was ill with teething troubles and in no fit state for travelling. But Shelley's peremptory summons clamoured to be obeyed and Mary, after talking things over with the Gisbornes, decided to go. The next two days were spent in packing. Then, taking Paolo with her, she set off in the intense heat on the uncomfortable four-day journey.

The effects on the baby Clara were almost immediately disastrous. Her illness turned to dysentery and the symptoms were not assuaged by uncomfortable delays over passports in Florence. When the little party finally arrived at Este five days later Clara was dangerously ill.

For several days they were all prisoners at Este. Shelley was unwell himself after food-poisoning with Italian cakes and Clara was too ill to be moved. The house, however, was delightful, cheerful and pleasant, built on the overhanging brow of a hill, with far-flung views and an attractive garden full of fruit. In spite of their anxiety over Clara's fever, literary work went on inexorably. Shelley established himself in the summerhouse as a study and started *Prometheus*. Mary read Dante and began some translations. In the meantime she had written to Mrs Gisborne, to tell her of their safe arrival, but adding that Clara was 'in a frightful state of weakness and fever' and that the doctor at Este was very stupid.

There were ups and downs in Clara's condition and Shelley eventually decided that she ought to see another and a better doctor either at Padua or Venice. He went on ahead with Claire to try to make some satisfactory arrangements. Eventually deciding on Venice, he wrote to Mary that she must come at once, bringing Clara, and instructing her to start at half past three in the morning to avoid the heat.

The folly of another exhausting journey for so young and

delicate a child, in the throes of severe illness, did not apparently cross his mind and, if it did, he dismissed it with a false optimism. It seemed sometimes that he had an extraordinary and fatal capacity for wrecking the lives and happiness of his family by pandering to some mad impulse which he, and only he, decided was the right course to pursue.

Mary, ever obedient, joined him with the sick child at Padua. From there on the journey became a nightmare, Clara growing worse and more desperately ill every moment. At one juncture it was found that they had forgotten their passports but Shelley's fiery determination to press on overrode officialdom. They crossed the lagoon by gondola with Clara in the grip of convulsions. When they arrived in Venice at last she was unconscious. Mary took her to the inn while Shelley went off to fetch the doctor. But when he returned it was to find Mary, still in the hall of the inn, and 'in the most dreadful distress'. During his absence still worse symptoms had appeared, another doctor had been fetched, only to tell the anguished parents that the situation was hopeless. In a very short time little Clara died in Mary's arms—'silently, without pain'. She died at seven o'clock in the evening, aged only one year and three months.

It was a tragic and bitter blow for the young parents. Mary temporarily, was reduced to a kind of despair. The Hoppners, ever solicitous, came at once and took both the Shelleys back to their house with them. Here Mary, trained by Godwin not to show emotion, made a great effort to control her grief. Whether or not she blamed Shelley for the calamity—an outcome in the first place of his preoccupation with Claire's affairs—is not known. There are indications in his poetry that it may have been the beginning of a subtle change in their relationship, undermining the first blissful trust and confidence. Putting up a brave front, Mary went sightseeing with the Hoppners in Venice. She also interviewed Byron and got him to agree that Allegra's visit to the villa at Este should be prolonged for another three or four weeks.

Byron at this time was fairly affable. Mary, who was never at ease with him, but who was impressed by rank and had a

weakness for titles, was flattered when he trusted her with some
of his poems to transcribe. Back at the peaceful Este villa, the
two children, William and Allegra, were happy together,
playing in the garden. Claire, with aching heart, tried to make
the most of the time that was left and Mary, determined to
stifle her grief, roused herself from despair. Later in October
she and Shelley again visited Venice to see both Byron and the
Hoppners.

On this occasion Shelley had more opportunity to see at
close quarters the kind of life that Byron was leading. He was
appalled by what he saw. Byron was, as he knew from *Childe
Harold*, a great poet. But as a man? 'He has a certain degree of
candour while you talk to him,' Shelley wrote to Peacock, 'but
unfortunately it does not outlast your departure.' It was with a
heavy heart that Shelley realized Allegra would soon have to
be handed back into his care. All efforts to persuade him to
prolong the visit to her mother were in vain.

At the end of October Allegra—and this time, without even
Elise—was sent back to Venice. On 5 November 1818 the
Shelleys, with what was left of their little retinue, left the villa
at Este and set off for Rome.

7

The baby Clara was dead. Little William was fragile and
delicate. But still the uncomfortable restless life of travelling
about the country, with no real resting place, no proper home,
was relentlessly pursued.

It was another exhausting journey that they undertook to
reach Rome. Paolo was driving and, so bad were the roads,
oxen were needed at times to help the horses to pull the
carriage. It was a fifteen-days journey through Ferrara, Bologna,
Spoleto. 'Sleep, or do not sleep,' Mary wrote resignedly in her
Journal, 'for we do not undress at a miserable inn.' After
contending with cheating innkeepers and other troubles, they

eventually arrived, on a rainy evening, in Rome. Here, to their relief, they found a comfortable hotel and here, before long, the sun shone.

Shelley wrote long descriptive letters of their travels to Peacock. Rome was a joy to them and seven intensive days were spent in sightseeing. The Vatican, the Forum, St Peter's, the Protestant Cemetery—all were explored at length. The next port of call was to be Naples. Again Shelley went on ahead to make arrangements and four days later he was joined by Mary, Claire and William—and the three servants, Paolo, Elise and Milly.

But the stay at Naples was not altogether a happy one. Perhaps partly in an effort to suppress thoughts of their recent griefs, they again overdid the sightseeing. Both Shelley and Mary were feeling the strain of events. The climate of Naples did not suit Shelley's complaint and he was undergoing a painful treatment from the local doctor with no encouraging results. Mary's fits of silent depression reacted on his spirits. The trouble, to increase as months went by, was aggravated by her determined stoicism. In her reserve, her suppression of grief, her abnormal self-control, she was becoming unapproachable. She gave the impression of coldness, of shutting Shelley away from her. She was not Godwin's daughter for nothing and even in Italy Godwin's influence was all powerful.

'I sincerely sympathize with you,' he wrote to her after Clara's death, 'the first severe trial of your constancy and the firmness of your temper that has occurred to you in the course of your life. You should, however, recollect that it is only persons of a very ordinary sort, and of a pusillanimous disposition, that sink long under a calamity of this nature—We seldom indulge long in depression and mourning, except when we think secretly that there is something very refined in it, and that it does us honour.'

Cold comfort—but Mary accepted it. All the passionate warmth of feeling, the loving impulses she had inherited from her mother, were crushed and suppressed. Inwardly she wept. Outwardly she appeared unmoved. Her nature, turned in on itself, was being poisoned at the source. She was losing something

of that candour and ardour which Shelley at the beginning
had found lovable. From now on there was no diminution of
that acidity in her turn of phrases which is a little repelling.
Courage remained. Sometimes, in the years to come, she must
have felt that, apart from courage, there was not a great deal
that was left.

Shelley, bewildered, himself longing for warmth and
support, and trammelled eternally with the burden of the past,
poured out his heart in poetry. Some of these poems written at
Naples were seen by Mary for the first time after his death. She
was puzzled by them and attributed them to the 'constant pain
to which he was a martyr'. But there was more—much more—
at the root of his depression than physical pain. The moving
'Stanzas Written in Dejection, near Naples' are heart-breaking
in their invocation of an anguish of spirit which defies all
attempts at healing:

> Alas! I have nor hope nor health,
> Nor peace within nor calm around,
> Nor that content surpassing wealth
> The sage in meditation found—
>
> Yet now despair itself is mild,
> Even as the wind and waters are;
> I could lie down like a tired child,
> And weep away the life of care
> Which I have born and yet must bear,
> Till death like sleep might steal on me,
> And I might feel in the warm air
> My cheek grow cold, and hear the sea
> Breathe o'er my dying brain its last monotony.

'Which I have born and yet must bear.' He did not give in.
Sometimes he thought longingly of England and friends at
home—of Leigh Hunt particularly, whose warm heart never
failed him in sympathy and support. He did indeed write to
Hunt and suggested that he should come to Italy. Byron, he
said, had made some suggestion of lending the money for the
journey. Whether he would want to bring *all* his family was

for his own decision. But Hunt was unable to make up his mind and, as yet, nothing came of this idea.

Meanwhile, still more problems were gathering. Claire was on tenterhooks and worried over Allegra's affairs as the news from Venice was not good. Mrs Hoppner wrote that the damp climate did not seem to suit her. Besides feeling the cold to an abnormal degree, so that her hands and feet were always icy, she was backward in speaking. Byron was no help as lately he had not been getting up until three o'clock in the afternoon when it was too late in the day for Allegra to visit him. Mrs Hoppner added that she did her best, but it seemed that Allegra was to be doomed 'always to live with strangers'.

It was a disturbing state of affairs but there seemed little that Claire and the Shelleys could do. They were now, too, about to lose the invaluable Elise. It was discovered that the Italian servant Paolo was not only a rogue and had been cheating them, he had also been carrying on a sexual affair with Elise for some time. It was a shock. Neither of the Shelleys were versed in worldly wisdom. In spite of their conviction that Paolo was a villain they browbeat the young couple into marrying. Paolo was dismissed from their service and Elise went with him. It was a tragic loss. As Mrs Marshall, Mary's early biographer, wrote: 'All three of the poor doomed children throve as long as Elise was in charge of them.'* There were too to be disastrous repercussions in other ways. Later Paolo, in revenge for his dismissal, spread scandal about the Shelleys' way of life, insisting that Claire was Shelley's mistress and that a child had been born in Naples and put into a foundling hospital. In months to come Elise was to regale the Hoppners with this same tale.

It seems to have been a garbled version of something which *did* actually happen in Naples and which has never been clearly explained. It is unlikely that it was anything to do with Claire but there *was* a child and, inexplicably, Shelley registered himself as the father. In Shelley's letters to the Gisbornes the child is alluded to more than once as 'my poor Neapolitan' or 'my Neapolitan charge'. Whose child was she? It is a strange

* Mrs Julian Marshall: *The Life and Letters of Mary Wollstonecraft Shelley.*

mystery and Shelley's own account of the little girl's history is more strange still.

In 1821 he provided his cousin Medwin, and an incredulous Byron, with an explanation. According to him, just before he left England he met a lady who conceived a violent admiration for him. The lady was married, of noble birth, and extremely beautiful. She had fallen at the feet of the author of *Queen Mab* and had wanted to become his mistress. Shelley had declined the honour, pointing out that his allegiance was to Mary. The lady, however, could not forget him. Instead of returning to her own home, she had followed the Shelleys abroad. In Naples she and Shelley met again. She now had a baby with her, and very shortly she died. In her last hours she entrusted the baby to Shelley's care.

Whatever the truth—and to many this odd-sounding explanation is yet another of Shelley's fabrications—the undoubted existence of the child in the foundling hospital was, at this time, another of Shelley's burdens. The mystery of her parentage remains without a solution and constitutes one of the strangest episodes in the Shelley story.

The time at Naples was now drawing short. The climate had never suited Shelley. There had been some social life but even here, at this distance from England, scandal would sometimes pursue them. Any hint of ostracism was painful to Mary. They felt they needed a change of scene and, in March 1819, they all made a leisurely journey back to Rome.

It was a particularly lovely spring and soon they were settled happily in comfortable lodgings. As ever, Shelley was fascinated by Rome. He wrote more letters to Peacock, describing in detail the grandeur of all they saw. The wonders of ancient art, the beauties of the natural scene, never failed to arouse in him an enthusiasm allied to ecstasy. It was the depredations of man which appalled him, causing in him, as he told Peacock, a 'conflict of sensations allied to madness'. It was inexpressibly painful, both to him and to Mary, to see the fettered criminals of Rome working in the streets, chained two by two, and watched by armed soldiers. The moral degradation of which men were capable in their treatment of one another never failed to rouse in him extreme anger. Evil, he felt, was an unnecessary adjunct to man and could be eradicated. He was writing *Prometheus Unbound*, his imagination at fever pitch, his physical health for the moment improved.

Claire and Mary too were revived by the better climate. Mary took up drawing again, always a favourite occupation, and had lessons from a master. Claire gave herself up to music and singing. She had professional lessons and practised assiduously for as much as seven hours a day. Such concentration of purpose was a far cry from the untrammelled emotional upheavals of her earlier youth.

A new friend at this time was Miss Amelia Curran, the daughter of Godwin's Irish reformer friend, whom they met one day in April in the Borghese Gardens. They all liked her, saw her constantly, and eventually sat to her for their portraits. Unfortunately the only two of these portraits to survive are those of Shelley and Claire. Claire's is disappointing. Her dark good looks are portrayed without her liveliness and animation. In the painting she looks heavy and dumpy whereas, in reality, we are told that she was tall, lithe and graceful. Shelley's portrait, which was unfinished, is the likeness of him with which we are most familiar. It is good in its way but only portrays the gentle, feminine side of his nature. The more masculine characteristics—his determination, courage and obstinacy, those characteristics which swept him forcefully through life, carrying others with him—are ignored. It was not considered a good likeness by either Mary or Peacock and, indeed, at one juncture the portrait was nearly thrown away, and only by a lucky chance survived.

As the spring advanced the Shelleys began to make plans for the summer months. They knew that they must leave Rome before the hot weather set in if only for little William's sake. 'He is,' Mary wrote, 'so very delicate that we must take the greatest possible care of him this summer.' Mary, however, was now pregnant again and they had arranged to return to Naples where she could be under the care of their former doctor, Dr Bell, a noted British surgeon. This arrangement was suddenly upset when Dr Bell changed his plans. They heard that, instead of going to Naples, he was to follow a wealthy patient to the Baths of Lucca. At the time they wanted him he would be either at Pisa or Florence.

By the end of May the Shelleys were still in Rome. Fatally dilatory, they were corresponding with the Gisbornes and making plans to meet them at Pisa. 6 June was the day eventually fixed for their departure. But the delay had been disastrous. On 2 June William had an alarming gastric attack and became desperately ill. They existed in a state of anguished suspense for several days. Shelley watched without sleep for sixty hours at William's bedside. Claire proved herself a patient and devoted nurse. The doctor paid repeated visits and momentarily William seemed to rally. Claire and Mary wrote a joint letter to Mrs Gisborne, postponing their arrival in Pisa. Mary added the last sentences: 'William is in the greatest danger—We do not quite despair yet—Yesterday he was in the convulsions of death and he was saved from them.' The misery of the passing hours were to her beyond calculation and, as she wrote: 'The hopes of my life are bound up in him.'

The child had a high fever. As Shelley wrote afterwards to Peacock, there was 'no hope from the moment of the attack'. On 7 June, the day after the one planned for their departure, William died.

⚜ 8 ⚜

This was the worst shock that had yet befallen them. 'It seems to me,' Shelley wrote in the letter to Peacock, 'as if, hunted by calamity as I have been, that I should never recover any cheerfulness again.' William had meant more to them than anybody else in the world. A gentle, affectionate, intelligent little boy, his early death is movingly tragic. He had silky hair, brilliant blue eyes, and a character of his own. So beautiful was he, that the Italian women used to bring each other to look at him when he was asleep. Already he was able to talk in three languages. Adoring his parents, and adored by them, he accompanied them everywhere.

Even poetry could not offer the release Shelley so badly needed to relieve the anguish of his pent-up emotion. There are poems he tried to write at this time to his little son but which he never succeeded in finishing:

> TO WILLIAM SHELLEY
>
> Thy little footsteps on the sands
> Of a remote and lonely shore;
> The twinkling of thine infant hands,
> Where now the worm will feed no more;
> Thy mingled look of love and glee
> When we returned to gaze on thee—

Or again, as he thought of the little dead body buried in the Protestant cemetery:

> Where art thou, my gentle child?
> Let me think thy spirit feeds,
> With its life intense and mild,
> The love of living leaves and weeds
> Among these tombs and ruins wild;—
> Let me think that through low seeds
> Of sweet flowers and sunny grass
> Into their hues and scents may pass
> A portion—

Again it breaks off. The grief was beyond words. And yet Shelley's agony of mind in this new disaster was more bearable, less irreparable in the end, than the torpor of despair that the loss had brought to Mary. Now at last her stoic façade was broken. But there was no blessed relief of tears or outward collapse. Instead she sank into a prostration of apathy and silent misery which defied help. With no children left to care for, her natural feelings stifled, exhausted by the strain of William's illness, she withdrew into a solitude of reserve where it seemed that nobody could reach her. 'I never shall recover from that blow,' she wrote to Miss Curran in June, 'the thought never leaves me for a single moment.' Everything had turned to dust and ashes, and she was unable to rouse herself.

Shelley tried fruitlessly to make some contact with her but now, still more than in the months after Clara died, he felt himself to be shut out. His own hold on reality was too tenuous for him fully to understand her desperate need of patient support, and his courage wavered:

> The world is dreary,
> And I am weary
> Of wandering on without thee, Mary.

Her withdrawal widened the subtle change in their relationship. Though still fundamentally devoted to each other they were somehow alienated. Mary's apathy defied comfort. Shelley's own depression went unsupported. All he knew was the danger. He knew that he could not afford to give way:

> My dearest Mary, wherefore hast thou gone,
> And left me in this dreary world alone?
> Thy form is here indeed—a lovely one—
> But thou art fled, gone down the dreary road,
> That leads to Sorrow's most obscure abode;
> Thou sittest on the hearth of pale despair,
> Where for thine own sake I cannot follow thee.

With a heavy heart he tried to gather together the remnants of their lives and to make plans for the future. The idea of going to Pisa or to the Baths of Lucca for the summer was abandoned. Instead they took a little country house at Leghorn for three months to be near the Gisbornes. It was the best thing that they could do under the circumstances but Shelley found himself longing intensely for England, for old friends, for familiar scenes. 'How we prize what we despised when present,' he wrote to Peacock. He turned for comfort and refuge to his work. At the top of the house was a glassed-in tower and this he made his study. There was a view of the sea and he could watch the storms and bask in the sunlight. It was here, as a new departure, that he wrote the main part of his drama *The Cenci*. Gradually his health and spirits began to revive.

The Gisbornes came every evening. It was a boon to Mary who liked Mrs Gisborne, but her husband they still found 'dreadfully dull'. In the household, however, Mary, Shelley and Claire were back to their old disastrous triangle. Mary's only bond with Claire had been broken. When Claire had become a mother, perhaps because her attentions were less concentrated on Shelley, Mary's hostility had appeared to lessen. A person of strong maternal feeling herself, Mary could sympathize with a woman of like instincts. For the first time she and Claire had had a fellow feeling which, in some degree at any rate, had helped to oil the workings of their difficult relationship.

Now there were no children. William and Clara were dead. Allegra was lost to them. Claire's presence began to irk and distress Mary in the same way that it had irked and distressed her in the old days in England. She longed to have Shelley to herself and could not conceal her irritation. Grief and strain broke out in quarrelling.

She wrote to Mrs Hunt: 'I never am in good spirits.' In August she started keeping the Journal again which had been broken off at William's death: 'I begin my Journal,' she wrote, 'on Shelley's birthday. We have now lived for five years together, and if all the events of the five years were blotted out, I might be happy; but to have won, and then cruelly to have lost, the associations of four years, is not an accident to which the human mind can bend without much suffering.'

Her state of mind was not improved by censorious letters from Godwin. He chided her for her depression: 'I cannot but consider it as lowering your character in a memorable degree, and putting you quite among the commonality and mob of your sex—What a falling-off is here!' There was much in the same strain—cavilling at her lack of gratitude for other blessings and 'all because a child of two years old is dead'.

Shelley was enraged at this paternal lack of sympathy. He wrote to Leigh Hunt explaining how he had himself written to Godwin begging 'this hard-hearted person' to write to his daughter more kindly. A still more heartless letter had come back, Godwin telling Mary that the only way to keep his favours was to make Shelley send him more money. 'He heaps on her misery, still misery.' Shelley's disillusionment with Godwin, his one-time idol, was devastating and complete. He poured out his anger to Leigh Hunt: 'I have bought bitter knowledge with £4,700.' It was the amount he had paid over to this insatiable father-in-law in the past. And still, apparently, Godwin expected more.

It was a relief when another past parasite, Charles Clairmont, arrived on a visit. Charles Clairmont's fortunes were looking up. At last he seemed prepared to stand on his own feet. After battening on Shelley for money he had been to Spain to learn Spanish and study literature, and now he intended to go on to Vienna to teach English. He was lively, attractive and hand-some—and also intelligent. Shelley found him a help over *The Cenci* and in the reading of Spanish. *The Cenci* now was Shelley's main lifeline. It was a tale of horror and revenge and he wanted Peacock to get it produced for him at Covent Garden. Peacock had now got a good job in India House and was a more influential person. But in spite of his efforts he could not get the play accepted.

While these negotiations were still going on arrangements were being made for Mary's coming confinement. It was now finally certain that the elusive Dr Bell would be available in Florence and accordingly Shelley, accompanied by Charles Clairmont, went there in September to look for lodgings. On the way they called on a Mr and Mrs Mason at Pisa. This Mrs Mason was later to be a good friend to them all, and a wise counsellor. Like Mrs Gisborne, she had once been a friend of Godwin's. At one time Mary Wollstonecraft had been her governess. Afterwards she had married unhappily Lord Mountcashell, and finally eloped with a Mr Tighe with whom she now lived in Italy. She was a woman of strong character, some eccentricity of appearance, and a capacity to command respect. Her liaison with Mr Tighe, long established and conventional, was accepted everywhere. They had two daughters. Later it was to be Mrs Tighe who was to have the insight to realize the extent to which Mary's life and happiness were being undermined by her own family, particularly Claire and Godwin. Mrs Tighe even managed to relieve the situation by her sensible advice.

In Florence Shelley was lucky enough to find pleasant lodgings which he booked for six months. 'We expect Mary to be confined towards the end of October,' he wrote to Leigh Hunt, and added hopefully: 'The birth of a child will probably relieve her from some part of her present melancholy depression.'

At the end of September Mary and Claire left Leghorn— a sad parting from the Gisbornes. The journey to Florence was undertaken in slow stages as Mary's pregnancy was so far advanced. October passed peacefully in the comfortable lodgings. Shelley haunted the Uffizi, shivering in the cold winds of Florence, but absorbed and entranced by all he saw. On 12 November 1819, after five 'hateful months' without a child, Mary's son, Percy Florence, was safely born.

9

Percy Florence was so named after his father and his place of birth. He was a small, healthy, attractive baby, something like William. The confinement gave Mary little trouble, she suffered only two hours' pain, and the next day, so Shelley wrote to Hunt, 'is now so well that it seems a wonder that she stays in bed'. It was, to Shelley, a great relief and comfort. 'Poor Mary,' he wrote, 'begins (for the first time) to look a little consoled.'

While Mary centred all her hopes on this new baby, looking after him with the help of Milly, and rapidly recovering her health, Shelley was making new friends. Just before the baby's birth a young woman, Sophia Stacey by name, had arrived in Florence with her Welsh travelling companion, a Miss Parry-Jones. Sophia Stacey came from Shelley's home county of Sussex. She was in fact connected with his family, being a ward of his uncle Robert Parker. After her father's death

Sophia had gone to live with Mr Parker at Bath. Here she had heard tales of Mr Parker's famous nephew and now, on a tour of Italy and just arrived in Florence, she was exceedingly anxious to make Shelley's acquaintance. Very soon she discovered the house where the Shelleys were staying and lost no time in calling.

Now began, for Shelley, a short but sweet 'romantic' friendship, a prelude to others which were to prove more serious. Shelley's estrangement from Mary after William's death had left him vulnerable. Impressionable at the best of times, and lacking in emotional stability, Shelley now could not fail to be flattered and comforted by the naïve attentions of a young woman who obviously adored him. To Sophia Stacey, the friendship was fascinating, dangerous, and of the greatest importance. She was spellbound by Shelley and anything to do with him. She admired his 'simplicity combined with refinement'* and his eyes, so she wrote in her Journal, were 'blue and large and of a tenderness unsurpassed'.† Mary too, she felt, looked 'very delicate and interesting'.‡

The Shelleys invited her upstairs to their rooms in the evenings where she sang to them and played the harp. Shelley gave her lessons in Italian and talked to her for hours of his early life in Sussex, of his family circle, of his sisters, of all the vicissitudes through which he had lived. He had been proud to show her the new baby, Percy Florence, and Sophia noticed a likeness in the baby to his grandmother, Lady Shelley of Field Place. Nothing that Shelley did for Sophia passed unnoticed. He had gallantly lifted her down a high step from her carriage and had been sympathetic when she had toothache. All was recorded in the Journal which she faithfully kept. The significance of seeing Florence and all its glories for the first time paled beside this far greater glory of meeting Shelley.

In return for this adoration Shelley was enthusiastic and attentive. He admired Sophia's looks and was entranced by the sweetness of her singing voice. Here was yet another peg on

* Mrs Rossetti Angeli: *Shelley and His Friends in Italy.*   † Ibid.
‡ Ibid.

which to hang his impossible dreams of the ideal woman. As fulfilment of a promise he wrote poems to her and gave her a pocket book in which some of these poems were transcribed. Some are moving, appearing to convey a wealth of emotion extravagant under the circumstances. After hearing her play the harp he wrote 'Thou art fair and few are fairer . . .'. There are others, too, written at this time, 'Time Long Past', 'Good-night', and the revealing:

> I fear thy kisses, gentle maiden,
>   Thou needest not fear mine;
> My spirit is too deeply laden
>   Ever to burthen thine.
>
> I fear thy mien, thy tones, thy motion,
>   Thou needest not fear mine;
> Innocent is the heart's devotion
>   With which I worship thine.

Shelley was discerning of his own nature. There are few of his biographers who even try to deny his essential innocence. There was little of the sensual man in his make-up. Instead he was obsessed by the romantic and the imaginative. 'I think,' he was to write later to Mr Gisborne, 'one is always in love with something or other; the error—consists in seeking in a mortal image the likeness of what is perhaps eternal.' It was the mistake he repeatedly made—seeking in a woman who attracted him the attributes of a goddess rather than the more human virtues of a flesh-and-blood human being. No woman could really come up to his expectations. He asked too much—not only beauty and graciousness and sympathy, but intelligence, philosophical understanding, perfection both in mind and body. Freud has said that the meagre satisfactions that man can extract from reality leave him starving. Perhaps it is true to say that most of Shelley's loves followed the pattern of this idealized *l'amour de tête*. And, as Somerset Maugham has written with truth: 'The love that starts in the imagination grows and thrives in the imagination and is apt to perish when it is consummated by sexual congress.'*

* W. Somerset Maugham: *Ten Novels and their Authors.*

N

This time Shelley's wavering of loyalty towards Mary was only slight. Sophia Stacey's appeal was momentary; she cheered him with her beauty and flattered him with her devotion. But he found her enchanting, young, sympathetic, and the relationship between them set a pattern. Later there was to be Emilia Viviani, and, later still, Jane Williams. The search as time went on was to become more meaningful. From now onwards too he was not attempting to discourage from his mind the accommodating notion that Mary had failed him.

Very soon, at the end of December of this year 1819, Sophia Stacey left Florence for the next stage of her tour. Shelley helped her with the preparations of departure and got up early to see her off. She and her companion were going on to Rome. It was the last that Sophia was to see of the god-like young poet with the eyes of 'unsurpassed tenderness'. Later she married someone else and the marriage was a happy one. The little note-book of poems which Shelley had given her remained one of her most dear possessions.

Meanwhile, the severe winter in Florence was telling on the Shelleys' endurance. Their rooms were lofty and stone-floored, with tiny fireplaces. Shelley wrote of the 'infernal cold' and his health began to suffer. Claire too was restless and ailing, worrying about Allegra. News from Venice was meagre and, when it did come, it was not consoling. Byron had now started his affair with the Countess Guiccioli and Allegra spent more time with him. A rich widow named Mrs Vavassour had taken a fancy to Allegra and had offered to adopt her if Byron would give her up completely, but Bryon had refused. His affection for Allegra was spasmodic. He enjoyed her sometimes as a plaything, at other times forgot her. And in the meantime the damp climate of Venice was taking its toll.

It seemed that there were problems and difficulties ahead on all counts. Financially Shelley was in a predicament. Unwisely, considering his other commitments, he had embarked with Mrs Gisborne's son, Henry Reveley, on an ambitious scheme for constructing a steamboat to run between Leghorn and Marseilles. Henry was to build the boat, Shelley was to provide the money. But for some reason there were delays over the arrival of Shelley's money from England. He now owed Henry Reveley £200 and the whole building scheme was held up because the £200 was not forthcoming.

Shelley began to have serious thoughts of going to England himself to settle his affairs. He was driven to distraction by Godwin who had been writing a stream of letters to Mary, demanding money. Godwin, apparently, had had a demand for accumulated rent of past years. He had no money to pay such a debt and the case had been taken to the courts. The ceaseless begging letters which he wrote to Mary had disastrous effects upon her health and spirits.

Shelley, at his wits' end, was prevented from going to England by a veto from the doctor. He was not well enough. Mary began to wonder if, instead, Godwin should be advised to leave England himself and come out to Italy. Very fortunately the sensible 'Mrs Mason' of Pisa, with whom they had been corresponding, strongly objected to this plan. 'Do we not seem,' wrote Shelley to Miss Curran late in 1819, 'like a knot of persons destined to ill?'

They had fully meant to stay in Florence for six months but instead they began to think that they must move elsewhere. The severe winter was undermining Shelley. He felt 'irritated to death for the want of a study' and was in continuous nervous pain. He stayed indoors and spent his time translating Spinoza and reading aloud, often from the Bible, to Mary.

Early in 1820 there was a still more freezing spell of cold. They thought longingly of Pisa. At Pisa the climate was milder and Shelley would be able to put himself under the care of a famous Italian physician named Vaccà. The Masons wrote sympathetically, urging them to come. Suddenly, with a change to 'lovely weather' on 24 January, they decided abruptly that they would go.

That day and the next were spent in packing. On the 26th, at eight o'clock in the morning, with their strange love of sudden departures and uncomfortable journeys, they set off by boat on the Arno. In mid-winter such a journey by river was cold and cheerless. After five hours, in which they covered thirty miles, they arrived at Empoli and took a carriage to Pisa.

There they found lodgings on the Lung' Arno: two bedrooms, two sitting-rooms, and servants' rooms, all nicely furnished, for four and a half guineas a month. Later, in March 1820, they changed to still better and more roomy apartments, 'very lightsome and spacious', on the top floor.

PART FIVE

LAST
ATTACHMENTS

Alas, that love should be a blight and snare
To those who seek all sympathies in one!
SHELLEY

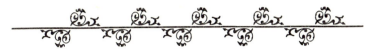

꯭ I ꯭

SHELLEY'S last years were spent mainly at Pisa. The climate was milder and his health benefited. The famous Vaccà advised him to rely more upon nature as a palliative and to give up medicines and drugs. He no doubt realized that there was little organically wrong with Shelley, but that most of his troubles were caused by the nervous tension and nervous exhaustion, inseparable from his highly strung and overwrought temperament. Shelley took the Italian doctor's advice and, though still describing himself in a letter to his cousin Medwin as 'a wretched invalid', managed to lead a fairly active life.

He and Mary at last, so he told Leigh Hunt, were living 'considerably within' their income. They found Italy a cheap country. 'A crown here,' Shelley informed Medwin, who was thinking of joining them, 'goes as far as a pound note in England.'

Their most congenial friends at Pisa were Lady Mount-cashell and Mr Tighe, unmarried, but still living, as they had lived for years, in the greatest respectability, as Mr and Mrs Mason. No breath of scandal touched them. They had won acceptance in a fashion followed in England in later years by George Eliot and George Lewes. Their faithfulness, propriety, integrity, impressed everyone. Later, in 1822, when Lord Mountcashell died, they married, and Mary remained friendly with them and their two daughters all her life.

The Shelleys now spent much of their time with Mrs Mason. With her capable and contented nature, large blue eyes, and brusque manner, she was a woman of immense kindness. Shelley, as so often on meeting a new acquaintance, was exaggeratedly impressed: he admired Mrs Mason and congratulated himself that she admired him in return. Charmed by her intelligence, he read Greek with her. 'You

189

will think it my fate,' he wrote to Leigh Hunt, 'either to find or to imagine some lady of 45, very unprejudiced and philosophical—with enchanting manners, and a disposition rather to like me, in every town that I inhabit.'

Shelley, however, was not Mrs Mason's chief concern. She realized with instinctive discernment that it was Claire, chiefly, who needed her friendship. It was imperative to her mind that Claire should be weaned away from her smothering dependence on the Shelleys, and encouraged to stand on her own feet. She persuaded Claire to have dancing lessons, to make her own amusements, and to take a more active part in social life. Her influence was practical and all to the good.

But it was Mary, chiefly, who hankered after women friends. When the Gisbornes announced their intention of going to England to settle their financial affairs Mary begged Mrs Gisborne to remain behind and to come to stay with them at Pisa. But Mrs Gisborne felt this to be impossible. She came instead on a farewell visit that April and Shelley wrote introductions for her to Hunt, Peacock, and all his English friends. Godwin, as usual, was the immediate problem. Godwin had lost his law action over the rent. Shelley, so he insisted, had promised him £500 but payment was not forthcoming. As a result Godwin was furious with Shelley for 'holding out false lights', a fury which as usual was vented on Mary. Shelley in his turn bitterly resented these attacks and spoke openly now of Godwin as his 'bitterest enemy'.

As was perhaps inevitable the Gisbornes, on their visit to England, became involved in the dispute. They visited Skinner Street where Godwin informed them that Shelley 'had treated him cruelly and would be the death of him'. Mrs Godwin's attacks were chiefly about Mary who was responsible, so she said, for the estrangement of her own daughter Claire, and all the misery attached to it. Whether the Godwins misrepresented the situation to such an extent as to make a deliberate breach between the Shelleys and Gisbornes is not altogether clear but it seems more than probable. 'I long for your English letters,' Mary had written hopefully to Mrs Gisborne at the outset, but she only received one meagre letter in reply. Mary had given her detailed shopping instructions: she could 'scratch out the stockings for Shelley', but what Mary wanted in particular was 'a handsome square black net-veil'. Mrs Gisborne wrote back, somewhat crushingly, that black net-veils had become vulgar and were only worn by nursery maids.

But black net-veils were of minor importance compared to the dilemma of whether or not to lend more money to Godwin. Godwin had asked Mr Gisborne for £400. Mary wrote, asking that the loan should be made, and promising that Shelley would repay it. Shelley himself wrote to Mr Gisborne telling him to use his own discretion in the matter. Mr Gisborne decided on a refusal. In August Shelley wrote to Godwin, rubbing in the fact that the £4,000–£5,000 he had already provided for Godwin might as well, to all intents and purposes, have been 'thrown into the sea'. Why, he asked pertinently, could not Godwin, a person of his 'extraordinary accomplishments', earn money for himself by writing another book?

Altogether the Shelleys had some painful problems to deal with during that year of 1820. While the unhappy correspondence with Godwin dragged out over many months, another hideous and unexpected complication turned their lives to nightmare. Their old servant Paolo, proved corrupt in the old days, and whom they had never liked, had turned up again and threatened them with blackmail. He would, he said, unless he received satisfaction, charge Shelley with 'most grievous crimes'—probably connected with the mysterious 'foundling' child at Naples.

In June the Shelleys moved into the Gisbornes' empty house at Leghorn, chiefly in order to be near the lawyer who was to deal with this new threat. 'The path of our life,' Mary wrote to Mrs Gisborne, 'is a very thorny one.' Her own depression over Godwin's affairs provided no comfort for Shelley who was made ill through worry. 'Domestic peace I might have,' he wrote, 'but have not, for Mary suffers dreadfully from the state of Godwin's circumstances.' The canker of this parasite of a father-in-law helped to undermine all serenity in their marital relationship. Paolo, fortunately, was crushed by the Leghorn lawyer and the threat of blackmail averted, one load off Shelley's mind; but a new anxiety had now arisen over the mysterious child at Naples.

The little girl was ill. On the subject of this child it would appear that Mr and Mrs Gisborne were Shelley's only confidants at this time. How much Mary and Claire had been told is doubtful. Shelley, in a postscript to a letter to the Gisbornes, asks that any letter on this subject should be addressed to 'Mr Jones', which suggests that there was a good deal of secrecy. He wrote now to the Gisbornes in great distress: 'My poor Neapolitan has a severe fever—I suppose she will die, and leave another memory to those which already torture me. I am waiting the next post with anxiety, but without much hope.' A few days later the blow had fallen and he wrote again: 'My Neapolitan charge is dead. It seems as if the destruction that is consuming me were as an atmosphere which wrapt and infected everything connected with me.'

The strange episode had ended in tragedy. Shelley, so he wrote, had taken 'every possible precaution' for the little girl, Elena Adelaide, but nothing could save her. It indeed appeared that any child connected with the Shelleys was doomed. The exception, mercifully, seemed to be the baby Percy. He was, so Mary wrote to Miss Curran around this time 'a thriving forward child', seldom ill, and giving very little trouble. Mary was still feeding him herself. In this baby's life, so Shelley had written to Godwin, 'after the frightful events of the last two years, her own seems wholly to be bound up'. But even with Percy, there had been an occasion when disaster had threatened. Mary had been so upset by her father's letters that her milk had been affected: her agitation of mind had produced in the child a similar upset to the illness which had killed baby Clara. Medical help had been called in. Percy had been saved. But Shelley, on Mary's authorization, told Godwin that no further demanding letters must be written to her—that, if they arrived, he would intercept them.

One way and another the household at Leghorn was not a happy one. All of the three inmates—Shelley, Mary and Claire—had too much on their minds for harmony. Shelley, after the recent shocks he had suffered, was unwell and irritable. Mary was unable to forget Godwin. And Claire now was faced with more trouble over Allegra.

2

Before leaving Pisa Claire had written to Mr and Mrs Hoppner. She had said that she would be 'willing to consider' the idea of Mrs Vavassour's adoption of Allegra. She had also asked the Hoppners to intercede with Byron to allow Allegra to be sent to Pisa for a short visit.

Byron, faced with this request, had written to the Hoppners a curt refusal. He disapproved, so he said, of the way children in the Shelley family were brought up. He added pertinently: 'Have they reared one?' And for good measure stated firmly that Allegra certainly should not leave him again 'to perish of Starvation and green fruit'. Or indeed, to be taught 'to believe that there is no Deity'.

This message was passed on to Claire by the Hoppners. She registered the arrival of their letter in her Journal as a letter 'concerning green fruit and God'. But this dispassionate cynicism concealed rage and anxiety. Weeks passed and she heard no more from Venice. Then in a further letter from the Hoppners she heard that Allegra had left Venice and been taken to Ravenna. Byron had removed himself there with his latest mistress, the Countess Guiccioli, and Allegra had accompanied them. He was thinking shortly of sending her to a convent.

If he carried out this convent plan he would be breaking the promise he had made to Claire that Allegra should remain with one or other of her parents until she was seven years old. Claire's first impulse was to rush off at once to Ravenna, taking Shelley with her, to confront Byron in the flesh. On cooler thoughts, she wondered if this would be a wise course to take. It was possible that Byron, who had a horror of seeing her, might become so exasperated that the situation might be still further worsened.

So instead she embarked on the fatal course of bombarding
Byron with letters. She demanded visits from Allegra, criticized
convents, found fault with all Byron's arrangements. Byron,
who considered that he was doing his best for the child, became
incensed. He wrote to Hoppner of Claire's 'bedlam behaviour'
and called her 'a damned bitch'. Allegra, he had discovered,
was already enough of a problem without Claire's 'insolent'
interference. He loved Allegra in his way, chiefly as a projection
of himself, but he found her a handful. She was pretty and
lively, the Countess Guiccioli petted her and took her for
drives, the Italian servants spoiled her. Byron gave her every
expensive care and attention and, in hot weather, sent her to a
villa in the country with two maids in attendance. But she
needed companions of her own age and every day she was
becoming more vain, spoilt, and unmanageable. A convent
near by, where she would have plenty of supervision, and other
children to play with, was beginning to seem the obvious
solution.

In spite of Shelley's efforts to make peace between Allegra's
parents, dissension grew. In August Byron wrote refusing to
have any further correspondence with Claire. Shelley, who
loved all children, was genuinely concerned for Allegra's
welfare. His patience over Claire's vagaries seemed now, as
ever, inexhaustible. He felt that at all costs, for the sake of
both mother and child, he must keep on friendly terms with
Byron. His letters, compared to the tempestuous exaggerations
of his more youthful days, are again models of tact:

Pisa. Sept. 17, 1820.

My dear Lord Byron,
    I have no conception of what Claire's letters to you contain—
One or two of her letters, but not lately, I have indeed seen;
But as I thought them extremely childish and absurd and
requested her not to send them, and she afterwards told me that
she had written and sent others in place of them, I cannot tell if
those which I saw on that occasion were sent to you or not—I
wonder however at your being provoked at what Claire writes;
though that she should write what is provoking is very probable.
You are conscious of performing your duty to Allegra, and your

refusal to allow her to visit Claire at this distance you conceive
to be part of your duty. That Claire should have wished to see
her is natural. That her disappointment should vex her, and her
vexation make her write absurdly is all in the usual order of
things. But, poor thing, she is very unhappy and in bad health,
and she ought to be treated with as much indulgence as possible. . . .
The weak and the foolish are in this respect like Kings: they
can do no wrong. . . . But, at present I do not see that you need
trouble yourself further, than to take care that she should receive
regular intelligence of Allegra's health, etc. You can write to
me, or make your secretary write to her (as you do not like
writing yourself) or arrange it in any manner most convenient
to you. Of course I should be happy to hear from you on any
subject—

Such patience under provocation was part of Shelley's self-
imposed creed of the healing power of reason and love. All
problems, he considered, should be met with in this spirit.
The effort at universal compassion must at this time have been
a taxing one in his home life. With the nerves of both Claire
and Mary on edge the relationship between them had again
deteriorated. There were constant irritations and bickerings,
duly registered by Claire in her Journal:

> Heigh ho, the Claire and the Maie
> Find something to fight about every day.

Shelley tried vainly to keep the peace—though still perversely ignoring the obvious solution. A letter to the Gisbornes
in July of that year shows the fundamental lack of realism which
vitiated his compassionate outlook. In this he stated that, if
only Mary was as wise as she would be at the age of forty-five,
or as wise as he had been made by misfortunes, she would live
peaceably with Claire.

As wise as he had been made by misfortune! Lately Shelley
had had his complacency rudely shaken by the famous and
irritating correspondence with his old idol, Robert Southey.
An article, offensive in criticism of *The Revolt of Islam*, had
appeared in the *Quarterly Review*. Shelley, for some reason,
became suspicious that Southey had written it and he wrote, in

somewhat high-handed terms, for assurance that this was not the case. Southey, in his reply, gave the desired assurance. But, disliking the tone of the younger poet's letter, he seized the occasion to admonish Shelley for the wrong-headedness of his opinions, and for the disaster these had brought to his life: 'Opinions are to be judged by their effects—and what has been the fruit of yours? Do they enable you to look backward with complacency or forward with hope? Have you found in them a rule of life conducive either to your own happiness, or to that of those who were most nearly and dearly connected with you? Or rather, have they not brought immediate misery upon others, and guilt, which is all but irremediable, on yourself?'

Irremediable guilt! In a moment all the anguish of the past, the haunting horror of Harriet's death, rose in Shelley's imagination. The criticism turned like a knife in the wound. For some weeks he did not answer the letter. When he did he began pleasantly enough, thanking Southey for his reassurances over the article. But fury grew with every line that he wrote:

> You accuse me, on what evidence I cannot guess, of *guilt*—a bald word, sir, this, and one which would have required me to write to you in another tone, had you addressed it to any one except myself. Instead, therefore, of refraining from 'judging that you be not judged' you not only judge but condemn. . . . You select a single passage out of a life otherwise not only spotless but spent in an impassioned pursuit of virtue, which looks like a blot, merely because I regulated my domestic arrangements without deferring to the notions of the vulgar—this you call *guilt*—I take God to witness—that you accuse me wrongfully. I am innocent of ill, either done or intended; the consequences you allude to* flowed in no respect from me. If you were my friend, I could tell you a history that would make you open your eyes; but I shall certainly never make the public my familiar confidant.

Southey wrote again, in no way relenting and, if anything, in a tone still more admonitory. He accused Shelley: 'You forsook your wife because you were tired of her, and had found another woman more suited to your taste.' Dismissing all

---

* Harriet's death.

Shelley's efforts at self-justification, he recommended him to Christianity, the Scriptures, and the book of Common Prayer. Even if Harriet herself had sinned, was it not, he insisted, because Shelley himself had corrupted her, robbing her of her moral and religious principles, debauching her mind. 'Ask your heart,' he continued, 'whether you have not been the whole, sole, and direct cause of her destruction? . . . Some men are wicked by disposition, others become so in their weakness; but you have corrupted in yourself an excellent nature.' The correspondence, he said, must now end and he inscribed himself, 'Believe me, sir, your sincere well-wisher, Robert Southey.'

Shelley, who was not unversed in the admonishment of others, did not take kindly to such blunt admonishments of himself. The self-righteous tone of his defence reveals something of the façade he had erected between himself and the truth. Southey's own tone, too, of self-assured superiority is in itself an affront. It was a relief probably to both when this painful correspondence ended as abruptly as it had begun. It was an episode for Shelley best forgotten—when remembered, only adding to the paranoiac feeling, from which he already suffered, of persecution and misunderstanding in an alien world.

The summer heat now at Leghorn was growing intense. Early in August 1820 they moved to the Baths of S. Giuliano di Pisa. Shelley, after house-hunting, had found a villa here, Casa Prinni, which he took for three months. Under two miles from the city of Pisa, the Baths provided a delightful place for a holiday, in beautiful surroundings, and with a pleasant and refreshing climate.

3

When the Gisbornes returned to Leghorn it was all too obvious that something had gone wrong in their relationship towards the Shelleys. Mary was hurt because a promised visit had not taken place; indeed the Gisbornes had actually passed through the Baths of Pisa without calling. She wrote, 'We do not *quite* understand your silence.' Her friendly invitations had been ignored. Instead Mrs Gisborne wrote what she herself described as a 'foolish letter' to Mary which had been in the nature of a bombshell. That the woman she considered to be her greatest friend had turned on her in this way caused Mary both distress and anger.

The letter she wrote back is overwrought but firm. She had called on the Gisbornes herself but had been made to feel that it was an 'inopportune visit'. She realized that something Mrs Godwin had said must have shaken Mrs Gisborne's loyalty. 'It is quite *impossible*,' she wrote, 'that we should visit you until we have first received you at our house'.

In spite of this ultimatum there was no visit from the Gisbornes until the following April. For the time being the relationship was in disarray and Shelley himself in a fury of rage and resentment against the entire family. Part of the trouble was the collapse of the steamboat project. He and Henry Reveley had failed to agree about fundamentals. Henry had blamed Shelley for wanting the engine of the boat to be built on much too large a scale. Shelley had found Henry dilatory. The requisite money had always been a problem. Finally the plan was abandoned altogether. Shelley decided he had been cheated and, forgetful for the moment of his creed of universal benevolence, complained bitterly of 'the vile treatment which I have received', and stigmatized the Gisbornes as 'most filthy and odious animals'. He would not, so he told Claire, remain in the house if they did come on a visit.

It was all rather a storm in a tea-cup. The machinery was sold and the proceeds handed over by Mr Gisborne to Shelley who found that he had not been cheated after all. Soon he was writing: 'My kindest remembrances to Mrs Gisborne and best wishes for your health and happiness.' But, all the same, something of the early joy in this friendship had been tarnished. Mary wrote in November of the 'inexplicable conduct' of the Gisbornes. And it was some months before the former confidence in her friend was in any way restored.

Lord Byron, from a miniature by James Holmes *(National Portrait Gallery)*

Claire Clairmont, from a portrait by Amelia Curran *(Curator of Newstead Abbey)*

E. J. Trelawny, from a
drawing by Bryan
Edward Duppa
(National Portrait Gallery)

Jane Williams, from a
portrait by George
Clint *(Bodleian
Library)*

Older women friends could, however, be very helpful. During that summer at the Baths of Pisa Mrs Mason came on a visit. An astute and understanding woman, she realized at once that the strained relations between Mary and Claire were worsening. The awkward, three-cornered household held undercurrents of extreme discord and tension. Claire might make herself very agreeable and sympathetic to Shelley, but to Mary she was often grumbling and ungrateful. The household was an unnatural one. Neither girl was particularly attached to the other. And both were people of strong individuality who knew what they wanted from life and preferred their own standards to those imposed by someone else.

Mrs Mason took Claire on one side and, in some way, persuaded her of the lack of wisdom in remaining with the Shelleys. Furthering her idea that Claire should learn to stand on her own feet, she now suggested a professor's family in Florence where she might go as a potential employee. A further argument in favour of her leaving the Shelleys was the fact that her presence caused scandal. The Shelleys had enough to live down already without any further suggestions of current misdemeanours. Paolo's shattering efforts at blackmail had been coloured by Claire's perpetual sharing of the household. How much better then, for all concerned, that they should separate.

Claire agreed—though it went against the grain. Mary was no doubt relieved though she said little. To Shelley the blow was severe. At the beginning he had sympathized with Mary over her feelings about Claire. He, too, had realized that the ambiguity of their position was likely to cause misunderstanding. Lately these aspects of the situation no longer bothered him. He enjoyed Claire's society. Some of his critics have even suggested that he could not be satisfied with only one woman but liked to enjoy the ministrations of *two*. He was unable, probably, to analyse his own motives. His own zealous protectiveness towards Claire—the ardent friendship, long letters, sacrifice of Mary's interests—could in his own mind be construed as part and parcel of his praiseworthy creed of universal compassion.

o

He now accompanied Claire to Florence on 20 October and settled her there with the family of Professor Bojti, with much misgiving. Even now he did not return alone but brought back with him his cousin, Thomas Medwin, to share with Mary the household of Casa Prinni. Medwin was an army captain, now on half-pay, and lately returned from India. He had been staying at Geneva with a friend, Edward Williams, and lately he had been anxious to see more of Italy, and of his cousin Percy.

Mary, faced with another triangular household, settled down to make the best of it. But as things turned out the holiday at the Baths of Pisa was cut short by the vagaries of nature. After a terrific downfall of rain the banks of the river broke. The Baths were flooded and finally overflowed. Water came into the house to a depth of four feet and the Shelleys, Medwin with them, were forced to escape by boat from the upper windows. It was an abrupt end to their holiday but, in any event, they had intended before long to return to Pisa. Now, on 29 October, they settled in new and comfortable lodgings on Lung' Arno. Shelley had a study of his own. 'Congratulate me on my seclusion,' he wrote to Claire, and, 'Mary has a very good room below, and there is plenty of space for the babe.'

His health was still bad: his illness, he was now convinced, a disease of the kidneys. He was sorry for himself and, inevitably, he missed Claire. She had always sympathized with him over his ailments and he had got into the habit of making her his confidante. Now that she was no longer there he idealized her in his overheated imagination, and wrote her long intimate letters which were kept secret from Mary: 'As to the pain I care little for it; but the nervous irritability which it leaves is a great and serious evil to me, and which, if not incessantly combated by myself and soothed by others, would leave me nothing but torment in life. I am now much better. Medwin's cheerful conversation is of some use to me, but what would it be to your sweet consolation, my own Claire.'

The emotional tone of these letters is difficult to assess. His indignation that Claire should have had to leave at all is revealed in his efforts to bring her back: 'Keep up your spirit, my best girl, until we meet at Pisa. But for Mrs Mason, I should say, come back immediately and give up a plan so inconsistent with your feelings.'

Or again, a few days later, in November:

Something indeed must be instantly decided respecting your present situation—unfit in every respect for you, and fraught with consequences to your health and spirits which I cannot endure to think of—The great thing now is, if possible, to come to Pisa before you shall stand engaged for another month, or perhaps another three months—You must take care of yourself this winter, and eat nourishing food, and try and receive care. How I long to see you again, and take what care I can of you—Adieu, dearest—be careful to tear this letter to pieces as I have written—[confidentially?]

He was, however, anxious not to offend Mrs Mason who took a tougher view. She had insisted that it would be 'weak and unreasonable' for Claire to give in so easily. Shelley had to tell Claire that Mrs Mason 'opposed strongly' the idea of her return. Later Mrs Mason had plans for helping Claire still further by more introductions in Florence. In the end Claire stayed with the Professor's family for the trial month as arranged, and then returned to Pisa for a few weeks, while planning to take up her abode in Florence for a further indefinite time, at the end of the year.

She returned to a more animated household than she had left behind at the Baths of Pisa. Medwin, a lively young man, with exaggerated views of his own literary importance, was much in evidence. There were, too, other more glamorous visitors. Never before in Italy had the Shelleys led such a social life with so many callers. The most ubiquitous was a somewhat shady Professor Pacchiani who knew everybody, introduced one to another, but was not universally popular. Through him before long the Shelleys had made the acquaintance of the spectacular and charming Prince Mavrocordato, later famous as the foremost statesman of the Greek revolution. He was two years older than Shelley, romantic in appearance, with thick eyebrows, bushy jet black hair and huge moustaches. Mary in particular was much attracted by this unusual visitor: a man, so she told Claire, much to her taste, and a great improvement on Medwin. 'Do you not envy my luck,' she wrote later to Mrs Gisborne, 'that, having begun Greek, an amiable, young, agreeable, and learned Greek prince comes every morning to give me a lesson of an hour and a half?' There is no doubt that the Prince's admiration and attentiveness towards her cheered her through the months that followed.

For, of all Professor Pacchiani's varied activities, the most momentous for the Shelley family that winter was to be the introduction to them of the beautiful, graceful, goddess-like young woman, Teresa Emilia Viviani.

4

Emilia Viviani was one of the two daughters of the Governor of Pisa, Niccolò Viviani. Pacchiani, a friend and confidant of the family, had once taught the two daughters languages and literature. Since then, however, their widower father had married for the second time, this time a woman thirty years younger than himself.

It was said that this young woman looked upon her two beautiful step-daughters as potential rivals and a threat to her own happiness. Under a covering story of 'completing their education' the two girls were both sent away from home to separate convents. In the meantime their father planned to search among his friends and acquaintances for prospective husbands who would take them, if possible, without a dowry.

Emilia, who was now about nineteen or twenty, had been at the Convent of St Anne for nearly three years. Pacchiani spoke of her with sentimental enthusiasm: 'Poverina, she pines like a bird in a cage—ardently longs to escape from her prison-house. She was made for love.'

The first to call on her were Mary and Claire. They were taken to the Convent of St Anne by Pacchiani himself and were fascinated by what they saw. Emilia Viviani was beautiful indeed: black hair, a marble brow, Grecian features, soulful eyes. Shelley and Medwin who followed later were, in their turn, struck forcibly with admiration. 'Lovely and interesting,' Medwin wrote, 'her eyes had the sleepy voluptuousness, if not the colour, of Beatrice Cenci's.'

There followed then one of the most violent and absorbing— if short-lived—passions of Shelley's life. There was everything here that he needed to transport him into fantasies of poetic imagination. A beautiful persecuted victim of oppression: a saint in need of help and protection: a 'caged lark' living in a cold, comfortless prison: she was all these things but, above all, a young girl, lacking love, lacking understanding, yet warm, responsive and sympathetic.

His relationship with Emilia Viviani gripped him to the exclusion of all else except poetry. She was, so he told Peacock, 'the only Italian for whom I ever felt any interest'. But 'interest' was a mild word to describe his feelings. The vision of Emilia which he conjured up in his imagination had, as usual, little resemblance to a flesh-and-blood human being. He idealized her as perfection, an object of worship, a creature without human failings, and worked himself up into a state of frantic indignation that so wonderful a creature should be kept incarcerated in a convent. He saw himself as her potential deliverer, her knight errant, and even had wild dreams of liberating her and fleeing with her to freedom.

Emilia in her turn, alive to her opportunities, played on his feelings and did her best to arouse pity for her predicament. They went for evening walks together. They exchanged letters. Mary invited her to stay. Emilia possessed all the ardour and warmth common to the Latin temperament and, in addition, a genius for self-expression. In contrast to the more reticent northerner's reserve, her eloquence was so vivid as to fire the imagination of her listeners.

At first Mary and Claire shared the universal homage. Mary

visited her frequently and Claire gave her lessons in English. But later doubts began to creep in. Could it be that the lovely Emilia was capable in more ways than one of exploiting the situation? Although complaining of persecution and imprisonment, she managed to achieve quite a number of diversions. It was not once, but often, that she walked alone with Shelley. She told Claire of her piety, praying always, so she said, to a saint. Claire, grown cynical, made a note in her Journal: 'And every time she changes her lover, she changes her saint, adopting the one of her lover.'

But for the moment Shelley's bondage was complete. With this latest passion taking possession of his entire nature, he gave vehement expression to his feelings in the poem *Epipsychidion*:

> Spouse! Sister! Angel! Pilot of the Fate
> Whose course has been so starless! O too late
> Belovèd! O too soon adored by me!
> . . . I love thee; yes, I feel
> That on the fountain of my heart a seal
> Is set, to keep its waters pure and bright
> For thee, since in those *tears* thou hast delight,
> We—are we not formed, as notes of music are,
> For one another, though dissimilar—

A vision of their life together in some haven, far from the cares of a mundane world, obsessed his imagination:

> The day is come, and thou wilt fly with me . . .
> Our breath shall intermix, our bosoms bound,
> And our veins beat together, and our lips
> With other eloquence than words, eclipse
> The soul that burns between them—
>
> Two overshadowing minds, one life, one death,
> One Heaven, one Hell, one immortality,
> And one annihilation. Woe is me!
> The wingèd words on which my soul would pierce
> Into the heights of Love's rare Universe,
> Are chains of lead around its flight of fire—
> I pant, I sink, I tremble, I expire!

He tried to write to her in her own language. Drafts of letters to her in Italian have recently been found. The tone is impassioned. He dreamed of feeling her lips pressed against his.

Mary, whose first generosity of feeling had been shaken by the extravagance of Shelley's infatuation, tried nobly to keep her composure. She could not fail to be aware that, as a goddess, she had long ago fallen from her pedestal, and that others were taking her place. The poem *Epipsychidion* was not helpful to her self-esteem: in it she is described as 'the cold, chaste moon' which 'warms but not illumines'. But she understood Shelley. She knew that, to a very large extent, his fantasies were essential as inspiration for the poetic genius which consumed him. She knew that, however ardent Shelley's desires, they were largely cerebral and that consummation, or even complete human involvement, was improbable. She might have agreed with a more modern poet writing today who has pointed out that 'to write poetry you have to be in an induced trance'.* She made allowances, counting doggedly on Shelley's fundamental loyalties.

But, all the same, it was a difficult situation. The gossip of other people must have reached her ears. She was still only twenty-two and Shelley was the husband she adored. Something of her uneasiness conveyed itself inevitably in her manner towards Emilia. And Emilia was enjoying herself in making a drama of the situation. 'Mary does not write to me,' she complained to Shelley; 'is it possible that she loves me less than the others do?' And to Mary herself: 'You seem to me a little cold sometimes, and that causes me an uncomfortable feeling; but I know that your husband said well when he said that your apparent coldness is only the ash which covers an affectionate heart.'

Emilia wanted it all ways—mopping up affection, deserving sympathy, yet essentially superficial in feeling. Her letters, exaggerated in their tone, frequent and copious, jar in their extravagance:

[To Shelley, 12 December, 1820] O my friend! my soul, my heart, can never be parted from my brother and from my dear

* Robert Graves: *Observer*, Supplement, 18 July 1965.

sisters. My person, once delivered from this prison, will attempt all things in order to follow my heart, and Emilia will seek you everywhere, even were you at the utmost boundaries of the world. I do not love, nor shall I ever be able to love any thing or person so much as your family; for it I would abandon everything—

Did she mean that she would abandon everything for Shelley? It is possible. Mary wrote generously about her in a letter to Leigh Hunt: 'Her only hope is a marriage which her parents tell her is concluded, although she has never seen the person intended for her.' Claire, back in Florence, was resenting the intrusion of Emilia into her own understanding with Shelley. She felt that she was being supplanted, that his letters to her were less affectionate, and she wrote to him, complaining that he no longer seemed to care about her welfare. One can sense something of her accusations by Shelley's replies:

> You do me injustice in imagining that I am in any degree insensible to your pleasure or pain—I see Emilia sometimes—She continues to enchant me infinitely—
>
> As much comfort as she receives from my attachment to her, *I lose*—There is no reason that you should fear any mixture of that which you call *love*—I think her tender and true—which is always something—how many are only one of these things at a time!

By the middle of February Shelley's own enthusiasm was waning. It was not long before he heard that Emilia, grown weary perhaps of awaiting rescue from the Shelleys, had agreed to marry the Italian suitor, Biondi, provided by her father. So, after all, this goddess, like all the others, had feet of clay. Looking back at his own rapt devotion Shelley felt disenchanted, and ashamed of his exaggeration of feeling. He was to write later to Byron about 'the great fuss' that had been made at Pisa about his intimacy with Emilia. He asked Byron not to mention anything he had been told as, if the whole truth came out, Mary might be 'very much annoyed'. He saw now, all too clearly, that Emilia was no better or worse than anybody else. After all, she was just an ordinary human being, not very constant, capable of guile, perhaps even rather uninteresting. How had he seen her in such an aura of ethereal perfection? Even the poem *Epipsychidion* made him feel uneasy. It represented, so he said, 'a part of himself already dead'. The poem, sent to Ollier for publication in February 1821, was described later to Mr Gisborne as 'an idealized history of my life and feelings'. All his excitement, his exaltation, had fallen away.

In spite of his disillusionment, however, he could not at the time entirely dismiss Emilia from his mind. There is allusion to her in his letters for many months to come. He could not refrain from keeping in touch with her, wondering about her fate:

[To Claire, 29 April 1821] I believe it is now certain that Emilia will marry—A great and painful weight will be taken off my mind by that event. Poor thing! she suffers dreadfully in her prison.

[To Claire, 14 May 1821] I go over about twice a week to see Emilia, who is in better spirits and health than she has been for some time.

[To Claire, 16 June 1821] Emilia's marriage is put off to September.

[To Mary, 10 August 1821] Have you heard anything of my poor Emilia, from whom I got a letter the day of my departure, saying that her marriage was deferred for a *very short* time on account of the illness of her sposo?

To Mary the end of the affair brought relief. She kept up a coolness and dignity through many months of strain and it was not until the March of 1822 that, in a letter to Mrs Gisborne, her true feeling emerged:

Emilia has married Biondi; we hear that she leads him and his mother (to use a vulgarism) a devil of a life. The conclusion of our friendship (à la Italiana) puts me in mind of a nursery rhyme which runs thus:

As I was going down Cranbourne Lane
    Cranbourne Lane was dirty,
And there I met a pretty maid
    Who dropt to me a curtsey.

I gave her cakes, I gave her wine,
    I gave her sugar candy;
But oh! the little naughty girl
    She asked me for some brandy.

Now turn 'Cranbourne Lane' into Pisan acquaintances, which, I am sure, are dirty enough, and 'brandy' into that wherewithal to buy brandy (and that no small sum *però*) and you have the whole story of Shelley's Italian Platonics.

There is bitterness here. And with it, perhaps understandably, some unfairness. It is true that Emilia had tried to get money from Shelley. It is true that in her character there was a strong element of self-seeking. But, in her defence, we are told that the money was not for herself but a loan for a woman friend. And in the venture of her marriage to her father's choice she met with little but misfortune. Biondi proved a brutal husband. She was taken to live in the Maremma district where malaria was rife and her health was undermined. In the first five years of marriage she lost four children. Eventually there was a separation and she returned in 1826 to her father's house in Florence. Biondi refused to return her dowry and, after her father's death, with no allowance, she was penniless, her only support a small provision from a philanthropic doctor who attended her.

Our last news of her is from Medwin who records a visit to he just before she died in 1836. All her beauty had vanished. She was living in the poorer quarter of Florence, lonely, undernourished, emaciated through illness. She had no hope left, her health ruined through malaria. Very shortly afterwards she died.

Mary, after all, in the end had little to envy.

༒ 5 ༒

In January there was a new addition to the Pisan circle. This was the arrival from England of Medwin's friend, Edward Ellerker Williams. With him were his 'wife', Jane, and their two children. Shelley himself in the old days had been at school with Williams at Eton. Afterwards Williams had joined the Navy and had later transferred to the Dragoons. In India he had met Medwin. And now, so Medwin said, he had 'allured' the Williamses to Pisa to 'chase Shelley's melancholy'.

Jane Williams was to play an important part in the last months of Shelley's life. She was a very pretty young woman, with a not uncalculated charm, and she had had a chequered history. Soon after her birth her mother, Mrs Cleveland, became a widow and frittered away the family fortune, playing cards. Jane's brother joined the army and Jane accompanied him to India. There she met a young officer whom she married, but the marriage was not a success. The young man was evidently a bad lot, for we hear in a letter of Medwin's later, of a life of crime which included theft and forgery. The marriage ended in separation but the legal tie remained, a millstone round Jane's neck, for the rest of her life.

Fortunately for her it was not long before she met Edward Williams, an uncomplicated person, who fell devotedly in love with her. As far as lay in her nature she returned his devotion and the two set up house together. After leaving India they had spent some time at Geneva, sharing a house with Medwin. Now, after a visit to England, they had come to Pisa, to find a peaceful life where they could remain together without too much comment. Also, after hearing Medwin's glowing accounts, they were very anxious to meet Shelley.

Shelley, almost immediately after their arrival, started writing about them in a succession of letters to Claire:

[To Claire, 16 January 1821] The Williams's are come and Mrs W. dined here today, an extremely pretty and gentle woman—apparently not *very* clever. I like her very much. I have only seen her for an hour but I will tell you more another time—I have not seen Mr W.

Later there were signs of uncertainty:

[To Claire, 14 May 1821] The Williams's come sometimes. W. I like and I have got reconciled to Jane.
[To Claire, 8 June 1821] We see a good deal of the Williams's —who are very good people and I like her much better than I did.
[To Claire, 16 June 1821] We see the Williams' constantly— nice, good-natured people; very soft society after authors and pretenders to philosophy.

Mary too had her reservations. She thought Jane very pretty but wanting in animation and sense. She wrote of her 'slow monotonous voice' and her very ordinary conversation— admitting, however, that she was good-tempered and tolerant. Later she was to describe her, somewhat ambiguously, as 'a violet by a mossy stone'. Williams himself she found congenial: like her, he was fond of drawing, and besides that had literary tastes, was good company, pleasant-natured and sensible.

Gradually, however, both the Williamses endeared themselves to her. Jane, she thought, improved on acquaintance. She began to find something stable and comforting about her amiable, unchanging serenity. Apart from having a lovely singing voice, Jane was not particularly artistic or cultured. It seems, however, that by tact and shrewdness she could cleverly conceal her limitations of intellect and feeling. She gave promise of a depth and capacity for affectionate response which she did not really possess. Somehow conveying this unfelt warmth, she managed to bind people to her in ties of passionate affection which, though gratifying to her vanity, left her comparatively unscathed.

The two families became more and more intimate. They

met almost daily, driving together and going for walks. It was a relief to Mary from an undiluted dose of Medwin. It also helped to alleviate the sadness of the coming parting from Prince Mavrocordato, who was shortly leaving them to fight for Greece's independence. 'Our amiable prince will leave us,' wrote Mary sadly. Shelley, less enthusiastic, was to write later: 'A vessel has arrived to take the Greek Prince and his suite to join the army in the Morea. He is a great loss to Mary, and *therefore* to me—but not otherwise.'

Shelley himself, not yet infatuated by Jane, as he was to be later, struck up a strong and undemanding friendship with Edward Williams. Their greatest bond was their mutual love of boating—the bond which, in the end, was to help bring about their deaths. Shelley now ordered for their use a flat-bottomed boat, ten feet long, which Harry Reveley undertook to obtain for them at Leghorn.

When the boat was ready Shelley and Williams went to Leghorn to fetch it, planning to return to Pisa by canal. Fortunately on this occasion Mr Gisborne insisted that Henry, more accustomed to the local waterways, should accompany them. Before long a stiff breeze sprang up and the boat became entangled among weeds. Williams stood up abruptly, clutched at the mast to steady himself, and the boat capsized. Shelley, who was unable to save himself, was saved by Henry Reveley. All managed to get safely to the bank where Shelley, saturated in cold wet clothes, fell flat on his face in a faint.

But nothing deterred them. The boat was repaired and there were still more voyages. They were often seen in it on the River Arno to the horror of the Italians who 'remonstrated on the danger'.

The boat, however, was certainly to prove very useful in the coming summer months. In May 1821 the Shelleys moved for a holiday again to the Baths of Pisa. The Williamses followed them and took a villa at Pugnano, four miles away. The two places communicated by canal—a safer canal this time, fed by the river and sheltered by trees, and even Mary was willing to accompany Shelley to and fro in the boat on frequent visits to their friends.

In many ways for Mary this was a happier time than usual. Claire was still with the Professor's family in Florence, apparently now settled and making new friends. The little boy Percy was flourishing. Shelley was better for leading a more open-air life though still often in pain, and sometimes irritable. These fits of depression alternated, as he explained in a letter to Claire, with 'moments of almost supernatural elevation'. His chief relief lay in writing poetry. He was now composing the beautiful *Adonais* in memory of Keats. When he had heard that Keats was so desperately ill and was coming to Italy, Shelley had written him a letter, hoping to intercept him at Naples, and inviting him to Pisa. But Keats had been unable to accept the invitation. All his plans had been pre-arranged for Rome.

And now, already, Keats was dead. Shelley, who had longed to be of service to him, was deeply shocked. He was one of the people who felt that Keats's death had been partly caused by the attacks of his critics, 'the assassins of his peace and of his fame'. Now in the poem *Adonais* he wrote passionately in Keats's defence. Strangely, it gives the impression that it was not only an elegy for Keats but, in many ways, an elegy for himself: a cry from the heart for all the misunderstanding which he felt had been meted out to him, for the disenchant-ment of life, and a welcome too for the release of death. After writing it he was conscious of having achieved something worthy of himself and of his subject. 'I should be surprised,' he wrote to his publisher, 'if *that* Poem were born to an immor-tality of oblivion.'

Mary, too, was writing. She was finishing her historical novel *Valpurgo* and wrote to tell Claire that she was feeling not gay but peaceful, and at peace with the world. To raise her morale there had been letters and farewell visits from Prince Mavrocordato. His admiration helped her in assuaging the doubts in her self-depreciating temperament, which had been nourished lately by Shelley's amorous adventures.

All might have been peaceful for a time if their calm had not been shattered by more worry over Claire and Allegra. Claire had heard earlier that Byron had carried out his threat.

He had sent Allegra to the convent of Bagnacavallo, twelve miles from Ravenna. He told the Hoppners that he wanted Allegra to be brought up as a Roman Catholic, he would give her a dowry, and he hoped eventually that she would marry. In the meantime it seemed that she needed discipline and a stable existence. She had become very spoilt, with dictatorial ways.

It does not seem that Allegra was unhappy in this new life. The nuns were kind and loving and she had apparently settled down without much trouble. It was only Claire who could not accept it. She was enraged. She felt that Byron had broken his word, and that she would not have a moment's peace until something drastic was done to alter the situation. She had written to Byron, again attacking Italian convents, and even suggesting a boarding-school in England. But Byron had not answered. Now she tried to enlist Shelley's help and support. But Shelley for once did not take her part. He considered that Byron was doing his best for Allegra and that there was no cause to interfere.

It was not until, in July, when the Carbonari revolution was suppressed throughout Italy, that matters came to a head. The suppression meant that many Liberal families were exiled from the Papal states. These included the Gambas, the family of Teresa Guiccioli. And now, exiled as they were, the whole family was on the move. They were thinking of crossing the border into Switzerland. If Teresa went, would Byron go with her? And, in that case, was Allegra to be left behind, far from all who belonged to her, stranded in the convent of Bagnacavallo? Now, indeed, Claire felt that she had just cause for complaint, and even action. Again she enlisted the help of Shelley.

Shelley too felt anxious. He corresponded with Byron who suggested a meeting. Shelley decided that he must leave for Ravenna immediately, leave the quietness and peace of his holiday with Mary at the Baths of Pisa, and do his best to deal with this new situation. Before his twenty-ninth birthday, 4 August, he had departed. Mary, alone again and anxious, made a prophetic note in her Journal: 'Saturday, August 4th.

Shelley's birthday. Seven years are now gone; what changes! What a life! We now appear tranquil; yet who knows what wind—but I will not prognosticate evil; we have had enough of it. When Shelley came to Italy, I said all is well if it were permanent; it was more passing than an Italian twilight. I now say the same. May it be a Polar day, yet that day too, has an end.'

⚜ 6 ⚜

Shelley went first to Leghorn. He wanted to discuss the problem of Allegra with Claire who was having a seaside holiday with the Gisbornes. It was probably during this holiday of Claire's that the son of the house, Henry Reveley, proposed to her and she refused him. She still avoided all compromise attempts at marriage as a feeble way out of her troubles, and she seemed to be unable to fall in love. She boated now with Shelley on his brief visit and they sailed together out to sea.

But Shelley was soon gone. He went on, travelling all night by road towards Bologna. At daybreak the horse stumbled and both Shelley and the *vetturino* were thrown over a hedge and on to a slope of meadow. Luckily no harm was done and they were able to proceed on their way to Ravenna, arriving at ten o'clock at night.

The Countess Guiccioli was away and Byron was alone—his only companions the servants and the usual menagerie consisting, so Shelley told Peacock, of 'ten horses, eight enormous dogs, three monkeys, five cats, an eagle, a crow and a falcon. And all these,' he added, 'except the horses, walk about the house!' Shelley was, however, pleasurably impressed by the change in his host. He found Byron 'greatly improved in every respect—in genius, in temper, in moral views, in health, in happiness'. The attachment to the Countess Guiccioli was evidently having the most desirable effect. His daily habits, on

Shelley's House at Lerici, from a water-colour painting (*Collections at Keats House, Hampstead, by permission of the Libraries and Arts Committee of the London Borough of Camden*)

Shelley's Funeral Rites, from a painting by Fournier (*Walker Art Gallery*)

the other hand, were still unorthodox. He breakfasted in the afternoon and Shelley had to alter his way of life to get up at midday. After that they talked for hours, sometimes all through the night, and until six o'clock in the morning.

The immediate problem of Allegra was almost at once overshadowed by Byron's revelations of Elise's treacherous disclosures to the Hoppners. Shelley was horrified. He wrote at once to Mary. It was the old Naples story, hinted at earlier by Paolo. Claire, so Elise told the Hoppners, was Shelley's mistress. At Naples she became pregnant. Shelley had given her violent medicine to bring about an abortion but, this having failed, the child was born and was promptly bundled into a Foundling Hospital. In addition, so Elise said, both Claire and Shelley treated Mary shamefully. Shelley neglected and beat her, and Claire 'never let a day pass' without insulting Mary violently, abetted all the time by Shelley. The Hoppners had, apparently, believed this story, chapter and verse. They had decided to have 'no further communication' with the Shelleys and had advised Byron to follow their example.

The Hoppners, in disclosing to Byron what had happened, enjoined him to secrecy. And Byron, with characteristic duplicity, made no effort to defend the Shelleys but wrote back: 'Of the facts—there can be little doubt: it is just like them.' Now, however, Byron not only revealed the entire slander to Shelley but seems to have assured him that of course he had never believed it. Mary wrote: 'I sincerely thank Lord Byron for his kind unbelief.'

The situation distressed the Shelleys inexpressibly. Shelley wrote to Mary of 'the filthy world, of which it is Hell to be a part' and 'imagine how it is possible that one of so weak and sensitive a nature as mine can run further the gauntlet through this hellish society of men!' He told Mary that she should at once write a letter to the Hoppners, denying the infamy, and proving that it was false. 'If you will send the letter to me here, I will forward it to the Hoppners—Lord Byron is not up, I do not know the Hoppners' address—and I am anxious not to lose the post.'

Mary did at once what he asked her. She wrote a letter at

P

white heat, so burning in its honesty and sincerity, that it is difficult to disbelieve it. She made it clear to Mrs Hoppner that there was not a word of truth in the slander, that Elise was a liar, and that her own faith in Shelley was unshaken and unshakeable. She marvelled that Mrs Hoppner could have believed stories so false, so wickedly untrue:

> You knew Shelley, you saw his face, and could you believe them? Believe them only on the testimony of a girl whom you despised—Claire had no child—the rest must be false—but that you should believe it—that my beloved Shelley should stand thus slandered in your minds—he the gentlest and the most humane of creatures, is more painful to me, oh far more painful than any words can express—Repair, I conjure you, the evil you have done by retracting your confidence in one so vile as Elise, and by writing to me that you now reject as false every circumstance of her infamous tale.

Whether Mrs Hoppner ever received this letter is doubtful. Shelley wrote to Mary: 'I have given it to Lord Byron, who has engaged to send it with his own comments to the Hoppners.' But after Byron's death the letter was found among his papers. Did he ever send it to Mrs Hoppner? True, the seal was broken: but it is also true that Mary never received an answer. The whole episode has provoked disagreement among biographers. Byron's defenders suggest that he must have sent it with the request that it should be returned to him. Others see in the episode yet one more proof of Byron's perfidy: he had broken his word to the Hoppners by regaling Shelley with the scandal—how unlikely then that he would give this away to Mrs Hoppner by sending her Mary's letter. The truth is still a mystery, though conjecture is damning to Byron. Mary could never have guessed for an instant that her letter would not be faithfully forwarded. She must have waited vainly, and in mounting indignation, for the reply which never came. In later years when the two women met each other accidentally in the street, Mary cut Mrs Hoppner dead.

There was still the question of Allegra's future to be settled.

Shelley remained at Ravenna for a few days trying to persuade Byron if he moved to take Allegra with him—or, alternatively, to allow her to be brought up with Percy. But Byron was in no yielding mood on the subject of Allegra. He complained that her temper had grown 'violent and imperious'. It transpired that he had not even accompanied her to the convent himself: he had instead sent her there with a servant and had never since visited her. His whole attention now was taken up by an effort to dissuade the Gamba family from moving into Switzerland. He had decided that he would prefer to remain in some other part of Italy and was thinking of Pisa. Shelley, whose tact and patience through these tiresome negotiations were wholly admirable, was persuaded to write to the Countess Guiccioli herself. In his letter, extremely polite, but written in 'bad Italian' he had to impress on the Countess that Geneva was highly unsuitable. He pointed out all the indignities that Byron had suffered there in the past: the scandals among the English residents and the way they had spied on his movements, often watching him through telescopes. There was, too, the lurid tale of the English woman who had fainted through horror when Byron entered a drawing-room.

The Countess was impressed. The Gambas changed their minds and decided that they would all go to Pisa. Shelley wrote to Mary telling her that Byron wished for 'a large and magnificent house' and telling her to inquire if any of the large Pisan palaces were to let.

The Shelleys themselves at this time were in favour of the idea of spending the winter in Florence. But gradually they too changed their minds and decided it might be wiser to stay in Pisa. They felt that the weight of Byron's social importance might give them a certain protection. Shelley was becoming genuinely frightened that the scandals and calumnies attached to his name might spread, making life entirely impossible for him and his family. In Pisa, besides Byron, they had other friends. 'Our roots were never struck so deeply as at Pisa,' he told Mary. Could not they form for themselves 'a society of our own class, as much as possible, in intellect or in feelings', and connect themselves entirely with the interests of that society?

But, before leaving Ravenna, Shelley was determined on two things—to see Allegra, and to come to some arrangement with Byron about the future of Leigh Hunt, who now wanted to come with his family to Italy.

The visit to Allegra was satisfactorily accomplished. Shelley travelled to the convent and stayed with her for about three hours. She had always been a favourite of his and, in default of her own father, Allegra found him a pleasing substitute. She led him all over the garden and all over the convent, 'running and skipping so fast that I could hardly keep up with her'. He described her changed appearance in a letter to Mary: the altered paler face, the slightness for her age, the contemplative seriousness mixed with her former vivacity. Her deep blue eyes were still beautiful and the dark hair 'beautifully profuse' hanging in curls on her neck. He gave her a gold chain which he had bought for her in Ravenna and a 'basket of sweetmeats' which, unlike the old Allegra, she insisted on sharing with the nuns. 'Her predominant foible,' he wrote, 'seems the love of distinction and vanity.'

Before he left she made him 'run all over the convent like a mad thing'. In spite of a strict discipline it seemed that the nuns could be lenient and even when, excited by Shelley's visit, she began to ring the bell, the 'tocsin of the convent' calling all the nuns to assemble, she was not scolded. Shelley disapproved of convents—'the talks and dreams of Paradise and angels', the 'prodigious list of saints' and perpetual talk of 'the Bambino'. 'The idea of bringing up so sweet a creature in the midst of such trash till sixteen!' Nevertheless, he did not feel that she was unhappy. But he still hoped to persuade Byron, when he moved to Pisa, to bring Allegra with him.

With regard to Leigh Hunt, here again the situation needed tact and diplomacy. At one time Byron had suggested lending Hunt the fare to come out to Italy but now his enthusiasm had lessened. The offer of the fare no longer held good. He did, however, tentatively put forward an idea that they should jointly publish a periodical in which their own compositions

could appear. This was enough for Shelley. He knew that the
Hunts were in serious difficulties with financial troubles and
ill-health. In January Mrs Hunt had written to Mary, begging
her to arrange for them all to come out to Italy. Shelley now
rushed off and wrote Hunt a glowing letter, inviting them to
come to Pisa at once. He himself would provide the journey
money, borrowing it from Byron, and giving Byron a bond in
exchange.

At first Hunt was doubtful. But his hesitation was short-
lived. He wrote back on 21 September saying that he and his
family—his wife and six children—would be setting off for
Italy in precisely a month's time. He was full of optimism
about the projected periodical. Money, as usual, was a
stumbling block. In this respect he hinted that he could not
manage without Shelley's 'kindness'.

Events were now moving swiftly. Mary had found that the
Palazzo Lanfranchi, 'the finest palace in Pisa', was to let.
Shelley immediately secured it for Byron, promising payment
of four hundred crowns a year, and signing the contract on
Byron's behalf. The Gambas were already in Pisa, accompanied
by the Countess Guiccioli, and Byron could be expected at the
end of September.

Perhaps for a moment Shelley had qualms. He wrote to his
friend, Horace Smith, of 'this humdrum Pisa' and at one
juncture wrote to Peacock asking if there was any chance that
he might obtain a diplomatic appointment in India. Peacock
quickly vetoed the suggestion. He did not think this 'Indian
project' would agree with Shelley either 'in mind or body';
besides which, such posts were only for the East India Company's regular employees. So instead the Shelleys settled in
'very nice apartments' opposite Byron's palace in Tre Palazzi
on the Lung' Arno. The Williamses, due back from Pugnano
in November, were taking the lower flat underneath. And the
Hunt family when they arrived were, it was foolishly decided,
to take up their abode on the empty ground floor of Byron's
palace.

Claire was already in Pisa. She was on holiday from Florence
and paying a visit to the Masons. She lived on tenterhooks

lest she should not get out of Pisa in time before Byron arrived. Whatever happened she felt that she must avoid a meeting but at the same time she was longing to know if he would really bring Allegra with him. Her nerves were on edge, she wrote imperious commands to Mary, demanding that some boxes of hers should be sent immediately: 'Don't delay and my band-box too', and asking if 'you could of your great bounty give me a sponge'. She planned to call on the Shelleys surreptitiously without being seen. But who could accompany her? 'Shelley won't do to fetch me because he looks singular in the streets.' All the same Shelley might be useful in other ways: 'I wish he would come now to give me some money.' Finally she left, returning to Florence on 1 November, and passing Byron's cavalcade on the way.

Byron's arrival in Pisa was a colourful event for the natives of that city. There were five carriages and the menagerie, besides a retinue of servants. But among the horses, dogs, cats, monkeys, peacocks, and birds of every description, there was no sign of Allegra.

7

Apart from the addition of Leigh Hunt, who was delayed by the weather, the 'Pisa circle' was now complete. They all met frequently. The Countess Guiccioli, who had been patiently awaiting Byron's belated arrival, was accepted and liked by them all. Mary particularly found her a pleasant companion and they went for day-time drives together. Otherwise most of the meetings took place in the evenings. Shelley read poetry and Jane Williams sang in her sweet magnetic voice.

Mary was unwell again. She suffered from rheumatism in her head and was unable to sleep. Shelley's health was better but he still felt weak and nervously irritable. He wandered off by himself in the day time, seeking 'intellectual solitude' but

unable to write anything but short poems. A restlessness consumed him. As Dowden, his early biographer wrote, it seemed
that he still pined 'for an ideal tenderness of sympathy and
love such as hardly belongs to this earth'.* The anticlimax
of the disillusioning affair with Emilia Viviani had left him
wounded and vulnerable. Again, perhaps for want of anyone
better, he turned to Claire.

Claire was back in Florence, all her future plans uncertain.
On 11 December Shelley wrote to her:

> My dearest friend
>   I should be very glad to receive a confidential letter from
> you—Do not think that my affection and anxiety for you ever
> cease, or that I ever love you less although that love has been
> and still must be a source of disquietude to me—Tell me
> ['dearest' scratched out] what you mean to do, and if it should
> give you pleasure come and live with us.

Again he harped on the old theme. Regardless of Mary's
feelings Claire should come back. With the memory of his
own misery and rage over Harriet's infliction on him of Eliza,
it is odd that Shelley never seemed to realize the unkindness
of inflicting Claire upon Mary. The two girls were not even
blood relations. Shelley knew Mary's views on the subject, he
knew what other people thought, Mrs Mason in particular,
and he knew of the scandal that was caused. Yet, right up to
the end in his letters, and even after Claire herself had summoned up enough resolution to accept independence, he was
continually urging her to return.

There is no doubt that it is this ambivalence in Shelley's
nature, this mixture of nobility with self-indulgence, which
has made his character so difficult to assess, and which has led
to such a difference of opinion among his biographers. Mary,
in his defence, and in extenuation of his behaviour, wrote that
'in all he did he, at the time of doing it, believed himself
justified by his own conscience'. John Cordy Jeaffreson, in his
somewhat caustic book *The Real Shelley*, took up this not very

* Edward Dowden: *Life of Percy Bysshe Shelley*.

convincing apologia: 'What makes this curious plea especially deserving of notice is its truth. As soon as Shelley wished to do a thing, it was manifest to him that he had a right to do it; and having done the thing (however wrong it might be) he could commend himself for virtue in having done it.'

Claire on this occasion did not respond to Shelley's overtures. She remained in Florence where she had found, surprisingly, that she was beginning to be a social success. Her liveliness, wit, ability to speak both French and Italian, and her attractive singing voice, brought a popularity which gave her more confidence to try to launch out on her own. Medwin, who called on her several times in Florence, described her as 'engaging and pleasing', her very dark hair and eyes making her look almost an Italian herself. It was only the nagging thought of Allegra which permanently harassed her happiness and serenity. The knowledge that Byron had broken his half-promise to bring Allegra with him to Pisa had plunged her into a seething unrest which defied comfort. Shelley had always been her champion. In later years as an old, old lady she was to describe Shelley as the one love of her life. But Shelley's 'love' for her was ambivalent. His first allegiance was obviously to Mary. And then lately had not there been this bizarre and consuming infatuation of his for the scheming Emilia Viviani? Such infidelity of soul had still further shaken Claire's faith in the constancy of man.

Shelley had to turn elsewhere for consolation. There was always Jane Williams whom he was beginning to like more and more. The Pisan circle was uniting now still further, closing its ranks in a mutual worry and apprehension because Leigh Hunt had not yet arrived. He and his family had set off on 15 November, but weeks of storms and gales had passed and they were still in England. Inevitably they were running out of money and Shelley again rose to the occasion. 'My dearest friend, I send you by return of post £150—How I am ever to assemble the constituents of such a sum again, I do not at present see,—but do not be disheartened: we will all put our shoulders to the wheel.'

In January 1822, instead of the expected Leigh Hunt, there

had been a new addition to the circle. This was the Cornish-
man, Edward John Trelawny, who had made the acquaintance
of Williams and Medwin in Switzerland. He was now
anxious to throw in his lot with Byron and Shelley, and hopefully planned that they should all spend a summer together,
boating in the Mediterranean.

Trelawny was a strange figure, in appearance flamboyant
and impressive, and in every way twice as large as life. 'A
kind of half-Arab Englishman' was Mary's description of him
or, as Shelley wrote, 'a wild but kind-hearted seaman'.
Already much travelled, with the history of two marriages
behind him, he was now twenty-nine, six feet in height, with
thickly curled raven-black hair, expressive eyes, thick brows,
and an infectious smile. There was something of the pirate
about him, exciting the imagination. Mary, particularly, was
impressed.

Later, in his *Recollections*, Trelawny wrote vividly of these
last months of Shelley's life. In spite of a questionable
veracity there is an authentic ring about his descriptions. Of
Mary he wrote: 'The most striking feature in her face was
her calm, grey eyes; she was rather under the English standard
of women's height, very fair and light-haired, witty, social
and animated in the society of friends, though mournful in
solitude.' Shelley, he described at their first meeting as
'blushing like a girl, a tall thin stripling' with 'a flushed,
feminine and artless face'. Later he wrote of 'the charm of his
simple, earnest manner' and added that 'to serve a friend, he
was ever ready to make any sacrifice'. Though friendly with
both Shelley and Byron, and much struck with Byron's 'mental
vivacity and wonderful memory', Trelawny much preferred
Shelley. 'I could not sympathize with Byron who believed in
nothing,' he wrote. And he was glad to cross the road from
the magnificent Palazzo Lanfranchi to the Shelley's more
congenial and hospitable flat.

Plans were afoot now for the whole of the Pisa circle, Byron
and Countess Guiccioli included, to move to Spezzia for the
summer months. Boating was to be the great attraction. Two
boats were ordered. They were to be built in the shipyards of

Genoa, by Trelawny's friend, Captain Roberts. The larger
was for Byron, the smaller for Shelley and Williams. The
wives, Mary and Jane, were apprehensive. While Shelley and
Williams pored over drawings and plans on the table, Jane
leaned over her husband's shoulder and remarked prophetically:
'You are sketching your death.'* Mary, who now distrusted
life completely, felt that the peaceful existence at Pisa was
only a 'lull between storms'. She was pregnant again and
would much have preferred to remain where she was, and not
to embark on yet another move. The doctor had advised her
to keep quiet before the baby's birth and so perhaps avoid her
usual depression afterwards. But again Shelley was restless.
Partly to inspire his genius, and with the egoism of the
dedicated artist, he liked to move from place to place, carrying
his family with him. The Spezzia plan aroused him to excitement and enthusiasm. And as so often—moved partly by a
feeling of inferiority, partly by an innate unselfishness—Mary
acquiesced.

But all the same in some little ways, probably more superficial than otherwise, it seemed lately that Mary and Shelley
were drifting apart. Though there was still a fundamental
bond between them, their tastes were showing more signs of
divergence. 'Poor Mary,' Shelley said later to Trelawny, 'hers
is a sad fate—She can't bear solitude, nor I society—the quick
coupled with the dead.' It was an exaggeration but, like most
exaggerations, held seeds of truth.

Mary now longed above all things for stability and for a
place in the sun. Years of vagabondage and ostracism had left
their mark. Ceaseless wandering, uncomfortable journeys,
seedy hotels, dirty lodgings—and, above all, despair at losing
her children—the strain had been too great. Always, secretly,
she had hankered after conventionality and had been impressed
by gracious living and nobility of birth. Lately there was a
curious ambivalence in her behaviour which revealed the
conflict in her mind. Though her loyalty to Shelley never
faltered she went out more now, tried to do what other people
were doing, went to the opera, to dances, even to church.

* Sylva Norman: *After Shelley*.

Outwardly she had become shallower, more 'respectable', less sympathetic to all that Shelley stood for. In years to come all the accumulated frustration of her life was to explode in one short sentence—'Let your son Percy learn to think for himself,' people advised her, only to be met with the swift, stinging retort: 'Oh, my God! Teach him to think like other people!' But now, at Pisa, she was still some distance from that revealing moment. There were still times when she inveighed against Pisan society, and longed for a quiet retreat with Shelley and her child alone, away from all worldly claims.

For Shelley, compromise was becoming a habit. He avoided disputes with Mary by avoiding the subjects on which they disagreed. He tried to guard her, to cheer her, but her dejection depressed him. Unconsciously, though held by unbreakable ties of habit, loyalty and—fundamentally—love, he sought a means of escape.

His chief consolation now was the friendship of Jane and Edward Williams. He basked in the soothing, benign influence of the enigmatic Jane and, gradually falling more and more under her spell, became infatuated. Her music and her sweet singing voice enchanted him. He wanted to give her an expensive harp but finally fell back on a guitar which he obtained for her from England. She was, so he told Mr Gisborne in January, 'a sort of spirit of embodied peace in our circle of tempests'. There are shades here of Miss Hitchener— 'the thunder-riven pinnacle of rock amid the rushing tempest and the boiling surge'. It was the old hopeless search 'in a mortal image' for impossible perfection. Jane now was the paragon: the feminine, predatory, limited, but very charming, Jane.

Fortunately Mary too was by this time devoted to Jane. She did not see her as a menace as, towards the end, she had seen Emilia Viviani. During Shelley's lifetime there is no sign that she ever consciously realized his growing infatuation for this other woman, whom she regarded as a particular friend of her own. In letters to Mrs Gisborne who had now, with her family, gone to live permanently in England, Mary wrote enthusiastically of her new friends: 'I like the Williams' exceedingly.' 'Mrs Williams is a miracle of economy, and, as Mrs Godwin used to call it, makes both ends meet with great comfort to herself and others.' Or again, earlier to Mrs Hunt: 'You should see me and my friend Mrs Williams poking about for violets by the sides of dry ditches.' She incited the ailing Mrs Hunt, waiting about in England for the weather to improve, to make haste to join them all in Pisa: 'Perhaps, as it was with me, Italy will not strike you as so divine at first; but each day it becomes dearer and more delightful; the sun, the flowers, the air, all is more sweet and more balmy than in the *Ultima Thule* that you inhabit.'

8

Shelley's happiness was considerably modified by the proximity of Byron. The two men were as poles apart in everything but their love of poetry. Now that they saw so much of one another this fact was painfully apparent. Shelley, who was forced into a 'weekly dinner' at Byron's palace, felt his nerves shaken to pieces watching his host and other guests 'making themselves vats of claret etc. till 3 o'clock in the morning'.

A bone of contention between them was, as ever, the problem of Allegra. Shelley did his best to alter Byron's views about her, but the effort was painful. Whenever the subject of Claire cropped up Byron appeared at his worst. He loathed Claire, having suffered so much at her hands. As a result, in his estimation, Shelley's obvious concern for her could only have one meaning. He did not hesitate by cynical innuendo to acquaint Shelley with what was in his mind. Shelley, disgusted and depressed, felt a longing to put an end to a friendship which was beginning to have so little meaning. Before long he was writing to Claire of this 'detested intimacy'. But too much was involved: all the negotiations over the Hunts, the promised flat for them on Byron's ground floor, the plans for the joint periodical, the money problems. And, before long, too, there were fresh difficulties over Allegra.

Claire, in Florence, had been making plans. She had heard that there were excellent opportunities for English teachers in Vienna, her brother Charles was there, and she resolved to join him. But before she left Italy she longed to see Allegra. Thoughts of the convent haunted her. She had bad dreams and could not sleep. What did she know of Bagnacavallo and what if conditions were so bad that Allegra should die? Secretly, and without telling the Shelleys, she sent her friend Mr Mason to Romagna to make investigations.

When Mr Mason reported back to her, her worst fears were realized. He had little to say in the convent's favour. It was, so he had heard, frequently scourged by fever infections from the near-by marshes, food was scanty, and there was insufficient warmth.

Claire wrote more frantic letters to Byron. She suggested that Allegra should be moved to a 'family in Tuscany'. There were no replies. Grown desperate, she wrote one last, abject, piteous letter in February, telling Byron of her plan to leave Italy, and insisting that she must be allowed to have a farewell meeting, and to embrace Allegra before she left.

When there was no reply to this letter either Claire, verging on despair, hurried to Pisa to consult her friends. The Shelleys did their best to soothe her. They were afraid that, if she became too persistent, Byron might move Allegra secretly to another convent as he had threatened, and they might lose all touch with her. But the Masons were not so placatory. Elizabeth Parker, an orphan girl living with the Masons, said that Byron's *death* was the only solution and that, if *she* had been the mother of Allegra, she would bring this about either by shooting or stabbing him. Mr Mason and Shelley were involved in fierce argument. Mr Mason wanted to horsewhip Byron while Shelley, who loathed violence, insisted that love was the only weapon. He made another effort to soften Byron's heart, but Byron said that Claire 'could not live without making scenes', and remained completely unmoved. Claire was now quite frantic and beginning to make absurd plans to rescue Allegra by subterfuge or force. Eventually, calmed down momentarily by the Shelleys, she was prevailed upon to return to Florence.

The Shelleys were much shaken. The violence of Claire's plans had appalled them and, as they aimed at embroiling Shelley, Mary felt that a duel with Byron might have resulted. Although she said of Byron that 'his hypocrisy and cruelty rouse one's soul from its depths', she wrote on 20 March a long letter to Claire in Florence, determinedly optimistic about the way things would turn out. Time, she said, was on their side. At any moment Byron might go to England. They should do nothing in a hurry but wait for the autumn. Shelley, in a postscript, backed her up: 'It seems to me that you have no other resource but time and chance and change.'

On 24 March he was writing to Claire again, but this time much more sternly:

> My dear Claire
> I know not what to think of the state of your mind, or what to fear for you—Your late plan about Allegra seems to me in its present form pregnant with irremediable infamy to all the actors in it except yourself; in any form wherein I must actively co-operate, with inevitable destruction—
> I am shocked at the thoughtless madness of your designs, and I wish to put my sense of their madness in the strongest light—
> Serious and calm reflexion has convinced me that you can never obtain Allegra by such means as you have lately devised—Lord Byron is inflexible. And he has her in his power—Remember Claire when you rejected my earnest advice (and treated me with that contempt which I have never merited from you) and how at Milan, and how vain is now your regret!—If you think well, this summer, go to Vienna; but wherever you go or stay let the *past* be past.

For once his patience was threatened. His own position was not so unassailable that he could risk any outbreak of trouble with Byron. It seemed, for a moment, that he hoped Claire would take herself off to Vienna, that he would be rid of her and her terrible problems for ever. But the hardening was short-lived. There were soon more letters. His heart melted and the old affectionate tone crept in again. He suggested that she should join them for the summer and accompany them

on their projected holiday to Spezzia. 'Come, my best girl, if
you think fit, and assure yourself that everyone—I need not
speak for myself—will be most happy to see you.'

Unexpected circumstances made this invitation possible.
Byron was no longer to be a member of the Spezzia party.
There had been a horseback fracas in Pisa which had caused
an outbreak of scandal and in which Byron, Shelley and Count
Gamba had all been involved. Shelley had been knocked from
his horse by a soldier accused of insulting behaviour, and later
the soldier himself had been severely wounded by Byron's
servant. Mary and the Countess Guiccioli, driving in a
carriage behind the riders, had seen part of the incident.
Williams, in his Journal, wrote a colourful account of the
aftermath: 'Lord Byron came in, the countess fainting on his
arm, Shelley sick from the blow; Lord Byron and the young
count foaming with anger; Mrs Shelley looking philosophically
upon this interesting scene, and Jane and I wondering what
the devil was to come next.'

As a result of this diversion the Gambas were again in
trouble. And for this reason among others, Byron and the
Countess abandoned the scheme of a 'summer colony' at
Spezzia and decided instead to go to Leghorn.

The Spezzia scheme anyhow was beset with difficulties
owing to the shortage of houses to rent. When Claire, accepting
Shelley's invitation, arrived from Florence on 15 April she was
sent off again almost immediately, with Mr and Mrs Williams,
on yet another house-hunting expedition. This time they
succeeded in finding one possible house, and one alone, the
unfurnished Casa Magni, situated between Lerici and San
Terenzo, in the Spezzia bay.

Just after their departure on this expedition the Shelleys
received terrible news of Allegra. Typhoid fever had ravaged
the convent and Allegra was dead. She had been ill for some
weeks. The nuns had nursed her devotedly and at one time it
was thought that she would recover. But when hope was given
up, and only two hours before her death, she was baptized.
There had been no thought of summoning her mother. Byron,
who had not seen her for a year, though informed of her

illness, did not visit her. She died on 19 April 1822, aged
five years and three months.

This shattering news was a terrible shock to the Shelleys.
Mary, already suffering from pre-natal depression, was
stunned. 'Evil news. Not well,' she wrote in her Journal.
After the recent dreadful scenes with Claire, and the advice
that she had given her to leave Allegra where she was,
Mary could not but feel guilty and involved. Added to
this, both she and Shelley had loved Allegra. The thought
of her short, tragic life—full of upheavals, fussed over
one minute, ignored the next, never really settled, so often
unwanted—was an aching grief. And how—and here apprehension quite sickened them—were they going to break the
news to Claire?

It was all a nightmare. With Byron living in such close
proximity, only just across the road, Shelley felt that before
they told Claire she must, at all costs, be got out of Pisa.
Otherwise she might make some terrible scene and cause a
public scandal. As soon as the travellers came back with the
news of the one house to let, he made his decision. They
must all move there at once. Mary, Claire and Trelawny,
with the baby Percy, must set off immediately for Spezzia
and make sure of renting the house. He would follow
without delay, transporting the furniture by boats to
Lerici. The Williamses too must come, bringing all their
furniture. If necessary they could all cram into the one house,
Casa Magni.

Shelley was in one of his positive moods; it was yet another
occasion when, whether wisely or not, he swept all before him
through sheer determination and forcefulness. It was, as Mary
described it afterwards, 'like a torrent hurrying everything in
its course'. Although suffering from illness and shock, she
obediently carried out his instructions. The house was duly
obtained; Shelley and the Williamses, after packing up the
furniture, left Pisa the next day. There was a problem of
getting leave to land the furniture from the boats. Shelley
wrote from Lerici on 28 April, with still more directions to
the unfortunate Mary:

Dearest Mary

I am this moment arrived at Lerici, where I am necessarily detained, waiting the furniture, which left Pisa last night at midnight—

How are you my best love and how have you sustained the trials of the journey?—Answer me this question and how my little babe and Claire are?—

Then to business. Is the Magni House taken, if not pray occupy yourself instantly in finishing the affair—send a messenger to me—*you* can come over in the same boat that brings this letter, and return in the evening—I am anxious to hear from you.

Finally all was settled. On 30 April the boats with the furniture arrived. The Shelleys moved into Casa Magni that same night. The Williamses, having made one last unsuccessful effort to find another house, joined them the next day. On Wednesday, 1 May, Edward Williams made an entry in his Journal: 'Cloudy, with rain. Came to Casa Magni after breakfast, the Shelleys having contrived to give us rooms. Without them, heaven knows what we should have done. Employed all day putting the things away. All comfortably settled by 4. Passed the evening in talking over our folly and our troubles.'

9

The Casa Magni was a strange and eerie white house, flat-roofed with arches, situated at the water's edge. Once a Jesuit convent, and now neglected, it was away from all civilization and far from comfortable. The ground floor was unpaved and only suitable for stowing boats. Two staircases led to the first floor which consisted of one immense dining-hall with four bedrooms leading off it. The walls were white-washed: Trelawny wrote afterwards of the 'splotchy walls, broken floors, cracked ceiling and poverty struck appearance'.

There was a communal kitchen and an outhouse for the

Q

servants. A long terrace stretched across the whole length of
the main building, with a magnificent sea view. On a calm
day the scene and situation were idyllic, breathtaking in
beauty. On a day of gales and squalls, the bay was swept with
foam, howling winds swept round the house, the sea roared
with the noise of guns going off, and the inmates felt as
though they were on board ship in a hurricane. The nearest
food supplies were three and a half miles away and even these
supplies were inadequate.

It was obvious from the first that they were going to be
uncomfortably overcrowded. Trelawny had left two days
before and Claire now, after a brief look round, announced her
intention of returning to Florence. Here, immediately, the
others were faced with a dilemma. Claire still did not know
the dreadful news of Allegra's death. It was impossible that
they could let her go without telling her.

They gathered together in Jane's room to discuss the situation. But Claire, sensing that something was wrong, burst in
on them. She realised at once from their faces that the trouble
was something to do with Allegra. As Shelley tried brokenly
to explain she guessed the truth.

At first her reaction was bitter and terrible. The news
seemed to plunge her into utter despair. In her first white-hot
rage and grief she sat down and wrote a blindingly scathing
letter to Byron, upbraiding him for all that had happened.
The letter later was sent by Byron to Shelley, as just one more
appalling example of all that he had suffered at Claire's hands.
Even Shelley was shocked at its tone. He explained to Byron
that he had no idea that she had written 'in that temper' and
that he would not 'have allowed such a letter to be sent' had
he suspected its contents. The letter was subsequently
destroyed.

But Claire's restoration to calm came sooner than the others
had expected. Now that the worst had happened, and all her
fears had been realized, she seemed strangely to acquire
strength. The conflict which had raged in her mind since
Allegra's birth was at last stilled. She had fought for Allegra
according to her own lights and it had been unavailing. She

had lived always under the shadow of her own past, the fear that the liaison with Byron should become common knowledge to her own detriment a continual nightmare. Now, bereft as she was, there was little left to fear. In the space of a few days she took a stumbling leap forward into maturity.

Shelley, exhausted with 'the scenes through which I have passed', did his best to act as a go-between in the subsequent negotiations with Byron. He asked that Claire might be allowed to have a portrait of Allegra and a lock of the child's hair 'however small', and these requests were immediately granted. The body was to be sent to England to be buried at Byron's behest. At first Claire had considered visiting the coffin at Leghorn but Shelley succeeded in dissuading her.

Byron's own feelings over the death of his little illegitimate daughter were pathetically chaotic. The news of her death had been broken to him by the Countess Guiccioli and at first it seemed that the shock had been great. He had grown visibly pale and strained, and had asked to be left alone. The next day he had appeared resigned. No doubt he had enough imagination to realize that Allegra's life could scarcely be a very happy one. He ascribed her death now to God's will— 'Let us mention it no more.' But, all the same, he did not forget her. A bitterness for all that had happened rankled in his mind for years to come. While she had been alive he had often neglected her. But the irrevocable burden of her death he found hard to bear.

He was anxious that she should be buried in Harrow Church where he had hoped one day to be buried himself. Harrow churchyard had been a favourite spot of his in his schooldays. But his plans, to include a fulsome tablet to her memory, were not considered seemly and burial inside the church was forbidden. In the end Allegra's last resting place was outside, under the trees in the churchyard, with no memorial stone at all.

It was the end of a sad chapter in all their lives. Claire stayed on at the Casa Magni for a little while longer and then returned to Florence, planning to come back later. Everyone's nerves had suffered. The death of yet another child enhanced

Mary's morbid depression to a degree that was almost unbearable to her. The howling of the wind and moaning of the waves round the house accentuated the tension in her mind, producing hysteria. She was beginning now to feel the after-effects of the frenzied exertion of leaving Pisa at such short notice. And now that the move had been accomplished, now that they were settled for the summer, there was still no comfort, no relaxation. The house was too small for so many inmates. The difficulties of housekeeping were endless. The servants quarrelled among themselves. Jane, obviously more domestically proficient than Mary, longed for her own house and saucepans and even Shelley was stung to criticism: 'It is a pity that anyone so pretty and amicable should be so selfish.'

His own nerves had suffered considerably. He and Williams longed daily for the arrival of their new boat from Genoa which would provide a welcome distraction. In the meantime, like Mary, he brooded over Allegra's death. On one occasion, walking with Williams on the terrace, he suddenly seized his friend by the arm: 'There it is again—there!' he exclaimed. He was quite certain that he had seen Allegra plainly, a naked child rising from the sea, clapping her hands, and smiling at him.

Six days later, after cloudy and threatening weather, to their intense relief the new boat arrived. Shelley and Williams were both delighted with her. 'We have now,' Williams wrote in his Journal, 'a perfect plaything for the summer.' The boat, twenty-eight feet by eight feet, cost Shelley eighty pounds. The name *Don Juan,* reminding them unpleasantly of Byron, was changed to *Ariel.* Charles Vivian, a young and inexperienced sailor-boy aged eighteen, was engaged to help them sail her. Williams, confident in his own skill, rejected Trelawny's advice to engage an experienced Genoese sailor. Shelley's own seamanship was extremely limited but this, to him, was a matter of no concern. He was perfectly happy steering the boat while reading a book: one, as he explained, was mental, the other mechanical. Danger did not apparently enter into it.

Now followed some idyllic days when, on all possible

occasions, Shelley escaped from all the domestic troubles at home by spending his life on the sea. 'This incessant boating,' Mary wrote unselfishly to Mrs Gisborne, 'does him a great deal of good.' Sometimes, on rare occasions, when she was well enough, she would go with him. They would drift away, and she would lie with her head on his knees, while he read aloud to her from Keats's poetry. More often he was with Williams or, on occasion, Jane. He and Williams together built a small boat of light canvas and reeds, which was useful for short journeys, and could be stowed easily on the schooner. Shelley liked, too, to paddle out to sea in it and drift. On a famous occasion he took Jane and her two babies with him a fair distance out to sea and then, turning to Jane calmly, suggested: 'Now let us together solve the great mystery!' Jane, horrified, wheedled him back to the shore where, under-standably, she got out in such a hurry that the boat upset.

In the evenings Shelley listened to Jane singing to the music of the guitar. He would make believe that all was well but at the back of his mind disaster seemed to threaten. His poems written during these last months reveal an all-pervading melancholy. He wrote to Trelawny asking him to obtain a small quantity of prussic acid: 'I need not tell you,' he wrote, 'I have no intention of suicide at present, but I confess it would be a comfort to me to hold in my possession that golden key to the chamber of perpetual rest.'

He was afraid of his own illness turning perhaps to incurable suffering. And he was depressed too by further threats from Godwin of imminent ruin. Mary's health was so bad now that he dared not discuss this trouble with her. Godwin had demanded £400, the alternative being that he would have to give up his home. Shelley had asked Horace Smith for the loan of the money and Horace Smith had refused.

It was difficult to know which way to turn for help and Shelley could only write a tactful letter to Mrs Godwin. 'Mary is at present about three months advanced in preg-nancy,' he told her, 'and the irritability and languor which accompany this state are always distressing and sometimes alarming.' He begged that care should be taken in involving her in Godwin's difficulties—difficulties which it was beyond her power to remedy. He himself could not 'enter into any further reversionary transactions'. He gave her news of Claire: 'Since the late melancholy event she has become far more tranquil.' But again a fear of the future seemed to haunt him. He stressed that it was best that Claire should make her own way in life and establish her independence because of 'the uncertainty of my own life and prospects'.

But, although he wrote in these terms about Claire to her mother, in reality he was still perversely trying to bind Claire to him. Mrs Mason, who had seen Claire since her departure, wrote him an outspoken letter: 'I wish she [Claire] had some determined project, but her plans seem as unsettled as ever, and she does not see half the reasons for separating herself from your society that really exist—I regret the loss of Mary's good health and spirits, but hope it is only the consequence of her present situation, and, therefore, merely temporary, but I dread Claire's being in the same house for a month or two—' Regardless of these warning hints Shelley could not forgo his own pleasure in Claire's society. Mary, he felt, had failed him. Of course he would be unfailingly kind, unfailingly compassionate, but at the same time he found it difficult to dispense with feminine sympathy and support. True, Jane was there, the incomparable Jane—but Jane was another man's wife and that man was his friend. He wrote to Claire on 28 May: 'Mary still continues to suffer terribly from languor and hysterical affections; and things in every respect remain as they were when you left us—I think that at least for the present you would be happier here than anywhere else.' And again, on 30 May: 'I think you would be happier here, and indeed always either with or near me.' His own health, he told her, was better but the palliative was to 'neither think or feel' or the old dreaded pain would return.

Claire accepted that her invitation to return to Lerici should stand. At the beginning of June she returned to her friends at the Casa Magni. Mrs Mason or no Mrs Mason, she would do what Shelley wanted. That month the weather changed, the storms died down, and there was an interval of overpowering heat, enervating to the inmates of the Casa Magni, particularly to the pregnant Mary. On 16 June, after a week of wretched weakness, she was taken violently ill.

⚜ IO ⚜

For some time now Mary had been living her life on the verge of a nervous breakdown. The enforced activity of leaving Pisa so hurriedly, the shock of Allegra's death, the harrowing scenes with Claire, the eerie terror of the wild surroundings of Lerici, the realization of estrangement from Shelley which she felt powerless to arrest—all had combined to produce in her a state of prostration verging on collapse.

The heat of the last days had added to her feverish state of mind. It was at this time of year, in the hot weather, that her children had died. She lived in haunting anxiety that Percy too might soon share their fate. Her lowered state of health and general debility, allied with her pregnancy, began to produce alarming symptoms and these culminated at last on 16 June with a dangerous miscarriage.

No medical help was immediately available and it seemed at first that she would die. She lay for seven hours nearly lifeless and the others began to abandon hope. Then Shelley took the law into his own hands. Rather than wait any longer for the doctor he took the ice which had at last been procured, and used it unsparingly. With the help of brandy, Mary revived. When the doctor at length arrived he found her well on the way to recovery and congratulated Shelley on his promptness and presence of mind.

The recovery of her strength and spirits was another matter. The situation was not improved when only a week later Shelley himself, his own nerves in shreds, had a violent nightmare. Mary awoke to hear him run screaming through the house. As he rushed into her room she got up in terror and, almost falling in her weakness, ran to call Jane Williams.

Edward went to soothe Shelley who at first said he had had no nightmare but a waking vision. In his 'vision' he had seen Edward and Jane, their bodies lacerated, the bones sticking through the flesh, their faces pale and stained with blood. They came into his room and Williams said: 'Get up, Shelley, the sea is flooding the house, and it is all coming down.' The nightmare had then changed and he had seen 'the figure of himself' strangling Mary. As soon as she had jumped out of bed it seemed that he had woken up and this proved it to have been a dream.

Mary comforted him by clasping him in her arms. The next morning however, he told her that, in the last few weeks, he had had several genuine 'visions'. On one occasion he had met the figure of himself walking on the terrace; 'How long,' the figure said to him, 'do you mean to be content?' As so often with him, as in the past at Keswick and at Tremadoc, reality warred with hallucination.

But strangely, so infectious was his odd psychic state, and so shattered were the nerves of the other members of the party after all that had happened, that they too were having similar unaccountable experiences. Byron told later of Shelley's friends at Lerici, sitting together one evening, having distinctly seen Shelley walk away out of sight into a wood—only to find afterwards that he had been nowhere in the neighbourhood at the time. And even Jane—the impassive, unimaginative Jane whose nerves had always been of the strongest—saw Shelley on one occasion walking on the terrace. She was sitting with Trelawny, and watched Shelley pass by the window, without a coat or jacket. A few minutes later she saw him again— passing *the same way*. She rushed out to look and, finding nobody there, called out: 'Good God! Can Shelley have leapt from the wall? Where can he be gone?' 'Shelley!' said Trelawny in amazement, 'no Shelley has passed.' Jane 'trembled exceedingly' when she heard this, which was indeed proved to be true. Shelley was miles away at the time she 'saw' him.

Gradually their nerves steadied. Shelley's greatest consola- tion was in Jane, his attachment for her growing daily. Here was yet another goddess, another projection of his fantasy, another peg for his idealistic dreams. He made love to her, tried to kiss her, but clear-headed, enjoying herself perhaps, but anyhow quite satisfied with her Edward, she kept him at bay. His devotion to her is portrayed in the poems he wrote to her at this time: 'To Jane—the Invitation', 'With a Guitar—to Jane', 'The Magnetic Lady to her Patient'. The poems had to be kept from Mary. There was one particular one 'The Recollection' with instructions: 'To Jane: not to be opened unless you are alone or with Williams.'

Earlier there had been the famous:

> I can give not what men call love,
>   But wilt though accept not
> The worship the heart lifts above
>   And the Heavens reject not,—
> The desire of the moth for the star,
>   Or the night for the morrow,
> The devotion to something afar
>   From the sphere of our sorrow.

Or, again, the illuminating 'The serpent is shut out from Paradise':

> Therefore, if now I see you seldomer,
> Dear friends, dear *friend*! know that I only fly
>   Your looks, because they stir
> Griefs that should sleep, and hopes that cannot die:
>   The very comfort that they minister
>   I scarce can bear, yet I,
>   So deeply is the arrow gone,
> Should quickly perish if it were withdrawn.
>
> When I return to my cold home, you ask
> Why I am not as I have ever been.
>   *You* spoil me for the task
> Of acting a forced part in life's dull scene—

'When I return to my cold home—' Mary's illness and subsequent lethargy of nervous exhaustion had done their work. For some weeks now he had been openly admitting that the want of sympathy between them was a source of bitterness. One of his most revealing letters was written to Mr

Gisborne on 18 June 1822, just after Mary's miscarriage. It
was in this letter that he admitted the mistake of 'seeking in
a mortal image the likeness of what is perhaps eternal'. But
he also added: 'I only feel the want of those who can feel, and
understand me. Whether from proximity and the continuity
of domestic intercourse, Mary does not.' He wrote too of
Jane: 'I like Jane more and more.' And of Claire: 'She is
vivacious and talkative—I like her.'

In many ways that summer he believed himself to be happy:
but it was a happiness hopelessly precarious and gnawed at
incessantly by spectres from the past. His armour of self-
righteousness had cracked irrevocably and he wrote of himself
now as 'a prey to the reproaches of memory'. He had achieved
momentarily a detachment from Mary and her troubles which,
though a palliative to his own nerves, had in it something of
inhumanity. He was, as he himself admitted, poised in time:
'If the past and the future could be obliterated, the present
would content me so well that I could say with Faust to the
passing moment, "Remain, thou, thou art so beautiful."'
But it was a position of danger: 'I stand, as it were, upon a
precipice, which I have ascended with great, and cannot
descend without *greater* peril, and I am content if the heaven
above me is calm for the passing moment.'

He was in a strangely elated state, over stimulated, fearful
of change. 'I still inhabit this divine bay,' he wrote on 29 June
to Horace Smith; 'we have some friends on a visit to us and
my only regret is that the summer must ever pass.'

It upset him that Mary did not share his passionate attachment to Casa Magni—poor Mary, who was to write of it
afterwards to Mrs Gisborne: 'No words can tell you how I
hated our house and the country about it.' Though aware of
its beauty, she was still driven frantic by the wildness and
the discomforts, the thankless efforts at housekeeping, the
crowded conditions, the frightening natives with their wild
noisy dances on the near-by shore, and the menacing roar of
waves and wind.

When at last news of Leigh Hunt's arrival in Italy reached
them, she was too ill to be left. Shelley and Williams had

meant to sail at once to meet the Hunts at Genoa but now, faced with Mary's relapse, they decided to postpone the meeting until the Hunts reached Leghorn. On 1 July at last they were prepared for departure. But even now Mary, filled with an inexplicable sense of calamity and dread, could not bear to be parted from them. She called Shelley back repeatedly, crying bitterly, begging him not to leave her. She swore that if they did not return swiftly she would take Percy with her and follow them to Pisa. But, in the end, she had to let them go and she never saw Shelley again.

II

Shelley and Williams sailed to Leghorn in the *Ariel*, taking seven and a half hours for the journey. Hunt with his family was waiting at a Leghorn hotel. At last the two friends met again. Shelley and Hunt rushed into each other's arms, embraced, and separated in tears. Hunt saw at once that, after four years, Shelley had changed. Instead of the smooth boyish face he had last seen, there were lines now, wrinkles in the forehead, grey hairs among the glossy brown locks.

But Shelley had grown in manliness and appeared to be still full of vigour and enthusiasm. He was determined to do what he could to make the Hunts feel welcome in Italy, particularly as he knew only too well that Byron had cooled off considerably and would probably show it. His worst fears on this score were soon realized. When he took the Hunts to the Lanfranchi Palace to install them in their new home on the ground floor, Byron could hardly be prevailed upon to greet them. Pre-occupied with his own problems—the Gambas had again been exiled after a brawl at his Leghorn villa—Byron felt, no doubt, impatient and depressed at his new commitments. Everything connected with the Hunt family seemed uncertain and un-satisfactory. Mrs Hunt was so obviously ill. He had expected them last November and this was July. What had possessed him to listen to the hot-headed Shelley and himself suggest the crazy project of embarking on this new periodical, the *Liberal*? He remained upstairs, and when Mrs Hunt was ushered into his presence, only bowed grudgingly and did not speak.

It was a bad beginning. Shelley tried to help matters by sending for the doctor, his famous friend Vaccà, to minister to Mrs Hunt who was almost prostrate with sickness. Vaccà examined her and took a gloomy view of her condition. Her case, he said, was hopeless: the wretched woman was in a decline, and could not live another year.

In the event Mrs Hunt was to live to the year 1857, thirty-five years distant. But poor Hunt was not to know this and Vaccà's gloomy verdict provided a miserable ending to an exhausting journey. Other problems loomed ahead. There were six children to feed. He had no money. Byron, agitated over his own affairs and anxious to leave Pisa immediately, seemed to take little interest in the projected journal. Hunt could only rely on Shelley and Shelley, though heartily sick of acting as a go-between, was determined before he left to pin down Byron into making definite agreements.

All this uncertainty meant more delay in returning to Mary at Lerici. Shelley had, in the meantime, been receiving from her letters 'of the most gloomy kind'. Williams, he knew, was anxious to start back without delay and was already waiting at Leghorn. Pressures were mounting. On 4 July he wrote the two last letters of his life—the first to Mary, telling her of his difficulties: 'I am detained unwillingly here—Things are in the worst possible situation with regard to poor Hunt—How are you, my best Mary?' The second letter was to Jane, dwelling on the hours they had 'lived together so intimately, so happily!' but alluding to them in the past tense—'Adieu, my dearest friend, I only write these lines for the pleasure of tracing what will meet your eyes.'

Byron finally offered the copyright of his poem *The Vision of Judgment* for the first number of the *Liberal*. So now, after all, the project could go ahead. Another day or two passed, while necessary arrangements were made. On Sunday, 7 July,

Shelley's last day was spent with Hunt, sight-seeing in Pisa. To Hunt, Shelley seemed to be looking better and in better spirits. But Shelley told Mrs Hunt: 'If I die tomorrow I have lived to be older than my father: I am ninety years of age.' He confided to Hunt a feeling that Mary had let him down.

Underneath his surface buoyancy there was a weight which never lifted. The succession of blows which life had dealt him had left him baffled and bewildered. Harriet's suicide, Fanny's suicide, Godwin's bloodsucking grip, the death of his two children, his family's ostracism, Byron's treachery, Mary's coldness—there seemed at times no ending to frustration and betrayal. On top of this his books did not sell, his poems made little impression, his efforts to reform the world to nobler ways had proved an empty dream. Although he kept up a courageous front, and did his best to act as a tower of strength to his friends, he was feeling as he went on a greater and greater weariness. So perhaps the next day, when the end was to come so suddenly, he may have welcomed the release of death and been glad to go.

He borrowed from Hunt his copy of Keats's *Hyperion,* visited Mrs Mason, and that evening left for Leghorn. At Leghorn Williams was still waiting. The Monday morning was spent in visiting the bank with Trelawny and shopping for the women at Lerici. Hunt had made Shelley promise that if the weather was bad he would postpone his departure and now a change was threatened. The heat wave was breaking, the priests had been praying for rain, and on the horizon storm clouds gathered. Trelawny's friend, Captain Roberts, advised the travellers to wait until the next day, to see if the weather became more settled. But Shelley knew that Williams was anxious to get back. In seven hours they could be at home! By midday they went aboard the *Ariel,* joining the young apprentice, Charles Vivian, and between one and two o'clock they sailed from the harbour of Leghorn on their homeward journey.

Trelawny watched them through his glasses. His mate pointed out the foolishness of their topsail, and the black clouds looming overhead. 'They should,' he said, 'have sailed at three or four a.m.' Captain Roberts, full of concern, climbed the lighthouse tower to watch them. He saw the topsail taken in and immediately afterwards the boat was enveloped in a sea fog. There was no air in the harbour and it was oppressive and sultry. Later it became very dark, the sea was smooth as a sheet of lead, until gusts of wind sprang up and there were crashing peals of thunder. Ships rushed for harbour to escape the fury of the storm. It lasted only twenty minutes and then Trelawny anxiously scanned the horizon for some sight of Shelley's boat. But nowhere was there any sign of the *Ariel*.

With *Hyperion* clutched in his hands, Shelley had found his own words, in elegy to his dead friend, of strange prophetic truth:

> The breath whose might I have invoked in song
> Descends on me; my spirit's bark is driven,
> Far from the shore, far from the trembling throng
> Whose sails were never to the tempest given;
> The massy earth and spherèd skies are riven!
> I am borne darkly, fearfully, afar;
> Whilst, burning through the inmost veil of Heaven,
> The soul of Adonais, like a star
> Beacons from the abode where the Eternal are.

12

At Casa Magni the three women waited. Jane had had a letter from her husband, written while he was awaiting Shelley at Leghorn, to say that they would start home on Monday. But on Monday at Lerici the weather was so bad that it was taken for granted their departure would have been postponed. But Tuesday, Wednesday, Thursday passed and there was no sign of the *Ariel* and no news.

On Friday, 12 July, at midday the post arrived. There was, however, only one letter and that letter struck fear and a terrible foreboding to both their hearts. It was a letter from Leigh Hunt at Pisa to Shelley, asking for news of his safe arrival after sailing in the bad weather of Monday.

Jane cried out in anguish: 'Then it is all over!' Mary would not accept disaster. She insisted that they must be off at once, without delay, to Pisa, to Leghorn if necessary, to find out what was happening. Anything was better than inaction. She could bear no longer to sit waiting for confirmation of the news which she knew in her heart must be the truth.

Leaving Claire with the children, they were rowed across to Lerici. There, for a moment, they were cheered by hearing that no disaster had been reported. They drove on to Pisa, arriving late at night, and were told that Hunt was asleep in bed. Instead they saw Byron and the Countess Guiccioli, who could tell them no more than they knew already: Shelley and Williams had sailed on Monday, and on Monday afternoon there had been a violent thunderstorm. By now they were exhausted. Mary was told afterwards that she appeared at Byron's palace looking 'more like a ghost than a woman', a strange light emanating from her features, her face white like marble.

But rest was impossible. She and Jane left Pisa immediately and pushed on to Leghorn, arriving at two o'clock in the morning. Here there was difficulty over finding the inn where Trelawny and Captain Roberts were staying. At the wrong inn where they had been taken, they threw themselves on the beds without undressing, and waited for the daylight.

Trelawny meanwhile had been making his own inquiries. None of the crews who had sheltered in the harbour from the storm could give him any news of the *Ariel*. 'They either knew nothing,' Trelawny wrote, 'or would say nothing.' On the third day he rode to Pisa to Byron's palace to see if any letter from Shelley had been received. Byron's 'lip quivered and his voice faltered' as he was questioned. There was no letter. Mrs Mason told of a dream she had had which seemed like an omen. Shelley had come to her, looking pale and melancholy. 'You look ill and tired,' she said, 'sit down and eat.' 'No', he replied, 'I shall never eat more; I have not a soldo left in the world.' 'Nonsense,' she said to him, 'this is no inn; you need not pay.' 'Perhaps,' he replied, 'it is the worse for that.' She awoke, slept again, and dreamed that Shelley was dead. Finally she awoke again, crying bitterly.

Trelawny sent Byron's yacht *Bolivar* to cruise along the coast and he himself rode off in the same direction. At Leghorn he and Captain Roberts met the two dazed and anguished women, Mary and Jane, and were unable to give them much hope. There was only a remote chance that the boat might have been blown off course, perhaps to Corsica or Elba.

Mary decided to return home and she and Jane set out for Lerici, accompanied by Trelawny. At Viareggio they drove into the town to inquire if there was any news. Here they were confonted by the first concrete signs of tragedy. A little boat and a water cask had been found five miles out to sea—both to be identified as having been aboard the *Ariel*.

They arrived back at the Casa Magni late at night on the Saturday. On the final stages of the journey Mary felt suffocated and gasped for breath. She struggled for control so that Jane should not notice. The next days were passed in an agonizing suspense. A *festa* was going on in the village and men, women and children spent nights screaming one monotonous air outside their doors, and dancing at the water's edge. The wind moaned its unceasing dirge, and the storm waves beat against the walls of the house.

Trelawny left them on the 18th and went back to Leghorn to see what next could be done. At Leghorn he was told that two bodies had been found, washed up on the beach, one near Viareggio, the other at the mouth of the Serchio. When he saw the body at Viareggio fear turned to certainty: 'The tall slight figure,' he wrote, 'the jacket, the volume of Sophocles in one pocket, and Keats's poems in the other, doubled back as if the reader, in the act of reading, had hastily thrust it away, were all too familiar to me to leave a doubt on my mind that this mutilated corpse was any other than Shelley's.' Later the third body, of the young sailor Charles Vivian, was washed up not far away.

At Casa Magni meanwhile the women waited for Trelawny's

return. When, during the day of the 19th, he did not come Mary tried to make herself believe that he had found nothing and therefore there was still hope. Claire, who had intercepted a letter from Trelawny, telling of the two bodies cast up on the shore, was in an agony of mind and felt incapable of breaking to the others such bitter news. She wrote to Leigh Hunt for advice and in the meantime, at seven o'clock in the evening of the 19th, Trelawny returned.

He appeared, speechless, in the upper room of the Casa Magni. After a terrible silence Mary managed to speak: 'Is there no hope?' Trelawny, unable to find words, turned away. He sent the children instead to the widowed women. Later, to Mary's comfort, instead of offering futile words of consolation, he 'launched forth into an overflowing and eloquent praise' of the Shelley he had so much loved and admired.

The next day they all left the Casa Magni, that unbearable house of roaring waves and howling winds, which now seemed only a habitation of nightmare, haunted by memories. Trelawny accompanied them back to Pisa where they would have the companionship of Hunt and their other friends.

There were still grim ceremonies to be carried out. By the laws of quarantine the bodies could not be removed from the shore until they had been reduced to ashes. Trelawny, Hunt and Byron were present when the funeral pyres were built on the sands. Williams's body was cremated on 15 August and that of Shelley at Viareggio on the day following. Byron could not bear to watch his friend's body consumed by the flames. He swam out to sea to the *Bolivar* and back. Hunt, overcome, sat in the carriage. Only the intrepid Trelawny, a tower of strength through these dreadful last days, stood stalwart to the end, put his hand into the flames and rescued Shelley's heart entire, and afterwards collected the ashes.

What had happened in the last tragic moments of Shelley's life and how had the accident come about? Various possibilities and conjectures have been discussed and argued over the years since Shelley's death and certainty is no greater than it was at the beginning. The boat was later raised off the coast of Viareggio and found to be partly broken and with the

R

masts gone. Roberts's first impression was that the boat had
not capsized but was probably swamped by a heavy sea. On
examining it closer, however, he thought that the broken
timbers to starboard indicated that the boat had been run
down by a felucca in the squall. It was known that Shelley
had money on board. It was rumoured that the *Ariel* was
immediately followed from the harbour by an Italian vessel.
Possibly there was a piratical plan for ramming the *Ariel*
and boarding her.

Whatever the final cause of the disaster Shelley's last few
minutes of life must have been nearly over when the crew
were seen by Captain Roberts to be taking in the topsail.
The boat foundered near this point. When found Shelley's
body was less emaciated than that of Williams who had
evidently half stripped, his shirt partly pulled over his head,
as though in the last cataclysmic moment he had meant to
fight for survival. Shelley's body was fully dressed. On more
than one occasion already he had fallen into the water and
made no effort to save himself. It looks now as though he
accepted death with resignation. Trelawny wrote later that
'the careless, not to say impatient, way in which the Poet
bore his burden of life, caused a vague dread amongst his
family and friends that he might lose or cast it away at any
moment'. Besides this, he had also 'always declared that in
case of wreck he would vanish instantly, and not imperil
valuable lives by permitting others to aid in saving his, which
he looked upon as valueless'. Williams was the only one of
the three who could swim and therefore it seems probable, as
Trelawny wrote, that Williams was the last survivor.

Shelley's heart, plucked from the flames by Trelawny, was
given to Leigh Hunt who later surrendered it—though under
protest—to Mary. When Mary died the heart, wrapped in a
silk shroud, was found between the pages of the Pisa edition
of *Adonais*. Later it was enclosed in a silver case and finally
buried in the grave of Shelley's son Percy at St. Peter's,
Bournemouth.

The oak casket containing Shelley's ashes was sent by
Trelawny to Rome to be buried in the Protestant cemetery.

It was not possible to find little William's grave so the ashes could not be buried at his side. A few people, including Joseph Severn, devoted friend of Keats, were present at the burial ceremony.

When, in 1823, Trelawny went again to Rome he felt dissatisfied with the position of the grave. Immediately he set about buying a new plot of land near the pyramid of Cestius in the New Protestant cemetery. Here he had two tombs made. One was for his own ashes in years to come. In the other Shelley's exhumed ashes were deposited and covered with solid stone.

On the stone was inscribed:

Percy Bysshe Shelley
Cor Cordium
Natus IV August MDCCXCII
Obiit VIII July MDCCCXXII

Nothing of him that doth fade
But doth suffer a sea change
Into something rich and strange.

PART SIX

AFTERMATH

A few survive who have felt life a desert since he left it.

MARY SHELLEY

I

'THE fine spirit that had animated and held us together was gone! Left to our own devices we degenerated apace.'

So wrote Trelawny after Shelley's death. It was an exaggeration, as were so many of his utterances, but it was not altogether untrue. If it is unfair to say that they degenerated it is certainly true that as human beings they were diminished. Shelley had been their inspiration, the king-pin who held them together, investing them all with the glamour of his genius. They had seen each other through his eyes—more desirable, more vital, more noble than they really were. Now their comparative ordinariness was more apparent. And as time went on a still more disillusioning aspect of their relationship made itself felt. There was between them a fundamental incompatability producing a clash of personalities.

It was not so obvious if they kept one another at a distance. At a discreet distance memory, nostalgia, an instinctive loyalty, could still bind them in some sort of comradeship. But efforts at closer fraternization ended only in disenchantment.

At first, the three bereft women clung together. 'We have one purse,' Mary wrote to Mrs Gisborne, 'and, joined in misery, we are for the present joined in life.' They stayed on temporarily at Pisa, supported by their friends. Byron and the Countess Guiccioli were kind and called twice a week. The Hunts were attentive and sympathetic. Mrs Mason was still a valued ally to be visited regularly. But all were agreed on one point which Mary more than once put into words: 'The friend to whom we are eternally indebted is Trelawny.'

But in the nature of things this temporary spell of numbed inactivity could not last. From the first the spectre of poverty haunted them. It was a spectre which was to follow Mary and Claire down through the years, wrecking their peace of mind, their health, and what little they had left of faith for the future. Only Jane managed in a comparatively short time to escape it.

At first Mary had borne up with a stoic endurance. She wrote to nobody, not even to her father. She built up in her mind a shrine to Shelley's memory, 'mine own Shelley', and clung to it as a talisman of past happiness. Godwin, the father who had failed so palpably to appreciate Shelley while he was alive, was pushed into the background.

Godwin felt the omission and wrote to her. It was only through a letter of Leigh Hunt's to a sister-in-law that he had happened to hear of Shelley's death at all. He felt himself ill-used: 'I shall hang in hope and fear on every post, knowing that you cannot neglect me for ever.' There was no word of personal sorrow in his letter to Mary, no real regret. Instead there was a clumsy effort at sympathy allied to a curious satisfaction because she was now fallen to his level. 'You are surrounded with adversity and with difficulty'; he could now, he assured her, not hesitate to confide in her all his own troubles and misfortunes. They must draw together in mutual consolation. 'I suppose you will hardly stay in Italy. In that case we shall be near to, and support each other.'

Mary was unable to decide what course to pursue. She wanted to return to England, chiefly to intercede with the Shelley family on behalf of her child, but at the same time she felt a sense of responsibility towards the Hunts. In August she wrote a letter of enormous length to her old friend, Mrs Gisborne, in England, recounting all that had happened and ending: 'All that might have been bright in my life is now dispoiled. I shall live to improve myself, to take care of my child, and render myself worthy to join him (Shelley).' And again, in September, something of her anguish of spirit was poured out to this old friend: 'I shudder with horror when I look back on what I have suffered—How long do you think I shall live?—Surely I am not long for this world.'

She decided finally to remain in Italy for the time being, sharing a house and expenses with the Hunts. Jane and her children departed for England to seek help from Edward's family. Claire, temporarily left behind alone at Pisa, while

the others went on to Genoa was, planning to join her brother
Charles in Vienna and to take a post as governess. The prospect
depressed her and the last letter that she wrote to Mary before
setting forth was, for her, unusually gloomy:

> My dear Mary,
>   You have only been gone for a few hours. I have been inex-
> pressibly low-spirited—Nothing new has happened—To me
> there seems nothing under the sun, except the old tale of misery,
> misery—I am to begin my journey to Vienna on Monday.
> Mrs Mason will make me go—If I should write you scolding
> letters, you will excuse them, knowing that, with the Psalmist,
> 'Out of the bitterness of my mouth have I spoken'.

But even here something of the true Claire breaks out in
this last sentence: something of the cynicism, the courage, and
the wit, which were to sustain her through the arduous years
which followed. At intervals Mary and Jane were to receive her
letters: from Austria, from Germany, from Russia, from
France: entertaining letters—despairing, lively, gay, venomous
in turns—as Claire grappled with her fate and grew old,
eccentric and worn-out with the years.

At Genoa Mary at first was busy house-hunting. Always
made use of by her friends, she had to find a palatial house
for Byron, besides a smaller one for herself and the Hunts.
She was struggling with a 'constant feeling of despair' but
found time to write encouragingly to Claire, hoping that she
would find happiness and perhaps find someone to whom she
could become 'really attached'. 'Adieu, my dear Claire: write
to me often, as I shall to you.' They still hoped to cling to each
other as companions in misfortune, persuading themselves that
the bond between them would outlast all adversities. 'God
bless you, dearest girl,' wrote Jane to Mary from Geneva, on
her way back to England. At Geneva, she added, there had
been a letter from Mary waiting for her, a letter from 'the only
friend who welcomes me'.

But realities piled up and the months passed slowly. Mary
stayed a year at Genoa, sharing the house with the Hunts.
Byron and his retinue were not far off. Trelawny came on

occasional visits. They were all that was left of the Pisan circle and soon they began to get on each other's nerves. The Hunt children, as a family, were noisy, out of hand and exhausting. Mrs Hunt, who drank more than was good for her, was slap-dash and sluttish in her methods, besides now being ill and awaiting yet another confinement. Hunt himself, gushing and charming, could also be moody, feckless and ineffectual. It was not a happy household, disintegration rapidly turning to squalor. Mary despaired. The climate seemed terribly cold after Pisa. Sometimes she tried to write in her bedroom, but as the stove smoked she dared not light it, and more often they all crowded round one fireplace.

They saw little of Byron. By now he was exasperated with the entire Hunt family and was only too thankful to have got them out of his house. The children, on principle allowed to do as they liked without reproof, were, he said, 'dirtier and more mischievous than Yahoos'. It upset him to feel that any-thing belonging to Shelley should fall into their clutches: 'What they can't destroy with their filth they will with their fingers.' As executor and proffered banker he attempted to help Mary with money and advice but his efforts were spasmodic, often half-hearted, not to be relied on. In his defence it must be added that Mary herself did not make things easy for him. Grief had made her touchily on the defensive and she was apt to suspect meanness and affront where none existed.

Her diary, which during Shelley's lifetime had only served as a laconic record of outward events, now became the chief outlet for her sufferings. She felt chilled and desolated by the lack of any companion in intimacy: 'I have no friend—Now I am alone—Oh, how alone!' Hunt, who had seemed to be her friend and ally, she was convinced no longer cared for her. 'For, after all,' she wrote despairingly to Claire, 'Hunt does not like me. It is both our faults, and I do not blame him, but so it is.' She felt that she and Shelley had understood each other in a way that the rest of the world could not begin to comprehend. Often, in the diary, she addresses Shelley direct: 'In spirit you will visit and encourage me. I know you will. What were I, if I did not believe that you still exist.' 'Mine

own Shelley! The sun knows of none to be likened to you—
brave, wise, noble-hearted, full of learning, tolerance and love.'
'Your gentle spirit was too much wounded by the sharpness of
this world.'

But, before long, she was to become obsessed with the
haunting feeling that by her coldness to him when he was alive
she had somehow failed him. She knew of this weakness in
herself, the fatal inability to show her feelings, so that her
natural warmth of heart was cloaked by a self-sufficient and
chilling reserve. How Shelley must have suffered from her
lack of response to his love! What had possessed her to inflict
on him this cruelty? She brooded incessantly, haunted by
remorse, and finally wrote a long and pathetic poem, *The
Choice*, in which she begged his forgiveness.

There was only one person who could rouse her from the
apathy of grief and that was Trelawny. Trelawny had always
liked and admired her. For the next fifteen years, until the
rot set in, he was to be her good friend and constant correspondent. 'There is not one now living,' he wrote, 'who has so
tender a friendship for you as I have.'

But he could too, if he thought it necessary for her good,
become astringently outspoken. It was time, he felt, as months
went by, that Mary was jolted from her self-absorbed mood
of introspective misery. Why did she always write of herself,
why not of others? 'You need not tell me that all your thoughts
are concentrated on the memory of your loss, for I have
observed it, with great regret and some astonishment. You tell
me nothing in your letters of how the *Liberal* is getting on?—
Does Hunt stay at Genoa this summer, and what does Lord
Byron determine on?—Where is Jane?—and is Mrs Hunt
likely to recover?'

She took the hint. Her subsequent letters gave him more
news of their mutual friends. She tried in future to confine
her outpourings of grief strictly to her Journal. Her child's
welfare and her literary work were her main standby. She had
earned £33 by writing an article for the *Liberal* and had sent
some of the money to Claire who had been ill. But now even
work was failing her: 'I cannot write. Day after day I suffer

the most tremendous agitation. I cannot write, or read, or think—I know not, but I am a wreck.'

She decided that she must go to England. She would stay at Genoa long enough to help Mrs Hunt through her coming confinement and then she would leave. Her father had written to her encouragingly. He had pointed out that she had great talents for writing fiction which should stand her in good stead. He had even, surprisingly, offered to help her financially: 'If it shall ever happen to you to be placed in sudden and urgent want of a small sum, I entreat you to let me know immediately; we must see what I can do.'

On all counts it seemed best to make the break with Italy, much as she loved it. For even at Genoa what remained of the Pisa circle was breaking up. The *Liberal* already was failing. Byron had joined a committee to help the Greeks in their fight for freedom. In July 1823 he set sail for Greece, taking Trelawny and Count Gamba with him. The Hunts—now her very good friends again, all irritations forgotten—were planning to go to Florence. She would like to have gone to Florence too, and lived somewhere near them. But for Percy's sake it seemed better to go back to her own country. On 25 July 1823 she left Genoa and started on the journey back to England.

2

After staying in Paris on the way to see Horace Smith and other old friends, she reached England exactly a month later. Her father, from his new home at 195 Strand, had written inviting her to his house 'to make shift with for a few days, but it would not do for a permanent residence'. She stayed with him for ten days and he and his wife apparently did their best to make her feel welcome.

The great event to Mary was, however, the reunion with Jane Williams. Before long she had settled herself near her beloved friend, in lodgings at Kentish Town. The two women met daily.

But Mary could not help realizing from the first that Jane's reactions to the tragedies of the past months had been very different from her own. Jane was unscathed, unchanged, almost buoyant. Her much shallower temperament had enabled her to push her grief to one side, in savouring the satisfactions of her new role. Mourning suited her, her beauty was untouched, her attractiveness to men, if anything, enhanced. 'A picturesque little woman', had been Godwin's verdict but, although attracted, he noticed that at their first interview she 'did not drop one tear' or fail to smile. Hogg, in his turn, meeting her for the first time, was bowled over completely. Here was yet another of Shelley's women—to him unfailingly magnetic. First there had been Harriet, afterwards Mary, now Jane. This time, his subjugation was complete.

Mary, observant and astute, realized all this but she clung to Jane with an almost hysterical affection. At this time in her life, as she confessed some years later, she felt 'afraid of men'. Yet there had to be someone in her life whom she could love with uncontrollable tenderness and entirely depend on—and Jane was chosen to fulfil that role. She had never agreed with Trelawny whose admiration for Jane had been qualified: 'I always dissented from your general voice of her being perfection', he had written to Mary at Genoa; 'it is impossible to dislike Jane; but to have an unqualified liking, such as I had for Edward, no—no—no!'

As time went on Mary was to realize the one-sidedness of her devotion. Her Journal again was to be her confidante: 'I love Jane better than any other human being, but I am pressed upon by the knowledge that she but slightly returns this affection.' And a few months later, as other friends seemed to drift away: 'Jane alone remains; if she loved me as well as I do her it would be much; she is all gentleness, and she is my only consolation, yet she does not console me.'

At the beginning on her arrival in England there had been a temporary boost to Mary's spirits when she discovered that *Frankenstein* had brought her an unexpected notoriety. A dramatized version had been produced which was shown at the English Opera House. On 29 August 1823 Jane, Mary and

Mary's half-brother, William, were escorted to the production by Godwin. Mary was entirely without conceit over her literary work and seldom spoke of it, but now she wrote excitedly to Hunt: 'Lo and behold! I found myself famous.'

She certainly needed something to cheer her for otherwise her prospects were bleak. Part of her intention in returning to England had been to try to establish some sort of rapprochement with Shelley's family. In this she soon found that she was to fail miserably.

Byron, on her behalf, had already written to Sir Timothy and had met with a rebuff. He had asked for an allowance for Mary and her child, pointing out that Mary was innocent of offence. Sir Timothy could not agree. 'On the contrary,' he wrote, 'I think that her conduct was the very reverse of what it ought to have been.' His condition for making himself responsible for Shelley's son was that the child should be removed from Mary's care and placed with 'a person I shall approve'. Mary, confronted with this ultimatum, had written back to Byron with indignant anger: 'I should not live ten days separated from him—I would never consent to it. I am said to have a cold heart; there are feelings, however, so strongly implanted in my nature that, to root them out, life will go with it.'

Now, back in England, Mary had written to Sir Timothy herself to tell him of her arrival but had received no reply. All negotiations, she was told, had to be carried out through the lawyer, Whitton.

It is hard to escape the conclusion that Sir Timothy had received the news of his elder son's death with a certain amount of relief. 'The Great Author of our Being', so he wrote to Whitton, had seen fit so to dispose of Bysshe and they must resign themselves to the situation. He had no sympathy with Mary, to him an undesirable young woman without principles, who had wrecked his son's marriage. Now all his hopes were centred in his second son, John.

Mary and her father had an unsatisfactory interview with Whitton. He advanced £100 to her, told her that Sir Timothy would probably pay this sum annually for Percy, but that anything further was uncertain. Harriet's son Charles was still alive. Percy was not the heir to the baronetcy. Mary was not to be accepted as a member of the family. She could consider herself, it seemed, an outcast.

It was a distressing verdict and the future that it conjured up was not a reassuring one. Mary realized that she would have to keep herself and Percy by literary work and struggle along as best she could. Courageously she decided that she would devote herself to collecting and editing Shelley's manuscripts. At the end of 1823 Shelley's *Posthumous Poems* were published.

But here again she fell foul of the implacable Sir Timothy who wished his errant son's memory to be forgotten. Mary was instructed that, during his lifetime, no biography of Shelley should be written by her and none of the works published. If this order was not strictly adhered to, he would immediately cut short the allowance.

Mary wrote to Hunt: 'Sir Timothy writhes under the fame of his incomparable son.' Nevertheless she did her best to placate her father-in-law. All copies of the *Posthumous Poems* that had not been sold were withdrawn from circulation. Sir Timothy, after all, could not live for ever. He was seventy now. Shelley's will had been proved valid which meant that eventually both she and Claire would be well off. When that time came, and she felt that it could not be far off, she would be able to write what she liked about her beloved Shelley. It was fortunate, perhaps, that she could not see into the future. In fact, Sir Timothy was destined to live for another twenty years, and not to die until the age of ninety-one.

Byron in the meantime—after the snub from Sir Timothy and some unpleasant disagreements with both Mary and Hunt before he left Genoa—had resigned his duties as executor of Shelley's will. He had also announced that he had no intention of accepting the £2,000 which Shelley had left him as a legacy. The more he had seen of the Pisan circle the less he had been impressed. There were too many people—Hunt being one of the chief offenders—casting envious eyes upon his money and expecting as a right that he should help them financially. He went to Greece, partly out of altruism, partly out of exhibitionism, but largely as a means of escape from a life which was beginning to exasperate him. Even the Countess Guiccioli had become a rather boring habit. In the swamps of Missolonghi he caught a fever, was bled mercilessly, and died.

His death made an enormous sensation. It was a sensation noticeable in contrast to the lack of interest taken when Shelley had been drowned. Byron's fame was world wide, Shelley in his lifetime had hardly stirred a ripple of adulation.

Byron's body was brought back to England and Mary and Jane, with feelings deeply stirred, watched the funeral procession as it went up Highgate Hill. Byron now was a hero, come back in death to the country which had spurned him. Mary forgot all the unpleasantness in their relationship and remembered only the times when Byron had been gay and generous and kind. Her attitude towards him had always been ambivalent, a strange mixture of uneasiness, repulsion and attraction. She wrote now to Trelawny of her affection for him and of his 'form of beauty which in life I often delighted to behold'. His loss, she added, 'makes me cling with greater zeal to those dear friends who remain to me'.

But through the years to come memory of Byron haunted her. He was to appear, over and over again, thinly disguised in the novels she wrote; handsome and 'honey-tongued' and fascinating, in contrast to the more sensitive, spiritual and delicate portrayal of Shelley. When she published *Lodore* Claire could stand it no longer: 'Good God! to think a person of your genius—should think it a task befitting its powers to gild and embellish and pass off as beautiful what was the merest compound of vanity, folly, and every miserable weakness that ever met together in one human being!' Claire's venomous bitterness towards Byron obsessed her more and more as years went by. She had had her 'ten minutes' of happiness and suffered for it for the rest of her life. Mary, ever emotional and impressionable, could never have analysed the ambiguities of her own strange brand of hero-worship. That her feeling for Byron had in it a strong streak of erotic fancy—of which she was unconscious—has more than once been recognized.

ꗨ 3 ꗨ

Peacock, Shelley's second executor, now took up the cudgels on Mary's behalf. He had never liked Mary, and they saw little of one another, but he was conscientious. He tried, through Whitton, to get Sir Timothy to advance a sum of money to Mary on her expectations from Shelley's will. This was no more successful than his subsequent effort to get her an annuity through an insurance company. However, he did get the allowance raised to £200 a year—all the money to be repaid to the estate on Sir Timothy's death. He also intervened to good effect when, on publication of Mary's novel *The Last Man*, Sir Timothy temporarily stopped the allowance—his grievance being that the book had been described as 'by the author of *Frankenstein*', thus bringing back memories of the Shelley name!

It is not surprising that Mary felt herself at times to be grappling with an adversity past all bearing. 'I cannot live without loving and being loved, without sympathy,' in September 1825 she poured out her distress in her Journal; 'if this is denied to me I must die. Would that the hour were come!'

Exactly a year later there was an important change for the better in her situation. The little boy, Charles Shelley, Harriet's son, died, and Mary's son Percy became the heir presumptive to the baronetcy.

Those two pathetic children, Charles and Ianthe, whose start in life had been so inauspicious, had drifted into the background of Mary's consciousness. At one time, to please Shelley, she had hoped to welcome them into her family life, to adopt them as her own. Instead there had been a period when they had lived with strangers, after which their paths had diverged. Charles had been taken into the home of Sir Timothy, and his grandfather had grown fond of him. Ianthe, after Shelley's death, was put under the guardianship of Harriet's sister Eliza, by this time Mrs Farthing Beauchamp.

s

Eliza was a kind and devoted aunt, her niece was later married advantageously to a Mr Esdaile, and they had two sons. Her life was a full and happy one, but little Charles was not so fortunate. Always delicate, he early showed signs of consumption. In September 1826, still not quite twelve years old, he died.

Percy now being in the important position of family heir, Mary hoped for a larger allowance. Poverty was an unending drag on her spirits and all her activities. She and Jane had a certain number of friends—they saw the Gisbornes, the Lambs, the Novellos, Coleridge and others—but, unable to any extent to reciprocate hospitality, their social life was limited. Mary could sympathize with Trelawny who was in the same dilemma. After leaving Byron, he had attached himself to an insurgent Greek chieftain, Odysseus, and narrowly escaped death in a fracas. Odysseus was murdered, Trelawny wounded. Now Trelawny, disgruntled, very poor, enfeebled in health, wrote to tell Mary he was returning to England. 'Poverty,' he wrote, 'haunts its victims to destruction—all the other calamities of human life—cannot compete with it'; and Mary wrote, in heartfelt agreement, 'I say Amen to all your anathema against poverty, it is beyond measure a torment and despair.' She added a note of affectionate solicitude for the only friend who, since Shelley's death, had really consoled her. 'Turning to you who are dearest to me—it makes me truly unhappy to find that you are hard pressed.'

She and Jane looked forward anxiously to Trelawny's arrival. The unwilling Sir Timothy, disappointed that Percy should have priority over his son John as heir to the baronetcy, had been prevailed on to increase Mary's allowance, but only to £300. However, this was an improvement in her prospects and Jane too was embarking on a change of fortune. Hogg had been in love with her ever since her arrival in England and now, in the summer of 1827, she decided to change both her name and place of abode, and to live with him as his wife.

This, inevitably, meant loss for Mary. She had envisaged that, when Sir Timothy died, she and Jane and Claire would all three return to live in her beloved Italy. She had even detailed her plans to Leigh Hunt: 'I shall not come without my Jane, who is now necessary to my existence almost.' But now, unselfishly, she welcomed Jane's new happiness and was determined to be pleased for her sake. She did not much care for Hogg, the provincial lawyer, who seemed to her to have developed into an odd and unattractive character, far from romantic. But he had at least been faithful. She wrote to Trelawny: 'He has loved Jane devotedly and ardently since she first arrived in England, almost five years ago. At first she was too faithfully attached to the memory of Edward—but his sincere and long-tried love has at last gained the day—We shall still continue near each other. I, as ever, must derive my only pleasure and solace from her society.'

But it was now, shortly after Jane's change of fortune, that Mary was to receive one of the worst blows of the many that life had dealt her. She discovered that Jane, whom she already feared to be lacking in deep affection for her, had even less sincerity of feeling than she could ever have imagined. No longer under Mary's sway, and secure in a new love, Jane made capital out of a friendship that had never meant very much to her. She joked and entertained her friends with stories of her past life with the Shelleys, dramatizing all that had happened. Shelley's infatuation for her was magnified into passionate devotion. She boasted of his attentions, his expensive presents, the poems and songs written for her. Mary was made to appear jealous and slightly ridiculous—a woman who had failed to keep her husband's affection. Loyalty, kindliness, friendship—all were sacrificed in order to make a 'good story': all being aimed at denigrating Mary, and at adopting for herself the role of Shelley's good angel, and adored confidante.

Mary had no inkling of foreboding that such a thing could happen. She had trusted Jane. She could not have believed her to be the type of woman who, less than a year after Edward's death, had, in fact, secretly embarked on a liaison with Hogg: a woman who mopped up admiration, set out to ensnare the devotion of others, giving little of herself in return.

The shock was quite shattering. Mary's anguish is apparent in her Journal: 'My friend has proved false and treacherous!

Miserable discovery. For four years I was devoted to her and earned only ingratitude. Not for worlds would I attempt to transfer the deathly blackness of my meditations to these pages. Let no trace remain save the deep, bleeding, hidden wound of my lost heart of such a tale of horror and despair. Writing, study, quiet, such remedies I must seek.'

It was a double blow. Not only had it proved Jane to be false, wrecking their friendship, it had poisoned the memory of those last years with Shelley which had been her safe refuge from grief. Nothing now could ever be quite the same.

At first she said nothing to Jane herself. She kept up the semblance of an intimacy which no longer had any reality, and later acted as godmother to Jane's daughter, Prudentia. She made some new friends, a family of sisters, the Miss Robinsons, and Tom Moore, the poet. Tom Moore was a comfort to her: 'I like him very much—I never felt myself so perfectly at my ease with anyone—he seems to understand and to like me.' Moore, in his turn, found her 'very gentle and feminine'. He visited her frequently and they had long, interesting talks of Shelley and Byron, and past happier days. She helped him with the book he was writing, a life of Byron. Finally she confessed to him her bitter grief at Jane's duplicity. Jane's stories, she knew, were being repeated and probably Moore himself had heard them. He took her part at once and advised her no longer to keep her indignation to herself but to tackle Jane.

At her next meeting with Jane, Mary tried to carry out this advice. But Jane was ready for her. With facile emotion she dissolved into tears and Mary, temporarily, was disarmed. Finally Mary wrote to her. The letter is a painful one, revealing a strangely fervid and exaggerated devotion from one woman to another, and yet startling in its sincerity of feeling:

> Could any but yourself have destroyed such engrossing and passionate love?—When first I heard that you did not love me, every hope of my life deserted me—How many hours this dreary winter I have paced my solitary room, driven nearly to madness —Do not ask me, I beseech you, a detail of the revelations made to me. Some of those most painful you made to several; others,

of less import, but which tended more, perhaps, than the more important to show that you loved me not, were made only to two—I have been an altered being since then—This explains my estrangement. While with you I was solely occupied by endeavouring not to think or feel—

It is the last we hear of this wretched correspondence. The friendship continued. Mary accepted Jane as she was and tried, by other distractions, to heal her heartbreak.

4

There were ups and downs in the years that followed. Soon after the breach with Jane, in 1828, Mary was unlucky enough to fall victim to an attack of smallpox while on a visit to Paris. Temporarily she lost her beauty. There were no scars fortunately, but her bright hair lost its lustre and her skin lost its delicacy and freshness. She bore the trial bravely but her feminine vanity must have been assailed when this temporary loss of looks coincided with Trelawny's home-coming.

The meeting had been eagerly looked forward to by both of them. Trelawny's letters had been affectionate: 'You are my dear and long true friend, and as such I love you, Yours, dear, Trelawny.' But somehow, when they met in the flesh, nothing quite came up to expectation. Trelawny's recent experiences had changed him for the worse: he was suffering from a slow, wasting fever, and was becoming crotchety, irritable and restless. Mary, much as she admired his flamboyant character and looks, had never really felt at ease with him. She could see now that, before very long, England irked him and he was anxious to be gone again.

By February 1829 he was back in Florence, and making excited plans for the autobiography he was going to write which was to include extensive reminiscences of Shelley and Byron. Mary, he insisted, must help him by providing him with memories and material. But Mary still clung to obscurity. She felt that it was too early yet to write a book about Shelley, and anyway she hoped one day to be able to write this book herself. Possibly she was afraid of Sir Timothy's reactions if she in any way associated herself with Trelawny's literary efforts. She refused firmly and Trelawny was incensed. It was their first serious clash of wills. Baulked of the assistance of the person likely to be most useful to him, Trelawny wrote angrily to Claire of Mary's unreasonableness and cant.

All the same he went ahead with his book, and insisted that Mary must vet it, and then find a publisher for him. He wanted £500 for a three-volume work and suggested it might be called *The Life of a Man.* 'My dearest Mary,' he wrote to her, 'for, notwithstanding what you may think of me, you every day become dearer to me,' adding that he sent her his book as 'the dearest friend I have'.

Whether his attentions were completely sincere, or whether he cultivated Mary as a useful adjunct to authorship, is open to question. He wrote to her lovingly, it is true, but alternated affectionate remarks with hints of conquests elsewhere: 'Florence is very gay and there are many pretty girls here, and balls every night.' In response Mary embarked on a somewhat heavy-handed flirtation, teasing him about 'pretty girls in Florence' and adding that, though not being the Lady of his love, she would not be marrying that year.

Trelawny, nothing loath, kept up the badinage. His next letter continued veiled hints which some biographers have construed as a genuine proposal of marriage: 'Do not abandon me—I should not wonder if fate, without our choice, united us; and who can control his fate? I blindly follow his decrees, dear Mary.'

The charade was taking a serious turn:

> [Mary to Trelawny. 14 June 1831] Do you think that I shall marry? Never—neither you nor anybody else. Mary Shelley shall be written on my tomb—and why? I cannot tell, except that it is so pretty a name—I never should have the heart to get rid of it.

> [Trelawny to Mary. 29 June 1831] I was more delighted with

your resolve not to change your name than with any other portion of your letter. Trelawny, too, is a good name, and sounds as well as Shelley; it fills the mouth as well and will as soon raise a spirit.

[Mary to Trelawny. 26 July 1831] My name will *never* be Trelawny. I am not so young as I was when you first knew me, but I am as proud. I must have the entire affection, devotion, and, above all, the solicitous protection of any one who would win me. You belong to womankind in general, and Mary Shelley will *never* be yours.

So that was final. Perhaps it was too blunt a finality. Mary, after all, had started up the hare herself. Some of her remarks at the beginning had been nothing if not provocative. It is certain that after this the relationship deteriorated.

Mary now was probably relieved to concentrate her mind on other matters. She had been making constant inquiries to Trelawny about Claire who was now in Florence. 'Have you seen Claire? How is she? She never writes except on special occasions, when she wants anything.' The news of Claire when it came was not good: 'Claire only remained in Florence about ten days—I saw her three or four times. She was very miserable, and looked so pale, thin and haggard. The people she lived with were bigots, and treated her very badly—Poor lady, I pity her; her life has been one of continued misery. I hope on Sir Timothy's death it will be bettered; her spirits are broken and she looks fifty.'

Mary, faced with this depressing and somewhat exaggerated report, was seized with a painful anxiety: 'Do whenever you write send me news of Claire—We are all excessively anxious about her—God knows when fate will do anything for us. I despair.'

She did her best for Trelawny's book but, rather to his disgust, could only get £300 for it, with £100 promised for a second edition. Published under the title of *The Adventures of a Younger Son*, it did not do well. Later, some years after Mary's death, the inimitable *Recollections of Shelley and Byron* was published. It is recognized as a brilliant, if not altogether truthful, picture of Shelley in his last days. Twenty years later there was a second edition. In the interval Trelawny's mind had become envenomed and warped, particularly against Mary. He made various alterations in the text. As Mrs Marshall indignantly points out, instead of the 'true and disinterested friend' Mary had been to him, she is now portrayed as 'conventional and commonplace, unsympathetic and jealous, narrow orthodox, and worldly'.*

Unlucky in her friendships, as in so much else in life, Mary struggled on with her efforts to make both ends meet. She was determined that she must carry out a wish expressed by Shelley to send Percy to a public school. Eton was vetoed by the family—Shelley memories of Eton were too painful—and Mary decided to send Percy to Harrow. She imagined that the Shelley family would be willing to pay some of the extra expenses involved but this was not to be. Whitton informed her that she must manage to pay the fees herself out of the £300 income.

It might have been wiser if Mary had accepted her fate with a good grace. It was so obvious that she was getting nowhere in her efforts to find acceptance with the Shelley family. But, instead, with an unfortunate lack of dignity, she persisted in her letter writing and her demands. Sir Timothy, stung to anger, labelled her as a 'very troublesome woman'.† He had not been altogether implacable. He had consented to see Percy and had, indeed, visited him at school and been pleased with the little boy. Occasionally he sent him a present. But, even over this, Mary behaved unwisely. She engineered Percy into writing some gushing letters to his grandfather, with insincere flattery, and veiled hints that he would like very much to be invited on a visit. Such efforts at ingratiation did not please Sir Timothy who condemned the letters as 'dictated artfully'.‡ He became all the more obstinately determined to have no personal dealings with Mary.

So there was no help for it. Mary faced a future of more and more hard work. In 1832 a cholera epidemic swept London. With all their hopes centred in Percy, Claire wrote frantic

* Mrs. Julian Marshall: *The Life and Letters of Mary Wollstonecraft Shelley.*
† Roger Ingpen: *Shelley in England.*   ‡ Ibid.

letters from abroad imploring Mary to save Percy from possible infection by removing him to the seaside. If necessary she, Claire, would pay the expenses from her meagre salary! Mary was assailed on all sides. She took Percy to Sandgate for several months at her own expense. Her father, short of money and ideas, demanded that she should supply him with material for his latest book. Claire sent a story, half-completed, begging Mary to finish it and to find a publisher. 'I want to gain money,' she wrote, 'the only key to freedom.' While Trelawny took advantage of her genuine kindness and unselfishness by asking her to accept his daughter on a long visit.

Mary stoically made the effort to fulfil all these demands. In a small way she was something of a literary celebrity now, though her novels were not very remunerative. However, she had been able to move to a better address in Portman Square and she enjoyed a certain amount of the social life which meant so much to her. She breakfasted with Samuel Rogers, gave occasional *soirées*, was seen at Ascot. Various people sought her acquaintance, puzzled and intrigued by the handsome, reserved young woman, who had lived through such shattering experiences. Lord Dillon, meeting her, could not reconcile her writings with her personality. In her books she appeared indiscreet, passionate, enthusiastic—in manner, by contrast, cool, quiet and feminine.

She was much admired but it is undeniable that to many she was an enigma. She had more than one proposal of marriage but refused them all, clinging almost morbidly to her widowhood. For her own sake it was a pity. More than most women she needed the care and protection of some man in her life. Although strong-minded and by no means weak in character, she was delicate, nervous and self-effacing. She knew her own temperament, describing herself to Mrs Gisborne as vacillating and a person in need of support. When Shelley died she was only twenty-five. Yet from the first she was determined: 'Mary Shelley shall be written on my tomb.'

5

Before long it was obvious that the boarding fees at Harrow were beyond her means. To keep Percy at the school of her choice she must go and live in the town near by and he would have to become a day boy.

It was a harsh decision to have to make. It meant giving up her London life and falling a prey once more to isolation and loneliness. She found Harrow a 'dull inhospitable place'. Too poor to rent a house, she lived in disagreeable lodgings, Percy her only confidant, and her literary work her only occupation.

Nothing could have been more unsuited to her temperament. As Trelawny wrote of her later, she detested solitude, and in the country 'was always complaining'. Her old friend, Mrs Gisborne, was again the recipient of long letters in which she dwelt obsessively on her woes. She had been made 'timid', she explained and 'benumbed by poverty'. Her health was affected by loneliness. Yet she could never now go beyond the garden gate: if she tried to get any farther she found herself weeping. Her sense of injury increased to bitterness: 'I have been so barbarously handled by fortune and my fellow creatures,' she told Mrs Gisborne, 'that I am no longer the same as when you knew me. I have no hope.'

There was but one blessing in her life and that was Percy. Successful at school—well-behaved, popular, easy-going, good-tempered—she admitted that she was proud of him. Harrow, at any rate, had been a happy choice for him, whatever miseries it entailed for herself.

In 1835 she published her society novel *Lodore*. None of her subsequent novels had the merits of *Frankenstein*. However, she was able to help her father financially and as usual she worried about his well-being. He was an old man now, over eighty. The death of his only son, William, in the cholera epidemic had been a fearful blow to him. Now, with Mary so far away, he missed her: 'Oh, this vile Harrow!' he wrote. 'We used to see each other two or three times a week—you might as well be at Timbuctoo!' In April 1836 he died, and something of her own life seemed to die with him. He had sapped her happiness, sapped her energies, but she had loved him devotedly.

In 1836 too, both the Gisbornes died, within a short time of one another. Friends were thinning in ranks. Trelawny was back in England but taken up with new conquests and new diversions. Jane's 'marriage' with Hogg was a success, Jane could not bear to be parted from him; but when Mary was ill she showed 'excessive kindness' and Mary was grateful.

Percy left Harrow in 1836, and, after a short period with a tutor, went to Trinity College, Cambridge. He was, so Mary said 'a child still, full of theatres and balloons and music'. There were no signs of his father's genius and no signs of his father's rebellious temperament. Perhaps it was a relief. Mary was growing increasingly tired and was thankful for any form of serenity. When she was asked to write a biography of her father she demurred and finally refused. Trelawny was scornful of such waste of opportunity. He wrote her sarcastic, scolding letters from Brighton and she was stung to bitter remonstrance: 'What has my life been?' she asked. 'What is it? My happiness, my health, my fortunes, all are wrecked—for Percy's sake I must battle on—My complaint is not against *persons* but *fate*.' His badinage, his lack of sympathy seemed to her the last straw: 'I am obliged to guard against low spirits as my worst disease, and I do guard, and usually I am not in low spirits. Why then do you awaken me to thought and suffering?'

It was the end of their intimacy, the end of their long correspondence. His last letter to her was written in November 1837. Later he married a friend of Mary's, a Mrs Augusta Goring, who had been divorced by her husband. The marriage was not a happy one. Before long Trelawny started an adulterous association with another woman and his wife was forced to leave him. Trelawny survived into great old age, dying in 1881, at the age of eighty-nine.

With the passing of the years other changes had come about. The unsympathetic lawyer, William Whitton, had died in 1832 and Sir Timothy now employed a Mr Gregson, who exercised a more benign influence. Mary at length obtained permission to publish a comprehensive edition of Shelley's poems, provided that she did not include a memoir.

She was over forty now. The work loomed over her as an undertaking of gigantic proportions but she felt, as she had always felt, that it was a sacred duty. The years from 1836 to 1840 were spent in laborious effort. To get over the memoir ban she wrote notes instead for each successive year of the poems. The notes are excellent—sincere, restrained and informative—the necessary compression effectually stifling a tendency to affectation, insincerity and over-dramatization which is apparent sometimes in her letters.

But the effort of transporting herself back into the past, and living through those momentous years once more in her imagination, was too much for her. She found herself 'torn to pieces by memory' and feared that illness might overwhelm her before she had finished. More than anything it was Jane's treachery which haunted her. As Mrs Marshall wrote: 'Nothing entered into her soul so deeply as the defection of this friend. Alienation is worse than bereavement Other sorrows had left her desolate; this one left her different.'* Now even her beloved Shelley's memory was warped and tarnished. But she was determined, if she could, to show Shelley as she had felt him to be: radiant, loving, innately noble, a being of such insight and genius that it was given to few to understand and appreciate him.

She finished the book at last and illness did ensue: 'What an illness! driving me to the verge of insanity!' But Shelley's reputation was growing. The publication of his poems in four small volumes, dedicated to his son Percy, was an event in the literary world. By 1840 Mary began to realize that at last she had money, her poverty-stricken days were over. From now on her life was to become more cheerful, immeasurably happier.

Not only was her poverty relieved but gradually she began

* Mrs Julian Marshall: *The Life and Letters of Mary Wollstonecraft Shelley.*

to realize that in her son Percy she had found what all her life
she had been looking for—staunch, dependable devotion. She
wrote in her Journal of his 'excellent understanding, his clear,
bright sincere spirit and affectionate heart'. Here at last was
somebody who did not betray her, who valued her for what
she was, who was consistently loyal. When Percy insisted that
she should accompany him and his friends on a continental
tour she was immeasurably touched. The holiday did her
good. Weary in body, she was refreshed in spirit. The following year their travels were repeated. They visited all the old
familiar places: Venice, Florence, Geneva. In Rome they saw,
for the first time, Shelley's grave. Afterwards Mary wrote
Rambles in Germany and Italy, published in 1844 in the form of
letters. Of Rome she wrote: 'The treasures of my life lie
buried there.' Shelley and little William! So long ago, it
seemed now, all those turgid, exhausting years of wandering,
all the suffering and ecstasy she had lived through, wearing her
out before her time, making her what she was.

But now at last—too late to save her health, but not too
late for her happiness—every year brought a new relief. All
her care in ensuring that Percy had a good education was
repaid when he took his degree at Cambridge in 1841. When
he became twenty-one his grandfather, mellowed at last, gave
him an allowance of £400 a year. Mary's new friend, Mrs
Norton, wrote to her: 'I hope it is the *dawn*, that your day of
struggling is over, and nothing to come but gradually increasing
comfort.'

In 1844 Sir Timothy died, aged ninety-one. Percy succeeded
to the baronetcy, and at last the legacies left by Shelley in his
will were paid.

6

Claire, hearing that Sir Timothy was dead, was incredulous.
Could it really be true that at last she was to get the £12,000
(believed to be double what was intended through a mistake

in a codicil) which Shelley had left her? Lately she had begun almost to believe that Sir Timothy would live for ever: that instead of growing older every year he was growing younger, his face filling out, his grey hair turning to brown, his step becoming brisker. Her agony had been so prolonged that she could be witty about her predicament. Year after year, she had slaved as companion, as governess, as school teacher—always waiting, waiting, for the release which never came.

At first, after Shelley's death, she had gone to Vienna to join her brother Charles. English governesses abroad were much in demand. But the climate did not suit her and she became ill. Trelawny, in Florence, wrote offering her the fare to return to Italy. He was at that time much in love with her and wanted to marry her. Failing that, he suggested that she should become his mistress. But Claire refused as she was to refuse all future male advances. Like Mary she turned her back on compromise, doomed herself to celibacy, and seemed determined to struggle on alone. A German, who paid her great attention, was, so she told Jane, 'not the being who could make life feel less a burden to me than it does'. But, all the same, as time went on, she was continually thinking of Trelawny. Had she done right in rejecting him? Yet somehow she knew that there was a fundamental antagonism between them. When they met again, on rare occasions, she was aware of this lack of sympathy. 'I admire, esteem and love him,' she wrote explainingly to Mary, 'but he likes a turbid and troubled life, I a quiet one; he is full of fine feelings and has no principles, I am full of fine principles but never had a feeling; he receives all his impressions through his heart, I through my head.'

It was unsatisfactory as a relationship but once, grown desperate, she thought that after all she would throw in her lot with his. In 1831 she wrote suggesting that she should come and keep house for him and his daughter by a sister of Odysseus. Trelawny rejected the suggestion. Grown thorny now, and less tractable, he felt that the tie might be too much for him. He had too, about this time, embarked on the flirtatious exchange with Mary. He and Claire kept up a casual correspondence, continued to be friends, but only saw each other occasionally.

Claire's behaviour now was always circumspect and correct. Instead of going to Florence after Vienna she went to Moscow. Her hatred towards Byron growing with the years, she lived in continual dread that her past should find her out. On one occasion she lost a lucrative post because her mother had been indiscreet to a woman who afterwards came to Moscow. There were few calamities, Claire felt, that she had not suffered. A governess's life was dull and hard. In Moscow all she seemed to hear was 'talk of cards, eating, and the different manner of managing slaves'. She was shut up with 'five hateful children' who gave her no peace. She grew more cynical, more resigned, more determined to become a stoic. 'I am now old enough,' she wrote, 'to know that misery is the universal malady of the human race'—adding, almost cheerfully—'I fashion my life according to this, and I often enjoy moments of serenest calm.'

It was undeniable that she kept up a brave front. Mary, receiving at spasmodic intervals, vivacious and entertaining letters—so much more lively than her own—was amazed at her courage. Claire made a point of always appearing gay in society, partly because she wanted to avoid 'odious curiosity'. In summer she felt well, but in winter her health suffered. Her anxiety that something might happen to Percy, and Shelley's will never bear fruit, almost paralysed her: 'It is frightful for the despairing to have their hopes suspended thus upon a single hair!'

She moved about restlessly: Moscow, Vienna, Carlsbad, Nice, Pisa. As companion to a sick woman in Dresden she dressed ulcers, applied leeches, gave mud baths. Fortunately she found 'a thousand alleviations to misery' in the glories of Dresden itself. The beauties of Nice later made her 'happy without happiness'. 'I think of England,' she wrote, 'and my friends all day long!' Or, more cynically: 'Pray write. The letters of my acquaintances (friends I have none) are my only pleasure.'

Her last post abroad was at Pisa. Here she lived with her

old ally, Mrs Mason, the one woman for whom she seemed to
have a real affection. 'Nothing can equal Mrs Mason's kind-
ness to me,' she wrote, 'hers is the only house, except my
Mother's, in which all my life I have always felt at home—
She understands me so completely.' But, even with the
Masons' house as her headquarters, her life was exhausting.
She took a job as a daily governess, left the house at nine
o'clock in the morning, returning at ten o'clock at night.

Finally in 1840 she came back at last to settle in England.
It was still necessary to work. She had no money except what
she earned. Mrs Godwin could not help her. Besides giving
Italian lessons, she took a governessing job, entailing so much
rush and travelling from place to place that she felt, so she
told Mary, that she might go out of her mind.

When, with Sir Timothy's death, at last this arduous life
was over, it seemed that her courage snapped. She had waited
too long, the strain had been too great. She became impatient,
bad-tempered, resentful of others' good fortune. It annoyed
her to see Mary in her new guise, châtelaine of Field Place,
her son a baronet. She felt that Mary had forsaken the ideals
of her youth—Shelley's ideals—and was now only preoccupied by her place in society. Determined not to appear to be
'paying court', Claire lost no opportunity of being rude and
snubbing.

She invested the £12,000 badly in a box at the Italian Opera
and lost a good part of it. Her chief interest in life was the
family of her brother, Charles Clairmont. Charles had done
well in Vienna, writing school books, and acting as tutor to the
Austrian royal family, including the young heir, Franz Joseph.
Here was a feather in Claire's own cap, a counterblast to
Mary's social successes. Mary invited her to Field Place but
Claire's rudeness and eccentricities were too much for her.
'Don't go, dear! Don't leave me alone with her!' Here was
that revealing cry from Mary's heart later to her daughter-in-
law; 'she has been the bane of my life ever since I was three
years old.' Finally the effort was abandoned and Claire was
no longer invited. After all, as Percy pointed out years later
when he refused to buy some papers Claire was anxious to sell

to him, Claire was no relation of the Shelley family. She had
already had Shelley's legacy of £12,000. And with that she
ought to be content.

Other minor pinpricks arose through the implementation
of Shelley's will. Hogg, who received a legacy, could not
prevent his envy and spleen overflowing in an impertinently
worded letter to Mary: 'You and your baronet-boy will do
well'—he was unable to conceal the sneer. Leigh Hunt was
more gracious but inevitably rapacious. He was to receive a
fixed allowance but later hinted that he would be grateful for
a capital sum. His affairs had not prospered and he was, as
usual, financially on the rocks. In 1825 he and Marianne and
their seven children had returned to England and later we hear
of them in Chelsea, living near the Carlyles, eggshells and
crusts of bread adorning the carpets,* squalor still prevailing.
Mary helped them over the years and, though unable to
produce the desired capital, remained on friendly terms with
them.

But fresh interests were cropping up in her life and disillusionment over old friends no longer had so much power to
hurt. In 1847 she met Jane St John, the young widow who
became her devoted friend, and a little later her daughter-in-
law. Jane adored Mary from the first. Mrs Marshall tells us of
Jane's description of Mary when, on entering a room, she
saw her for the first time: '. . . the fair, lovely, almost girlish-
looking being "as slight as a reed" with beautiful clear eyes,
who put out her hand as she rose, saying half timidly, "I'm
Mary Shelley".'†

Percy, besides being an ideal son, appears to have been an
ideal husband. His career, however, had been something of a
problem. He did not fancy the Army or the Church; most of
his interests were artistic, the theatre being his chief passion.
Eventually he ran a private theatre of his own, painting his
own scenery and composing his own music, a hobby which
absorbed him increasingly as the years went by.

He and Jane were both agreed when marrying that Mary

* Thea Holme: *The Carlyles at Home*.
† Mrs Julian Marshall: *The Life and Letters of Mary Wollstonecraft Shelley*.

T

should never leave them. She had only three more years of life but these years were serene and happy. She had always been an unselfish woman and the miraculous affinity between herself and her daughter-in-law ruled out any suspicion of discord over Percy. At last too the torments of the past seemed to have lost their sting. She seldom talked now of the people who had hurt her and of the wrongs she and others had suffered. Instead Shelley was almost always in her thoughts. She had meant to write his Life and she did in fact begin to collect together all the relevant material. But she was too tired, the effort of writing the book was beyond her.

As time went on, her health deteriorated. Her strength ebbing, she fell a victim to nervous complaints and towards the end she lost the power of movement in one side of her body. Field Place had been given up on health grounds: the climate and soil did not seem to agree with the Shelleys. Instead, Sir Percy bought, as his country home, Boscombe Manor at Bournemouth. But Mary was too ill to be moved from their London house in Chester Square. On 21 February 1851, twenty-nine years after Shelley's death, she died. Her grave is in Bournemouth churchyard. Later her father and mother were moved to her side.

7

The spell that Shelley cast on each and every one of the dream women in his life is undeniable. After his death, or for the remainder of their lives, each liked to think that she alone was the one who had really mattered to him.

Which of them was right?

Was it Jane Williams, the last of the 'goddesses', who survived Hogg by twenty-two years and lived to the age of eighty-six: Jane, who claimed that Shelley had loved her in those last dramatic days at Pisa and Lerici?

She was a vain woman and a beautiful one. Even in old age,

grown vague and absent-minded and forgetting to powder one side of her face, we are told that she was still handsome and magnetic. The liaison with Hogg had been a pedestrian affair but it had satisfied her, bringing her a feeling of domestic security which she valued. After Hogg's death she shared a house with her nephew, Henry Cleveland. Her health failed as she grew older. But she kept up her piano playing, and played the guitar to her grandchildren to remind her of those past magical days in Italy. She still kept Shelley's guitar, the strings broken, and portraits of both him and herself when young, side by side on the wall. Her feeling for him was something which never left her. She bowed reverently to his portrait and cherished to the end the flattering conviction that he had loved her.

Or there was Claire: Claire, whose life was also a long one, and who lived to the age of eighty-one.

Claire, full of eccentricities and, at the end, far from truthful, is, of all the women in Shelley's life, the greatest enigma. What exactly was her relationship with him? In view of the intense indignation and distress shown by both Shelley and Mary at the time of Elise's revelations to the Hoppners, it is almost impossible to believe that Claire was Shelley's mistress. And yet that they meant a good deal to one another, and at times became emotionally involved, is undeniable.

When, in 1878, Claire was an old lady of eighty, living with her niece Paula in Florence, an attractive and ambitious young writer, William Graham, went to visit her. He was much captivated both by her appearance and her intellect. In spite of having lost money in the Opera House disaster, she was still living in apparent affluence and comfort and, with her lovely white hair, light eyes and willowy figure, 'There was in the lady,' he wrote, 'a charm which old age could not kill— a charm that must once have been all powerful.'* He ingratiated himself with her, saw her every day, and, so he tells us, 'gained her confidence'.† On the subject of her past life she was, however, full of teasing hints and innuendoes.

* William Graham: *Last Links with Byron, Shelley and Keats.*
† Ibid.

About her affair with Byron she was superficially straight-
forward. 'I was young,' she excused herself, 'and vain and
poor. He was famous beyond all precedent.' All Europe, she
explained, was obsessed by him. Adoring young women wrote
to him every day. When she met him, and he took notice of
her, her 'head was turned'. It was not a question of love, she
insisted: she had been dazzled by the glamour which surrounded him. It was true that she had hoped to marry him.
The Shelleys too had hoped for 'their lasting union'. But now,
she knew better. In her 'charming, melodious voice'* she
castigated the Byron she had once known in no uncertain
terms. True, he was a poetic genius, an able man, and a man
of the world, but he was too 'utterly selfish, utterly false,
and utterly spoiled and vain, while, as the French say, he was
always playing to the gallery'.†

William Graham, fascinated though he was by these revelations, was not satisfied. What he wanted to find out if he could,
was the true state of feeling between Claire and Shelley. On
this, Claire was far more evasive. If Graham asked too many
questions she retaliated by boxing his ears. All the same, in
roundabout ways, Graham drew his own conclusions. He
noticed that when he drew attention to Shelley's poems, 'To
Constantia, Singing' and others which had been obviously
dedicated to Claire, she became self-conscious. 'Well,' she
said, 'it was not my fault that men fell in love with me.' She
went on to rhapsodize over Shelley in a way which was in
marked contrast to her disparagement of Byron: 'Shelley,' she
said, 'had an irresistible attraction for all women: his nature
was so pure and noble—Instead of holding with Byron that
woman is inferior to man, he looked up to women as something
higher and nobler.'‡

Graham, bracing himself to boldness, asked her if she had
ever loved. She blushed.

'Shelley?' he murmured.

'With all my heart and soul,' she replied.§

So there, in Florence, Claire lived on into old age, nourished

---

* William Graham: *Last Links with Byron, Shelley and Keats.*   † Ibid.
‡ Ibid.   § Ibid.

by her memories of Shelley's kindness and tenderness, dwelling on the man who was, according to Graham, the 'one love of her life'.

She had become a Roman Catholic, at one time she entered a convent, for a short time she had had a mental collapse. Now, living alone with her niece Paula, she had outlived all the old friends of her youth except Jane and Trelawny. There were some new friends. People were curious. Henry James was fascinated by her story and *The Aspern Papers* is based on Claire's history. She herself would like to have written a book of her reminiscences of the two poets, but was unable to bring herself to the task. In March 1879, at the age of eighty-one, she slipped peacefully away into unconsciousness and her stormy life was over. The little shawl which Shelley had given her was, as she had requested, buried with her in her coffin.

It is obvious that Claire, like Jane, felt herself to have been of a very special importance in Shelley's life. There were others too: Miss Hitchener, the 'Brown Demon', who carefully preserved all his letters: Sophia Stacey, who all her life cherished the little notebook he had given her inscribed with his poems: Emilia Viviani, dying of neglect and unhappiness after a miserable marriage, and remembering the adoring young poet and *Epipsychidion*, one of the most passionate love poems ever written.

There was poor Harriet Westbrook, who had believed so implicitly in Shelley's love and whose heart had broken when he deserted her: Harriet Grove too, the schoolgirl love of his youth, who had finally allowed caution to over-rule ardour and, by doing so, had possibly saved herself from a similar heartbreak: and the pathetic Fanny Imlay, who buoyed herself up with the conviction that Shelley had singled her out for special friendship—only to fall into a stupor of desolation when she found that she had been mistaken.

Lastly, and most important of all, there was Mary, the woman who had devoted her life to him and who, gazing at his portrait after his death and looking back at their marriage, had written in her Journal: 'That dear look assures me that thou wert mine, and recalls and narrates to my backward looking mind *a long tale of love and happiness*'—but who, nevertheless, had apparently disappointed him in the end.

At the final assessment it is surely impossible to judge the relative importance of these women in Shelley's life. In a way they were all important. In a way they were of little importance. Shelley lived the vital part of his life in his imagination and, particularly in the early years, his hold on reality was tenuous.

The chief accusation of his critics is that his anti-social principles combined with his emotional instability brought misery to many people connected with him. All true enough. Yet, strangely, his motives were good, even noble. He believed in universal love as the panacea of all evil and in the sharing of all life's benefits. In many ways he successfully practised these convictions. He had read enormously, absorbing himself in intellectual thought, and some of his liberal ideas were decades ahead of his time. But his theories were often too idealistic—too remote from humanity—to belong to this world. As a consequence, especially at the beginning, he made some terrible mistakes. He did not realize that few people could share his more high-flown precepts and that to inflict them upon the uninitiated could be sheer cruelty. He treated women badly because he was incapable of accepting them as human beings with ordinary human feelings and failings.

His nearest approach to a normal relationship was probably his relationship with Mary. But even Mary who at the beginning seemed to have everything that he desired—beauty, intellect, idealism, understanding—wilted under the strain of his impossible demands. She too was only a 'mortal image'. Inevitably he was disenchanted. As he himself illuminatingly explained: 'Some of us have in a prior existence been in love with an Antigone, and that makes us find no full content in any mortal tie.'

Yet, in spite of this lack in himself, there seems to be no doubt that women found him irresistible. It was not sensual desire that he aroused in them so much as a passion of gratitude for his tenderness, gentleness, reverence towards them as superior beings—the very characteristics, particularly the last, which in the end proved to be their undoing.

What they all failed to realize was that he lived in his own world of genius and imagination and that it was a world to which none of them had entry. In the end therefore, as an inevitable consequence of this fundamental divergence, he could only elude them all.

MAIN BOOKS CONSULTED

ANGELI, MRS ROSSETTI, *Shelley and His Friends in Italy* (1911).

BAILEY, RUTH, *Shelley* (Duckworth, 1931).

BLUNDEN, EDMUND, *Shelley* (Collins, 1946).

BOAS, LOUISE S., *Harriet Shelley* (Oxford University Press, 1962).

BROWN, FORD, K., *The Life of William Godwin* (Dent, 1926).

CAMERON, KENNETH NEILL, *The Young Shelley* (Gollancz, 1951).

—— *Shelley and His Circle*. Vols. I and II (Oxford University Press, 1961).

—— *The Esdaile Notebook* (Faber, 1964).

CHESSER, DR EUSTACE, *Shelley and Zastrozzi: Self-Revelation of a Neurotic* (Gregg Archive, 1965).

CHURCH, RICHARD, *Mary Shelley* (Gerald Howe, 1928).

DOWDEN, EDWARD, *The Life of Percy Bysshe Shelley*, 2 volumes (Kegan Paul, Trench, 1886).

EMDEN, CECIL S., *Poets in Their Letters* (Oxford University Press, 1959).

FREEMAN, MARTIN, *Thomas Love Peacock* (Secker, 1911).

GRAHAM, WILLIAM, *Last Links with Byron, Shelley and Keats* (Leonard Smithers, 1898).

GRAY, AUSTIN K., *Teresa: The Story of Byron's Last Mistress* (Harrap, 1948).

GRYLLS, E. GLYNN, *Mary Shelley* (Oxford University Press, 1938).

—— *Claire Clairmont* (John Murray, 1939).

HEWLETT, DOROTHY, *Adonais: A Life of Keats* (Hurst & Blackett, 1937).

HOGG, THOMAS JEFFERSON, *The Life of Percy Bysshe Shelley* (1858).

HOTSON, LESLIE, *Shelley's Lost Letters to Harriet* (Faber & Faber, 1930).

HUNT, LEIGH, *Autobiography* (1850).

INGPEN, ROGER, *Shelley in England* (Kegan Paul, Trench, Trubner, 1917).

JONES, FREDERICK L., *The Letters of Percy Bysshe Shelley*, 2 volumes (Oxford University Press, 1964).

Keats-Shelley Memorial Association Bulletins.

LOVELL, ERNEST J., JR., *Captain Medwin* (Macdonald, 1963).

MARSHALL, MRS JULIAN, *The Life and Letters of Mary Wollstonecraft Shelley*, 2 volumes (Bentley, 1889).

MAUROIS, ANDRÉ, *Ariel* (Bodley Head, 1924).

MOORE, DORIS LANGLEY, *The Late Lord Byron* (John Murray, 1961).

NORMAN, SYLVA, *After Shelley* (Oxford University Press, 1934).

ORIGO, IRIS, *Allegra* (Hogarth Press, 1935).

—— *The Last Attachment* (Cape & Murray, 1949).

PEACOCK, THOMAS LOVE, *Memoirs of Shelley*, ed. by H. F. B. Brett-Smith (Frowde, 1909).

RAYMOND, ERNEST, *Two Gentlemen of Rome* (Cassell, 1952).

TRELAWNY, E. J., *Recollections of Shelley and Byron* (Moxon, 1858).

WOOLF, VIRGINIA, *The Common Reader*, Volume 2 (Hogarth Press, 1932).

INDEX

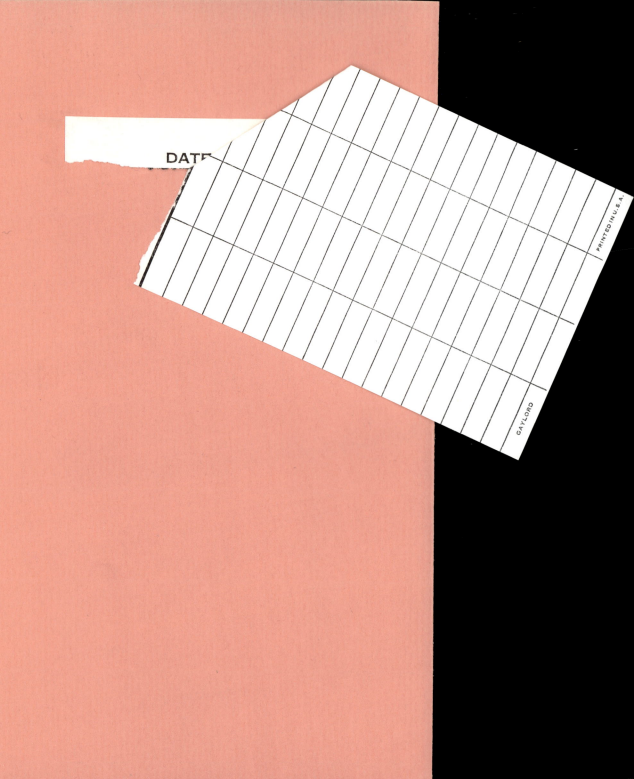

DATE

PRINTED IN U.S.A.

GAYLORD